Sports Law in India

Sports Law in India

Mohammad Naseem
Saman Naseem

This book was originally published as a monograph in the International Encyclopaedia of Laws/Sports Law.

Founding Editor: Roger Blanpain
General Editor: Frank Hendrickx
Volume Editor: Michele Colucci

Wolters Kluwer

Published by:
Kluwer Law International B.V.
PO Box 316
2400 AH Alphen aan den Rijn
The Netherlands
E-mail: lrs-sales@wolterskluwer.com
Website: www.wolterskluwer.com/en/solutions/kluwerlawinternational

Sold and distributed by:
Wolters Kluwer Legal & Regulatory U.S.
7201 McKinney Circle
Frederick, MD 21704
United States of America
E-mail: customer.service@wolterskluwer.com

ISBN 978-94-035-0036-2

e-Book: ISBN 978-94-035-4775-6
web-PDF: ISBN 978-94-035-4785-5

The Authors

Mr Mohammad Naseem born and brought up in Sardarnagar, District Pilibhit, India, is a Science Graduate and a Master of Laws with a specialization in Commercial Law from Aligarh Muslim Univcrsity, India. He is ex-Deputy General Manager (Legal) of Oil and Natural Gas Corporation Limited (ONGC) Limited, where he joined in 1985. He was also Vice President, ONGC-Videsh Limited for seven years. At present, he is the Chairman and Managing Partner of Global Law and Liaison Services, New Delhi. In his professional career spanning more than three decades, he has dealt with a large number of high-value commercial matters, domestic and international arbitration and litigation. He has been part of a large number of negotiation teams, having successfully negotiated deals worth billions of dollars including acquisitions of petroleum properties in a number of countries.

He is the author of monographs and books on Energy Law, Environmental Law, Medical Law, Islamic Law of Contracts and Religion Law of India. He has also authored Energy Law International, Environmental Law International and Medical Law International. All these are published by Wolters Kluwer, the Netherlands. A number of articles have also been published in national and international journals of repute. He is the co-author of *Fuel and Energy II (Petroleum and Natural Gas)* of Halsbury's Laws of India Series (Volume 21) published by LexisNexis Butterworths India Limited. Edward Elgar Publishing Limited has published an article authored by him on 'World Petroleum Regimes' in the *Research Hand Book on Energy Laws of the World*. His article on 'Natural Gas Provisions in Host Government Contracts – Regulatory and Contractual Aspects in India' is published by Oil, Gas and Energy Law Intelligence (OGEL), United Kingdom (UK).

He is the visiting faculty and guest expert speaker of the Indian Academy of International Law and Diplomacy, University of Petroleum and Energy Studies, Dehradun (UPES) and Indian School of Petroleum, New Delhi. He is a member of Consultative Committee of Faculty of Law, UPES. He has travelled extensively throughout the world in relation to negotiation and delivering lectures. He has spoken in Seminars organized by IBC Asia Limited at Singapore, Oil and Gas IQPC at Bangkok, Thailand, Kuala Lumpur, Malaysia and Tehran, Iran in a seminar conducted by OIPF, Iran. For conducting negotiations, he has visited Myanmar, Singapore, Vietnam, Japan, South Korea, Hong Kong, Thailand, Iran, UAE, Iraq, Jordan, Syria, Turkey, Egypt, Libya, Sudan, South

Sudan, Italy, Russia, Kazakhstan, Denmark, Netherlands, Switzerland, France, UK, USA, Canada, Ecuador, Venezuela and Uzbekistan. He is the life member of Indian Society of International Law. With more than thirty years of varied practical and on the job legal experience in negotiation, drafting, interpretation and vetting of legal documents and dealing with arbitration and litigation on the one hand and acting as a trainer, speaker and author, Mr Naseem has been part of an exclusive team of trainers, negotiators, advisers and legal strategists of eminence and is a legal luminary of international repute in his own right.
Email – naseem_md@yahoo.com.

Ms Saman Naseem is a Law Graduate from Symbiosis International University and a Postgraduate in Commercial Law from Aligarh Muslim University, India. She is an active participant in seminars and conferences and has presented various research papers. She is the co-author of monograph on Energy Law, Environmental Law, Religion Law and Medical Law, all pertaining to India; Energy Law International, Environmental Law International and Medical Law International published by Wolters Kluwer, the Netherlands. Edward Elgar Publishing Limited has published a chapter co-authored by her by the title, 'World Petroleum Regimes' in the book named *Research Handbook on Energy Laws of the World*. A research paper on 'Natural Gas Provisions in Host Government Contracts: Regulatory and Contractual Aspects in India' has been co-authored by her and published in e-journal *Oil, Gas and Energy Law Intelligence* (*OGEL*), UK. She is associated with Global Law and Liaison Services, a firm providing professional legal advice in India. She is also associated with various NGOs like the Madad Foundation, Leprosy Eradication Drive by Indian Leprosy Foundation and in social causes such as collection of funds for Help Age India, poor, needy and for the blind.
Email – saman1492@gmail.com.

Table of Contents

List of Abbreviations

AAF	Adverse Analytical Findings
AAFI	Amateur Athletic Federation of India
ADAP	Anti-Doping Appeal Panel
ADDP	Anti-Doping Disciplinary Panel
AIFF	All India Football Federation
AIR	All India Reporter
AO	Assessment Officer
ASCI	Advertising Standards Council of India
BCA	Bombay Cricket Association
BCCI	Board of Control for Cricket in India
BRR	Broadcast Reproduction Right
CAS	Court of Arbitration for Sport
CBA	Collective Bargaining Agreement
CBDT	Central Board for Direct Taxes
CBI	Central Bureau of Investigation
CCI	Competition Commission of India
CCI	Convention on the Elimination of All Forms of Discrimination Against
CEDAW	Women
CIT	Commissioner of Income Tax
CPC	Civil Procedure Code
Cr.P.C	Criminal Procedure Code
CVO	Chief Vigilance Officer
DD	Doordarshan (A Government TV Channel)
DDCA	Delhi District Cricket Association
DG	Director General
DMA	Disaster Management Act
EDA	Epidemic Diseases Act
EPO	Erythropoietin
FDI	Foreign Direct Investment
FIFA	Federation Internationale de Football Association

List of Abbreviations

FII	Foreign Institutional Investor
FINA	Federation International Association
GST	Goods and Services Tax
IAF	International Athletic Federation
ICAS	International Council of Arbitration for Sport
ICC	International Cricket Council
ICL	Indian Cricket League
IFA	Indian Football Association
IGST	Integrated Goods and Services Tax
IHF	Indian Hockey Federation
IOA	Indian Olympic Association
IOC	International Olympic Committee
IPC	Indian Penal Code
IPL	Indian Premier League
ITBP	Indo-Tibetan Border Police
ITO	Income Tax Officer
LIC	Life Insurance Corporation
MAR	Minimum Assured Revenue
MCA	Maharashtra Cricket Association
MYAS	Ministry of Youth Affairs and Sports
NABL	National Accreditation Board for Testing and Calibration Laboratories
NADA	National Anti-Doping Agency
NBA	News Broadcasters Association
NCOE	National Centres of Excellence
NDTL	National Dope Testing Laboratory
NGO	Non-governmental Organization
NPFAI	National Playing Field Association of India
NRI	Non-resident Indian
NSA	National Sports Academy
NSDC	National Sports Development Code
NSDCI	National Sports Development Code of India
NSDF	National Sports Development Fund
NSF	National Sports Federation
NYKS	Nehru Yuva Kendra Sangthan
ONGC	Oil and Natural Gas Corporation Limited
PCC	Padiham Cricket Club
RAT	Rapid Antigen Test
RTI	Right to Information
SAI	Sports Authority of India

SAIL	Steel Authority of India Limited
SGL	Sanspareils Green Land Limited
SIMCON	State Information Minister Conference
SOPs	Standard Operating Procedures
SSCB	Services Sports Control Board
UNESCO	United Nations Educational, Social And Cultural Organization
UT	Union Territories
WADA	World Anti-Doping Agency
WFI	Wrestling Federation of India
YMCA	Young Men's Christian Association

List of Abbreviations

Acknowledgements

We would like to thank and express our sincere gratitude to Mrs Rana Naseem and Mr Faraz Naseem who have not only spared to take time out of their share but also helped in collection of scarce material on sport law, typographic help and in all other respects so that this task could be completed successfully.

Mohammad Naseem
Saman Naseem

Acknowledgements

General Introduction

Chapter 1. General Background

1. India has a very rich and ancient tradition of awareness of physical fitness and sports from early historic periods. In the field of sport a value system evolved, according to which a special relationship of faith existed in between the disciple and the teacher (Guru and Shishya). The finest example of this relationship is Arjuna, the archer par excellence as the '*Shishya*' (meaning disciple or student) and Dronacharya as *Guru* (teacher). Swamy Vivekananda has aptly remarked that 'You will be nearer to Heaven through playing football rather than studying Gita.'

2. Therefore, sports and physical fitness are vital components of civilization of India evident from a highly evolved system of yoga and a range of developed indigenous games, including martial arts. In India, the history of sports can be traced back to the epic of Mahabharata which narrates an incidence where a game called *Chaturang* was played between two groups of warring cousins Pandavas and Kauravas.

3. There are various viewpoints as to the origin of the term 'sport'. As per one such view, the term 'sport' is derived from the French determined English word '*sportem*', i.e., to divest and also the Latin term 'desporto', i.e., literally to carry away. The emphasis is on sport being a distraction or something that gives pleasure. Sport in fact began as fertility magic, to ensure birth, growth and return of spring. It is the child in a man that is the source of his curiosity, creativity and uniqueness and the playground has been considered the most favourable milieu for the unfolding of inherent potential, latent capacities and talents.

4. Sports play a major role in shaping the personality and are integral to all-round physical and mental development of the human being and are the basis for developing a sense of achievement in collective national conscience. Achievement in sports is considered a matter of national prestige, pride and a morale booster.

5. Besides, in present-day world, the sport is not only an activity of physical development of body or an activity of entertainment but has acquired a professional approach along with a business proposition with huge financial implications. With high salaries, ticket prices and profits, professional sports are no longer just a game, but a big business worth billions of dollars.

6. Unfortunately, sports and physical education in India to some extent took a back seat under the British rule, as for long periods starting from the first war of independence in 1857 till its achievement in 1947, whole generations were involved and participating in the freedom struggle.

7. In the Constitution of India (enforced on 26 January 1950), sports fall under the Schedule VII (Seventh Schedule), State List (only States can legislate on items included in this list), Entry 33 and is a State subject. This has come in the way of the evolution and enactment of a nationwide and overall sports legislation. Efforts were made to bring sports under Concurrent List (both State and Centre can legislate on the items in this List) so as to give the centre more legislative powers. Since the twelfth Lok Sabha, a Bill aimed at transferring the subject of 'sport' from the State List to Concurrent List remained under consideration in the Parliament but the States strongly opposed it and ultimately it was withdrawn. On 31 July 2013, the Ministry of Youth Affairs and Sports (MYAS) came up with a Draft of National Sports Development Bill, 2013 but same is still pending.

In this background sport in India is regulated and monitored by Government of India through sports federations and associations. These bodies control domestic matches or games in the country. They also field national teams representing the country for participation in international competitions. These bodies also give telecasting and broadcasting rights to the successful bidder for hefty sums and also earn revenues from advertisement in sports events. They take disciplinary action against the erring players including debarring them from the game. These associations and federations have monopolistic character in respective sports field. The issue of accountability and transparency of National Sports Federations (NSFs) has been raised from time to time. There has been public and even judicial scrutiny over the functioning of the sports club conducting sports event particularly of cricket. The domination of sports club by business giants and politicians has also been a cause of concern.

8. The sports law is new in India and despite having several federations and independent bodies, lacks a good sporting regulatory system. Being a State subject, there is no precise and uniform law for sports throughout the country. Sports in India is governed by the National Sports Development Code (NSDC), 2011 and administration falls within the realm and remit of various autonomous bodies like Board of Control for Cricket in India (BCCI), Indian Olympic Association (IOA) and Hockey India, etc.

9. In the past, dark sides of the competitive world have come out in public which depicts the maladministration of sports, such as the Olympic Games Scandal, the Indian Premier League (IPL) scam, Federation Internationale de Football Association (FIFA) scandal and allegations of sexual assault, etc.

10. The major issues in sports law include labour and employment problems, drug use, broadcasting rights, sports injury and the concurrent liability, harassment in sports, etc. Looking into the large population India has, the performance in different sports events has not been satisfactory for which non-availability of proper facilities and infrastructure is mainly responsible.

11. Given the close relation of sports with national pride and the influence it has on the minds of people, the State has the most important role to play. It is clear that the existing model has not succeeded in achieving its objective and a new model is to be evolved. But, any change has been resisted by the State governments in India.

12. As sports is a State subject and some States have passed legislations on Sports. The States of Rajasthan, Himachal Pradesh and Uttar Pradesh made efforts to enact legislation on sports activities. The Himachal Pradesh Sports (Registration, Recognition and Regulation of Association) Bill, 2015 was passed by the Himachal Pradesh Assembly on 9 April 2015. This is a re-enactment as the 2005 Act was repealed. Rajasthan had enacted the Rajasthan Sport Act, 2005. These enactments regulated activities including registration, regulation and recognition of sports associations. Uttar Pradesh has already repealed the Sports Act which was earlier enacted.

Chapter 2. Sources of Sports Law

§1. Introduction

13. The sources of sports law in India are legislation, rules and regulations of various sporting federations, other bodies, institutions and clubs; sports policy; judicial decisions, etc. The Constitution of India gives power of making laws to States relating to sports but, there is no major legislative enactment by a large number of States regulating the field of sports. MYAS framed and issued guidelines known as 'National Sports Development Code of India' in 2011 in pursuance of successive National Sports Policies. The sport code is published in Gazette of India for wide publicity. Some States like Rajasthan, Uttar Pradesh, Himachal Pradesh and Haryana have exercised legislative power in their respective jurisdiction and have enacted laws on regulating sports activity including registration, regulation and recognition of sports associations (Uttar Pradesh has since repealed the Act).

§2. Constitution and Other Laws

14. The Constitution of India, promulgated on 15 August 1950, contains and deals with matters related to sports and games. In general, it has also been provided for in the Fundamental Duties that, 'It shall be the duty of every citizen of India to strive towards excellence in all spheres of individual and collective activity so that the nation constantly rises to higher levels of endeavour and achievement' (Article 51A, Part IV A). The Constitution, in Entry 33 of the State List (Schedule 7) includes sports, entertainment and amusement. Hence, States have power to legislate on matters of sports, entertainment and amusement.

15. There is no separate codified or unified body of law in India which could be termed as sports law. So the Central Government brought draft National Sports Development Bill, 2013, to take care of sports at national level. In addition, another draft Bill namely the Prevention of Sporting Fraud Bill, 2013 was also brought to prevent and combat sporting frauds affecting the integrity of sports and fair play in relation to national and international sporting events and for matters connected thereto or incidental therewith. The Anti-Doping Bill, 2021 has also been introduced in the lower House of the Parliament. But all these efforts have not resulted in any of the above bills maturing in enactment. Therefore, up till now, sports law has emerged mainly out of the application of various disciplines of law to sports and situations where sport or sportsmen are involved. The application of general law to sports activity and connected activity by the courts including the Supreme Court, the highest court in India, has helped in development of sports law in certain areas like broadcasting and telecasting of sports events, match-fixing, spot-fixing, functioning of Board related to cricket, etc. The main sources of rules and regulations and guiding principles have been National Sport Policy, Regulations framed by sports federations, Anti-Doping Rules and Sports Code. The two legislations, which to some extent deal with sport activities, are Sports Broadcasting Signals (Mandatory Sharing with Prasar Bharti) Act, 2007 and Narcotics Drugs and Psychotropic

Substances Act of 1985 which *inter alia* deals with drugs used for doping. The provincial sports bodies work as non-profit making organizations registered under the Company Law or under the Society Registration Act. Rules and regulations like statutory orders act only as secondary legislations supplementing laws.

16. However there is a void in the field of legislation for sports and subjects like doping, match-fixing, welfare of sportspersons has assumed importance and need of a comprehensive legislation was being felt and the proposed legislation may fill up some of the void.

17. After the issue of 2001, NSDC guidelines, several major initiatives were taken by the government, which included declaration of NSFs availing of government grant as a public authorities under the Right to Information (RTI) Act, 2005; implementation of age and tenure limit in respect of office-bearers of NSFs; notification and implementation of National Anti-Doping Agency's (NADA) Anti-Doping Rules; introduction of guidelines for prevention of age fraud in sports, and guidelines for holding fair and transparent elections to NSFs. These guidelines are aimed at promoting good governance among NSFs so as to strengthen their autonomy for discharging their functions and duties in accordance with the Olympic Charter and the basic principles and rules that govern the Olympic movement.

18. The existing instructions relating to sports have been compiled in the form of a single document namely NSDC, 2011 to enable better compliance with the basic universal principles of good governance in sports, which has promoted a strong sporting culture and sports excellence. The RTI Act, 2005 has been another legislation enabling access to information about functioning of NSFs receiving grants from the Central Government.

§3. Rules and Regulations Derived from the Sports Bodies

19. The sports law and rules and regulations are also derived from the charter documents and functioning of the following:

(1) National Sports Policy.
(2) Sports Law and Welfare Association of India.
(3) Sports Authority of India (SAI).

I. National Sports Policy

20. In view of importance of sports in the country, government has formulated National Sports Policy. A Resolution on the National Sports Policy was laid in both Houses of Parliament in August 1984. The National Sports Policy was formulated with the objective of raising the standard of sports in the country. The policy provided, *inter alia*, that the progress made in its implementation would be reviewed every five years to determine the further course of action, as may be necessary, following such review. In 2001, the National Sports Policy was implemented which was reviewed in 2007 and a comprehensive draft National Sports Policy 2007 was formulated but it was resisted by NSF's and IOA and hence was not implemented.

21. The draft National Sports Development Bill, 2013 was brought to encourage and coordinate sporting activities which envisaged formulation of an Athlete Commission for each sport for advising the NSF and National Olympic Committee on the need of the athlete's development and training (section 42(2) of the Sports Development Bill). The National Sports Policy also aims to pursue inclusion of 'sports' in the Concurrent List of the Constitution of India and introduction of appropriate legislation for guiding all matters involving national and interstate jurisdiction.

II. Sports Law and Welfare Association of India

22. The Sports Law and Welfare Association of India is a national non-profit and professional organization working with the goal of understanding, advancement and ethical practice of sports law in India for the promotion of sports, by bringing legal experts and sportspersons together. The association provides consultancy on regulation of sports governing bodies, general sport and legal issues, intellectual property issues in sport, online advocating in legal disputes of sports in court on behalf of sportspersons and sports bodies, etc. The association aims to further the discussion of legal problems affecting sports and promotes the exchange of a variety of perspectives and positions of sports law. It also provides a forum for lawyers representing athletes, teams, leagues, conferences, civic recreational programmes, educational institutions and other organizations involved in professional, collegiate, Olympic, physical education and amateur sports. The deliberations of this body provide material which may with time mature into regulations and later on in law through enactment.

III. Sports Authority of India

23. The SAI was established to fulfil the need of an apex body to coordinate various sports activities in India. SAI lays down rules, regulations, guidelines and this functioning gives rise and result in evolution of norms. It has gradually extended its operations to promote broad basing of sports.

§4. The Sports Broadcasting Law

24. The Sports Broadcasting Signals (Mandatory Sharing with Prasar Bharti) Act was passed in 2007 with the objective to provide access to the largest number of listeners and viewers, on a free-to-air basis, of sporting events of national importance through mandatory sharing of sports broadcasting signals with Prasar Bharti.

The Act provides that any content right owner or holder, television or radio broadcasting service provider shall not carry a live television broadcast on any cable or Direct-to-Home network or radio commentary broadcast in India of sporting events of national importance, unless it simultaneously shares the live broadcasting signal, without its advertisements, with the Prasar Bharti to enable them to retransmit the same on its terrestrial networks and Direct-to-Home networks in such manner and on such terms and conditions as may be specified.

§5. Sports and Competition Law

25. The Competition Law, 2002 promotes competition in the market, forbids abuse of dominance and anticompetitive agreements. However, it is desirable to promote competition in all spheres of life, and in the case of sports, it is the soul of the game and basic motivating and moving force. The Competition Act, 2002 prevents practices adversely affecting competition, promotes and sustains competition, protects the interests of consumers, etc. The Act prohibits agreements, practices and decisions that are anticompetitive. A department of the government carrying on economic activity falls within the ambit of the Act (section 2(h)). The broadcasting rights, single federation per sport, denial of stadiums, sports merchandising collusion among bidders, etc. raise serious legal issues concerning competition. Other issues relate to barriers for new entrants acting as driving out competition and thereby violating the Competition Act, 2002. In India, unlike in the United States (US) and some European countries, there has been a monopoly of the government in the area of broadcasting and telecasting. The Indian Telegraphing Act, 1885 has created this monopoly and vests the power of regulating and licensing broadcasting in the government. Further, the Cinematograph Act, 1952 empowers the government to pre-censor films. However, the power given to the government to license and to pre-censor under the respective legislations has to be read in the context of the Article 19(2) of the Constitution containing the parameters of reasonable restrictions which can be placed on the right to freedom of speech and expression. The power to pre-censor films and to grant licences for access to telecasting has to be exercised in conformity with the provisions of Article 19(2).[1]

§6. Judicial Decisions

26. Litigation has been a good source in the evolution and development of sports law. It has been fuelled by increased monetary stakes as well as promotion of products in the sports industry giving rise to a business-like and commercial approach to sports. Therefore, a multitude of law including torts, criminal law, contract law, etc. has been applied by the courts to sports activity and would continue to be applied. Thus, judicial decisions become a very important source of law. The case of *Ajay Jadeja v. Union of India* (95 (2002) DLT) began a new era of legal developments. It was held in this case that as the sporting bodies perform public functions and

1. *Ten Sports v. Citizen Consumer and Civic Action Group* (2004) 5 SCC 351 para. 48.

therefore, are subject to the writ jurisdiction of High Court. This principle was upheld in the case of *Zee Telefilms and Others v. Union of India & Others* [(2005) 4 SCC 649] by the apex court. This case is referred as the Magna Carta of Sports Law in India. The question that arose in this case was BCCI's arbitrary termination of broadcasting rights agreement. Here, the aggrieved party, Zee Telefilms filed a writ petition under Article 32 of the Constitution of India before the Supreme Court. Although, a writ under Article 32 can only be filed against the authorities which fall under the definition of 'State' under Article 12 of the Constitution. The Supreme Court held that BCCI did not fall within the ambit of 'State' as per Article 12 of the Constitution but government has certain control over it. Justice Sinha (minority opinion) opined that BCCI constitutes to fall under 'State'. There are numerous other decisions which contribute to the jurisprudence of Sports Law in India. As in the case of *K. Murugan v. Fencing Association of India, Jabalpur* (1991 SCC (2) 412), the Supreme Court discussed the significance of sports in India. The issue was regarding the election of the members to executive council of the IOA. The Supreme Court held that this does not appear to be a matter where individual rights in terms of the rules and regulations of the society should engage courts attention. Sports in modern times have been considered to be a matter of great importance to the community. International sports have assumed greater importance and has been in the focus for over a few decades. Sports in India remains ungoverned as there is an absence of enthusiasm of States. Hence, the sports bodies come in to play their part of role in governing the same.

27. There are several sports bodies and federations, such as BCCI for cricket, All India Football Federation (AIFF) for Football, Indian Hockey Federation (IHF) for Hockey, SAI and IOA at the apex. This shows that there is no focal sports authority to govern all the sports game other than the Ministry of Youth and Sports, which also works externally to administer these sports bodies. This issue was discussed in the case of *Zee Telefilms v. Union of India* [(2005) 4 SCC 649], it was said that, 'the Sports bodies largely remain unaccountable to the State or any other central body inside the territory of India, which however should not be the case considering the importance of sports in the modern arena'.

Therefore, a specific enactment is required, though there are certain regulations such as the NSDC, 2011 which governs the NSFs, but as sports is in the State List of Seventh Schedule of the Indian Constitution, its validity was challenged. The Code's validity was upheld in the case of *Indian Olympic Association v. Union of India*[2] by the Delhi High Court.

2. (W.P. (C) 2310/2012, CM APPL.4946 & 17545/2012).

Chapter 3. Specificity of Sports

28. The sports entities and their business organization are significantly different and peculiar than other business organizations giving rise to specificity. The 'specificity of sport' refers to its inherent characteristics which distinguish it from other economic and social activities. The sport has specific nature as its structure is based on voluntary activity and its social and educational function. The 'specificity of sport' has evolved into a legal concept developed through the rulings of the courts and through practice as regards competition rules. The monopolistic nature of sports organizations and the need for maintaining a competitive balance between teams resulted in the emergence of many forms of economic restraints like revenue-sharing, spending caps, drafts, non-tampering clauses. Although these restraints are common in modern sports, they have inevitably attracted the attention of competition law which aims to protect markets from anticompetitive restraints.

§1. Competition Law and Specificity

29. In India cricket is financially the most money-generating sport; however, other sports like football and hockey and recently even Formula 1 races have also become popular and generate revenue. Their viewership has increased manifold with large corporates showing interest in sponsorship and willing to invest in building brands and acquiring popular clubs.

30. The sport events worldwide are organized in a pyramid structure, under which a particular sport is governed and regulated by a single International Federation (IF) with various NSFs affiliated to it. The IF governs the regulatory aspect, i.e., laying down the rules of the sport, eligibility criteria and playing conditions. The IF also makes the annual calendar for that sport and conducts the world championship(s) and other international events. A corollary at the national level would be that the NSF would follow the regulations of the IF as a condition of its membership and have exclusive powers to make the annual calendar, develop the sport and conduct tournaments and training camps. Integrity, uniformity and strict control over regulations ensure that non-discriminatory and uniform rules in all aspects of the game are applied worldwide and encourage proper growth of the sports across the globe. It may even include sporting sanctions like disciplinary action, suspensions, fines and bans for behaviour contrary to the spirit of sports.

31. The IF/NSFs' rules restricting rival tournaments and release of players for these tournaments may come under the scanner of competition/antitrust laws like abuse of dominant position and anticompetitive agreements, amounting to unreasonable restraint on trade. The sports industry is unique as its pyramid structure ensures the monopoly which is essential in maintaining the integrity of sport. Unlike other industries, the sport industry thrives on competition rather than from the lack of it. Thus, certain sporting activities are required to be excluded from the purview of the competition laws.

32. Pure sporting activities like laying down the rules of the sport, defining the size and weight of the ball and dimensions of the playing field are generally excluded from the ambit of competition laws. But activities of the IF/NSF having substantial economic impact are within the purview of the competition law. The regulatory power of the IF/NSF if used to gain commercial and financial advantage would fall within this ambit provided the following conditions are satisfied:

(i) that the agreements are not anticompetitive, i.e., they do not attempt/cause appreciable adverse effect on competition; and/or
(ii) that they are not abusing their dominant position and are not imposing unfair or discriminatory conditions.

33. So with respect to competition law, there is a need to recognize the specificity of sport and carve out exceptions. It will have a huge impact on sports industry as many corporate bodies await a chance to start their own breakaway leagues and commercially gain from the revenue so generated.

Sport bodies in India are organized with a single governing body controlling most regulatory and commercial aspects of each sport. Such governing body is generally de facto 'dominant' and therefore there are allegations of the abuse of monopoly. For example, the BCCI may attempt to preserve its sole ability to regulate the sport and to organize events. In order to prevent the development of rival organizations, they tie players by prohibiting them from competing in other events, otherwise will be excluded from 'official' events, and such rules have been the subject of challenge under competition law.

34. When Zee launched Indian Cricket League (ICL), the BCCI sacked Kapil Dev as chairman of the National Cricket Academy for aligning with ICL and barred all other forty-four defecting players from playing for India in international events or at the domestic level. This act on part of the BCCI may attract liability under the provisions of the Competition Act, 2002. As per section 4(2)(c) of the Act if any enterprise 'indulges in practice or practices resulting in denial of market access in any manner', it shall be liable for abuse of dominant position. Thus, the practice of banning players from domestic tournaments on account of joining the rival leagues may face a challenge on the grounds of abuse of dominant position.

35. The denial of stadiums by the BCCI can also attract liability for abuse of dominant position under section 4(2)(c) of the Competition Act, 2002 as by denying the use of facilities under its control it raises the barriers to entry in the market for its competitors, resulting effectively in denial of market access. Operating from just one stadium in Panchkula (in Haryana near Chandigarh), the ICL missed out on one of the integral aspects of leagues sports, i.e., a fan base, since it was unable to capture home crowds for matches on account of non-access to the stadiums.

36. In June 2018, the Competition Commission of India (CCI) found a prima facie case of abuse of dominance against the BCCI for restrictions imposed on the ICL. Under the Competition Act, 2002 which came into force in 2009, several high-profile disputes relating to business of sports have been adjudicated by competition regulators. Proliferation of professional sports leagues in cricket, hockey, football, badminton, kabaddi has resulted and drawn attention to issues on assignment of media rights, restrictions on players and on rival leagues, that have raised questions on potential violations of section 3, which prohibits anticompetitive agreements, and section 4 of the Competition Act, outlawing abuse of dominance.

37. A high-profile competition case on sports pertained to a complaint filed by Dhanraj Pillay former great India hockey player, against Hockey India (HI), which claimed that the restrictive conditions imposed by HI through its revised Code of Conduct (CoC) Agreement with its players, on participation in private professional leagues resulted in undue restrictions on mobility of players and on prospective private professional leagues. The CCI ruled that while HI was in a position of dominance, it had neither abused its dominant position nor entered into any anticompetitive agreements with the players. Even though CCI found no violation of the Competition Act, it called upon HI 'to put in place an effective internal control system' to 'ensure that its regulatory powers are not used' for 'deciding on any matters relating to its commercial activities.'

Thus, there is no exception for sports from scrutiny of competition regulators in India. Yet, the CCI also recognized 'the right of self-regulation of sports bodies with regard to issues, which are purely and exclusively sporting, such as selection of teams, formulation of rules of the sport, etc. or, even the issues which have economic aspects such as grant of various rights related to sports events or organization of leagues, etc.'.

I. Indian Cricket League

38. A complaint was filed by proprietors of the ICL against the BCCI in 2013. The ICL a privately owned league alleged that the BCCI imposed a number of restraints on them as they saw them as a rival. These restraints included ban on players, directives to affiliated entities to terminate employment of players associated with ICL, denial of access to cricket facilities. In addition, eligibility conditions for allocation of media rights for the IPL specifically excluded any bidder 'involved in any litigation proceedings of any kind' with the BCCI, resulting in exclusion of proprietors of ICL and denying them market access.

The CCI ruled that the BCCI enjoyed a dominant position in relevant market of organization of professional cricket leagues in India and had systematically excluded the complainant from participation in this market by not recognizing the ICL. With regards to blacklisting of proprietors from bidding for the broadcast rights for IPL, it observed that the sequence of events and the nature of restriction reveals that the conditions were specifically targeted against the company which ran the ICL and the modifications in the eligibility conditions for allocation of broadcast rights were intended to prevent the company from bidding for the media rights for IPL. Therefore, the CCI held that there was a prima facie case of abuse of dominance as defined by section 4(2)(c) of the Competition Act and directed the Director General (DG) to carry out an investigation.

II. Athletic Federation of India

39. There was a complaint against the Athletic Federation of India (AFI) relating to the decision taken in one of its 2015 Annual General Meeting (AGM) to act against its State level member-associations, their officials and athletes who encourage unauthorized marathons without the permission of AFI as anticompetitive. The CCI initially took the view that there existed a prima facie case of contravention of provisions of section 4 of the Competition Act by AFI and directed the DG to investigate the complaint. In its final order, however, the CCI did not find any violation. It ruled that the complaint was based on the Draft Minutes of the 2015 Annual General Meeting and that the final minutes of the said meeting does not contain anything which can amount to abusive in terms of section 4 of the Act.

III. Restraint on Mobility

40. The fact remains that while some rules governing the players and the organization of sport events/tournaments may create a restrictive environment for the economic activities that are related to sport but they could be justified in the context of the sport. So the mere fact that some of the rules of the sporting organizations have a restrictive impact on mobility of players or freedom of competition would not make those rules violating the principles of competition law. The test would be to assess whether the restraint on competition is a necessary requirement to serve the development of sport or preserve its integrity.

The use of judicial review by constitutional courts to monitor Sports Governing Bodies (SGBs) is fairly routine in India with writs being issued in several different sports by the Supreme Court and High Courts. The dominant position of SGBs does not by itself render restraints imposed by SGBs as illegal, the legality of such restraints are determined on the basis of their purported sporting justification. Thus, CCI has strengthened its flexible case-by-case approach that allows consideration of the specificity of sports.

§2. Single Federation per Sport

41. The National Sports Development Bill, 2013 provides that the government shall not recognize more than one NSF for each sport discipline, which will cater to both men and women, to all age groups, including veterans and also be responsible for different variants of that sport discipline. The constitution of IOA provides that the membership of the NSFs or Associations, within their particular field of specialization, is confined to the corresponding State and other special units affiliated to the NSFs or Associations and that where any of the NSFs or Associations that grant membership to individual clubs or individual persons, such membership does not confer on such members the right to vote in any of the federation or association meetings. For any one game, only one sports association is permitted in one State. It implies, therefore, that in the field of sports, it will be ‘One State, One Unit’. No

NSF or association shall affiliate a sports unit of any State or department that has not been affiliated or recognized by the State Olympic Association which is affiliated to the IOA.

§3. Restrictions Arising from Players' Transfer Rules

42. A federation can put reasonable restrictions on the right of the sportsman to join another federation or sporting club. The transfer rules must not unreasonably restrict the principle of free movement and competition rules. In case a sportsman has entered into an agreement, he shall be bound by the terms of such agreement and the rules of the federation or club as the case may be. But terms of a contract cannot impose absolute restrictions which violate his freedom to employment. However reasonable restrictions can be imposed on this right.

§4. Rules Restricting Activities of the Participants in Professional Sports

43. The sports bodies like IOA and SAI promote amateur sports and not professional sport. The Memorandum of Association of IOA provides that it is to develop and promote Olympic movement and amateur sport; to educate the public as to the value of amateurism in sports. IOA to guard and enforce amateur rules in connection with NSFs or Associations and to maintain the highest ideals of amateurism and to promote interest therein. Thus there is very limited scope for professional sport.

Chapter 4. Certain Sports and Mental Exercises Specific to India

§1. YOGA

44. From time immemorial, Yoga occupied an unparalleled and distinct recognition in the cultural history of India, as a practical system of physical, mental, moral and spiritual culture. Yoga has been one of the fundamental doctrines devoted for attaining perfect health and mental poise. Hieun Tsang, the famous Chinese traveller, visited Nalanda University to learn the 'Yogasastra'. A statue excavated from the Indus valley civilization shows a man in a yogin attitude which proves the old age of yoga. In the later Vedic and post-Vedic period, yoga was an integral part of the ancient civilization which is illustrated in the verses of the Yajurveda. In the post-Vedic times, the practice of Yoga was developed into a formal system with detailed textbooks. Now Yoga has become very popular throughout the world and considered a great exercise for harmonizing the body and mind.

§2. CHESS

45. The Mahabharata story throws light on the fact that a game similar to chess was played in ancient India. The Mahabharata is variously dated around 800 and 1100 BC. Thus, this game was known in India nearly 3,000 years ago. It is the view of some historians that this game was also used in the allocation of land among different members of a clan when a new settlement was being established.

46. The Indian origin of the game of chess is supported by the Encyclopaedia Britannica, according to which: 'About 1783–1789 Sir William Jones, in an essay published in the second Volume of Asiatic Researches, argued that Hindustan (India) was the cradle of chess; the game was known as chaturanga, that is, the four angas, or members of an army, which are said in the Amarakosha (an ancient Indian Dictionary – S.B.) to be elephants, horses, chariots and foot soldiers. As applicable to real armies, the term chaturanga is frequently used by the epic poets of India. Sir William Jones' essay is substantially a translation of the Bhawishya Purana, in which is given a description of a four-handed game of chess played with dice.' Sir William, however, grounds his opinions as to the Hindu origin of chess upon the testimony of the Persians and not upon the above manuscript. He lays it down that chess, under the Sanskrit name 'Chaturanga' was exported from India to Persia in the sixth century of our era; that by a natural corruption, the old Persians changed the name into Chatrang; but when their country was soon afterwards taken possession of by the Arabs, who had neither the initial nor the final letter of the word in their alphabet, they altered it further into Shatranj, which name found its way presently into modern Persian and ultimately into the dialects of India.

47. According to the Encyclopaedia Britannica, Wander Linde, in his exhaustive work, *Geschichte and Litteraturdes Schachspiels* (1874), has much to say of the origin-theories, nearly all of which he treats as so many myths. He agrees with those who consider that the Persians received the game from India. The outcome of his studies was that chess certainly existed in India in the eighth century, and that probably that country is the land of its birth.

48. According to thc Encyclopacdia Britannica, 'Wc find thc bcst authoritics agreeing that chess existed in India before it is known to have been played anywhere else.' In this supposition they are strengthened by the names of the game and some of its pieces. Shatranj, as Forbes has pointed out, is a foreign word among the Persians and the Chaturanga is obvious.

49. With respect to introduction of this game into Persia, the Encyclopaedia says that 'The Persian poet Firdousi, in his historical poem, the Shahnama, gives an account of the introduction of Shatranj into Persia in the reign of Chosroes I Anushirwan, to whom came ambassadors from the sovereign of Hind (India), with a chessboard and men asking him to solve the secrets of the game, if he could; or pay tribute. The king asked for seven days' grace, during which time the wise men vainly tried to discover the secret. Finally, the king's minister took the pieces home and discovered the secret in a day and a night.' According to Firdausi, the minister even went further and better and invented a new game called 'nard' which was more baffling.

50. The Encyclopaedia Britannica concludes that 'Other Persian and Arabian writers state that Shatranj came into Persia from India and there appears to be a consensus of opinion that may be considered to settle the question. Thus we have the game passing from the Hindus to the Persians and then to the Arabians, after the capture of Persia by the Caliphs in the seventh century, and from them, directly or indirectly, to various parts of Europe, at a time which cannot be definitely fixed, but either in or before the tenth century.

51. The other term 'Astapada', meaning eight steps, was also used to describe this game in ancient India, and it was perhaps a description for the eight steps (squares) which the modern chessboard has. The modern chessboard is chequered with 64 (8 × 8) squares in all, with eight squares on each side. The old English word for chess which is Esches possibly stems from this eight squared aspect of the game as did the Sanskrit word 'Astapada'. H.J.R. Murry in his monumental work *A History of Chess*, has come to the conclusion that chess is a descendant of an Indian game played in the seventh century.

§3. Game of Cards

52. The popular game of cards originated in ancient India and was known as Krida Patram. This game was one of the favourite pastimes of Indians in ancient times, patronized especially by the royalty and nobility. This game was known in ancient times as Krida Patram, in the middle ages, it was known as Ganjifa. In medieval India, Ganjifa cards were played in practically all the royal courts. This game is recorded to have been played in Rajputana, Kashyapa Meru (Kashmir), Utkala

(Orissa) the Deccan and even in Nepal. The Mughals also patronized this game, but the Mughal card sets differ from those of the ancient Indian royal courts.

53. Some scholars are of the opinion that this game was in fact, introduced into India by the Mughals. But according to Abul Fazal, author of the *Ain-e-Akbari*, the game of cards was of Indian origin and that it was a very popular pastime in the Indian Royal courts when the Muslims came into India. Abul Fazal has given a description of the cards used. The first was Ashvapati which means 'lord of horses'. The Ashvapati, which was the highest card in the pack, represented the picture of the king on horseback. The second highest card represented a General (Senapati) on horseback. After this card come ten other with pictures of horses from one to ten.

54. Another set of cards had the Gajapati (lord of elephants) which represented the king whose power lay in the number of elephants. The other eleven cards in this pack represented the Senapati and ten others with a soldier astride an elephant. Another pack has the Narpati, a king whose power lies in his infantry. We also had other cards known as the Dhanpati, the lord of treasures, Dalpati, the lord of the squadron, Navapati, the lord of the navy, Surapati, the lord of divinities, Asrapati, lord of genii, Vanapati, the king of the forest and Ahipati, lord of snakes, etc.

55. On the basis of the description of Abul Fazal, it can be said that the game of playing cards had been invented by sages in ancient times that took the number twelve as the basis and made a set of twelve cards. Every king had eleven followers, thus a pack had 144 cards. The Mughals retained twelve sets having ninety-six cards. These Mughal Ganjifa sets have representations of diverse trades like Nakkash (painter), Mujallid (bookbinder), Rangrez (dyer), etc. In addition, there were also the Padishah-i-Qimash (king of the manufacturers) and Padishah-izar-i-Safid (king of silver), etc.

56. The pre-Mughal origin of the game of cards is evident from the pattern of paintings on the cards. Despite the observation of Abul Fazal that Akbar introduced the pack with eight sets, even earlier, in Indian (Hindu) courts there were packs with eight, nine and ten sets apart from the usual twelve. The numbers were derived from the eight cardinal directions Ashtadikpala, for the pack with eight sets, from the nine planets Navagraha for the one with nine sets and from ten incarnations Dashavatara of Vishnu for the pack with ten sets.

57. Themes from the Ramayana and Mahabharata are painted on these cards. The largest number of such cards is to be found in Orissa. The painters from Orissa have represented various illustrations like the Navagunjara, a mythical bird-human animal which was the form assumed by Sri Krishna to test Arjuna's fidelity, illustrations from the Dashavatara of Vishnu are also portrayed.

§4. THE MARTIAL ARTS: KARATE AND JUDO

58. India is also the originator of the martial arts of Judo and Karate. Whereas general perception is that it was the countries of the Far East, China, Korea and Japan who have given these arts to the world. The finest exponents of Karate and Judo come from these countries, schools like Shaolin and Ninja that have nurtured these arts are from the Far East. But in the distant corners of India a dying martial art exists which comes significantly close to Karate. This art form is called Kalaripayattu. The practitioners of Kalaripayattu have to develop acrobatic capabilities and use swords or knives to attack an opponent. Even an unarmed exponent of Kalaripayattu presents an invincible adversary.

59. This art form seems to have travelled from India to the countries of the Far East along with the Buddhist religion. Buddhists monks who travelled barefoot and unarmed to spread the gospel of Buddha seem to have accepted this art with alterations suitable to the philosophy of non-violence. Such a technique of defence would have been necessary for them as they travelled individually or in small groups in foreign lands during which they were exposed to dangers from bandits and fanatics from other religions. The aim of a Karate practitioner is mainly to disarm and disable his opponent without mortally wounding him. This can be taken as a reflection of the Buddhist attitude towards life. Thus it is quite possible that these martial art forms originated in Southern India and were transmitted to China, Korea and Japan by Buddhist monks.

Part I. The Legal Framework

Chapter 1. Public Law and Fundamental Rights

60. Before independence, India being under British Rule, the basic objective of education was to train people for service under the British Government. Hence, the educational system did not address itself to wholesome physical and mental development of the people. After independence, the importance of physical discipline was realized and a large number of sports organizations were established in the country.

§1. Right to Practice Sports

61. 61. International Charter of Physical Education Physical Activity and Sports by United Nations Educational, Social And Cultural Organization (UNESCO) suggest that sports is a fundamental right for all. Right to play or right to sports impliedly exists within the right to freedom enshrined in Article 21 of the Constitution of India. Sports have always been an integral part of school education. A petition has also filed by a law student in the Supreme Court to recognize sports as a fundamental right under Article 21 A of the Constitution which has led to issuance of notice.[3]

§2. Freedom of Association

62. 62. Article 19 (1) (c) of the Constitution of India guarantees to all its citizens the right 'to form associations, or unions or Co- Operative Societies'. Under clause (4) of the Article 19, however, the State may by law impose reasonable restrictions on this right in the interest of public order or morality or the sovereignty and integrity of India. So sportspersons can form trade unions. However, this right is not absolute and can be regulated. This fundamental right shall not affect the operation of any existing law insofar as it imposes, or prevents the State from making any law imposing, in the interest of sovereignty and integrity of India or public or morality, reasonable restrictions on the exercise of the right to form associations or unions.

---

3. (Reported in TOI dated 30 Aug. 2018).

§3. PERSONALITY RIGHTS

63. 63. Personality rights are protected under Article 21 of the Constitution of India which provides for the right to privacy and publicity under the right to life. Additionally, the Copyright Act, 1957 (Copyright Act), and the Trade Marks Act, 1999 (Trade Marks Act) in general protect personality rights. Section 14 of the Copyright Act states that 'copyright' means the exclusive right subject to the provisions of the Act, to do or authorize the doing of any of listed acts in respect of a work or any substantial part thereof, which safeguard the rights of the creator of the work. The Copyright Act under sections 38, 38A, and 38B also provides for performers rights according to which they have the right to be given credit or claim authorship of their work and have a negative right, restraining others from causing any kind of damage to their work which consequently affects their reputation. Section 14 of the Trade Marks Act restricts the use of personal names of persons living or recently dead, thereby preventing misuse of a person's name or representation of the said person. Personality rights under intellectual property law are therefore interpreted in a manner where personality rights are the property of well-known personalities and hence cannot be misused or misappropriated by anyone else. However, there is no specific or comprehensive statute or legal provision dealing with personality rights in India.

I. Right to Privacy

64. The personality right has two components namely Right to Privacy and Right to Use one's identity in publicity like a trademark. The essence of right to privacy is that it signifies keeping one's image and likeliness from being exploited without permission or contractual compensation. Right to privacy has been declared as right to live with dignity which is covered under Article 21 of the Constitution of India which states that no person shall be deprived of his life or personal liberty except according to the procedure established by the law. The line of demarcation between right of public to intrude into the privacy of sports celebrity and right of such celebrity to his private life not to be exposed to public gaze, is very thin. As per section 37(2) of the National Sports Development Bill, 2013, the quality of performance of an athlete at an athletic competition; injuries suffered by an athlete; medical health and fitness of an athlete; the whereabouts of an athlete and test results and information that are treated as confidential under the NADA Code, have been kept out of the purview of the RTI Act, 2005. The National Olympic Committee and NSFs shall not be deemed to be public authorities in respect of above-stated matters.

II. The Right to Use the Image of Sportsperson

65. An advertiser is required to take permission for using the image of sportsperson. So, nobody, particularly an advertiser has any right to use the image of sportsperson to promote his product as such sportsperson is deprived of his earnings by using his image to promote other products. Photos and images have become very important nowadays, as social media is at an all-time high and even single pictures of personalities from the sporting world sell for huge amounts. Therefore, having a right over thousands of such pictures, a part of endorsements, and all other things that fall under personality rights is extremely valuable. So using the image of a sportsperson without consent is violation of the right of the sportsperson to use it for some gain.

III. The Right to Name and the Right to Personal Identity

66. A sportsperson who has gained fame has a right to name and image, and others owe a duty that they should not use it for commercial purposes. There are various attributes of personal identity like voice and cap, glasses, hat frequently used and which are identified with a person and these are also protected. For example wearing a specific type of cap and nose ring may be a style statement of a sportsperson and may get protection. The IPL has opened a new vista for cricket players to earn huge money. In various instances, if the player's name, image, or likeness has been registered, been copyrighted, or used as a trademark, the said copyright or trademark can be licensed. Sachin Tendulkar, for instance, has trademarked his name across various classes and so has Kapil Dev.

IV. Right to Gender Equality

67. The women participating in sports face issues like gender equality and verification, homophobia, media coverage for the wrong reasons, etc. In Olympic Games a test of testosterone levels is implemented which may disqualify athletes from women's events if they have testosterone levels equivalent to the normal male range, which is 7 to 30 nanomoles per litre in the blood.

68. India is a signatory to the Convention on the Elimination of All Forms of Discrimination against Women (CEDAW). Article 10(g) of the CEDAW guidelines contains a provision which explicitly, addresses sports:

> States Parties shall take all appropriate measures to eliminate discrimination against women in order to ensure to them equal rights with men in the field of education and in particular to ensure, on a basis of equality of men and women … . The same opportunities to participate actively in sports and physical education.

Further, Article 13 of the CEDAW states that:

> States Parties shall take all appropriate measures to eliminate discrimination against women in other areas of economic and social life in order to ensure, on

> a basis of equality with men and women, the same rights, in particular ... . The right to participate in recreational activities, sports and all aspects of cultural life.

69. There are a number of laws in India against gender discrimination in education and employment, and many other general laws eliminating discrimination against women, but laws with specific focus on sports are still not there. Article 14 of the Constitution mandates equality before law. Article 15(1) prohibits discrimination on the grounds of religion, race, caste, sex and place of birth. Article 16 provides equality of opportunity for all. Article 39(a) talks of equal right to adequate means of livelihood. Despite all of this, gender equality in sports still takes a backseat. The National Policy for the Empowerment of Women, 2001 aims to bring the advancement, development and empowerment of women. The objectives include creation of an environment where women can realize their full potential, enjoyment of all human rights and fundamental freedoms in all spheres of life, equal access to participation and decision-making in healthcare, quality education, employment, elimination of all forms of discrimination against women, changing social attitudes, elimination of all forms of violence against women and building and strengthening partnership with civil society, particularly women's organization.

§4. Other Rights

I. Right to Strike

70. Striking is an important and effective tool in collective bargaining and has been considered as part of the freedom of association and forms part and parcel of freedom to form associations. But, sportsmen are bound by their associations with respect to right to strike for fulfilment of their demands.

II. The Right to Publicity

71. Right to publicity refer to rights related to personality of sportsperson such as certain characteristics, personality traits and their commercial use and exploitation. These rights are available to those who have attained a certain level of fame where the said personality traits are associated with them or are unique to them and may be used to monetize items that are attached to their names. The business aspect of the sport industry has seen the most exponential growth. Various franchises and individual players have started merchandizing items related to them and their personality traits. Sports celebrities market and sell merchandise bearing their image and personality rights to further commercially exploit their fame. It is therefore essential that the personality rights of these celebrities are not used for the wrong reasons.

72. These rights aim at the prevention of misuse of the said person's name, image, resemblance and any other identifying aspect of the personality of sportsperson. The right to publicity no doubt emanates from the right to one's name and fame but is subject to public interest, and that is why information about and associated with facts, events, ceremonies, etc. is not considered as protected. The right to publicity may also be restricted by membership of a club which might be having its own rules and regulations to deal with the publicity of its members.

III. Personal Rights of Sportsman and as Part of Team

73. The mere association of the name of a team, their logo, or a team player, could offer unprecedented mileage to the person or entity using such name or logo. It is a loss to the team, team owner, the player and an unwarranted gain for the entity associating such name or logo for their commercial benefits, without taking any permission or paying any licence fee or royalty. Hence, having a clear line of demarcation between the sportsmen's personality rights and his image as a part of the team is very important. Any such unauthorized use of the trademark would amount to unfair trade practice, unfair competition and also dilution of goodwill and reputation of the respective proprietor.

74. In *ICC Development (International) Ltd. v. Arvee Enterprises and Ors*,[4] the plaintiff contended that the commercial persona and identity of events held by the International Cricket Council (ICC) vest wholly and exclusively with the plaintiff and that they own publicity rights in all events held by the ICC that have any commercial value. The defendants in the case were wrongfully exploiting the persona of the plaintiff's events and thereby making wrongful gains. The court observed that despite all forms of appropriation of a legal entity's property being protected under various laws including the Copyright Act, granting personality rights to a corporate entity would defeat the concept of 'persona'. The court held that the right of publicity has evolved from the right of privacy and can inhere only in an individual or in any indicia of an individual's personality like his name, personality trait, signature, voice, etc. and no persona can be monopolized. The right of publicity vests in an individual and he alone is entitled to profit from it. For example, if any entity, was to use Kapil Dev or Sachin Tendulkar's name in connection with the 'World Cup' without their authorization, they would have a valid and enforceable cause of action.

75. In the case of *Gautam Gambhir v. D.A.P & Co. & Anr.*,[5] the plaintiff contended that the defendant's chain of restaurants could not use his name in their tagline as he is a famous cricketer and therefore his name is protectable as a well-known trademark. The plaintiff argued that due to his name being used, confusion was being caused in the minds of the general public as to the plaintiff's association with the said chain of restaurants amounting to deception and personality rights of

---

4. indiankanoon.org/doc/358048.
5. https://indiancaselaw.in/gautam-gambhir-v-d-a-p-and-co-and-ors/.

the plaintiff being illegally violated. The court declined the plaintiff's contentions and held that as the defendant did not use the plaintiff's image or in any other way portray to the public by using his photo or poster in his restaurant or on his social media pages, there was no intention on the defendant's behalf to confuse. Therefore, unless there is unjust enrichment of one by using a famous personality's name, image, or likeness, the suit will fail to stand the test of personality rights.

Chapter 2. Governmental Conditions and Permits (Quotas and Work Restrictions)

76. There is general law in India to deal with professional aspects of and with respect to employment and labour matters. It is interesting to note that the rules of IOA through voluntary surrender take away the right of all NSFs, Associations, State Olympic Association affiliated to IOA, to go to the court for redressal of the grievances and settlements of disputes.

77. The National Sports Development Bill, 2013 also provides that no Civil Court shall have jurisdiction to entertain any suit or proceeding in respect of any matter which the Appellate Sports Tribunal is empowered by or under this Act to determine and no injunction shall be granted by any court or other authority in respect of any action taken or to be taken in pursuance of any power conferred by or under the Act (section 32).

78. With respect to individual sportsman, it is applicable to expulsion and so far as relationship of sportsman with their sponsor or sports federation is concerned, it is governed by the contract which a sportsman has with the sponsor or sports federation. The Rules of IOA also deal with the nature and type of remuneration, which a sportsperson as competitor in international games can accept.

§1. Status and Definition of Sportsmen

79. Sportsmen carry out a sporting activity for remuneration or as amateur. The IOA Eligibility Code term it as competitor. According to the rules of IOA, to be eligible for participation in the Olympic Games and other international competitions and tournaments a competitor has, *inter alia*, to observe and abide by the rules of the International Olympic Committee (IOC) and, in addition, the rule of International Federation, as approved by IOC, even if the federation's rules are more strict than those of the IOC, as well as Asian Games, Commonwealth Games and any other international competitions, recognized by the IOC, Commonwealth Games Federation and Olympic Council of Asia.

§2. Relationship with Employer

80. The status of the sportsperson vis-à-vis employment is extremely varied and every sport as well as relationship of sportsperson with its employer has peculiar characteristics. Sometimes a sportsperson plays for his employer and sometimes represents his or her nation individually or as part of a team. The employment may be full time and sportsperson is considered and treated for all practical purposes as employee. In case he is with some club or federation, it is generally based on term contract basis or membership basis as the case may be.

§3. Service Contract

81. In the case of *Md. Azharuddin v. Dr A Muthaiiah and Others* (AIR 2002 AP 409) wherein the matter related to a life ban imposed by BCCI on the cricketer, the High Court of Andhra Pradesh at Hyderabad dealt with the nature of contract which a cricketer has with the sporting association and held that 'On behalf of the petitioner-plaintiff it is contended that there is a service contract between the plaintiff and the first defendant and therefore, the plaintiff is entitled to move the Civil Court seeking redressal of his grievances for violation of his rights under Article 311 of the Constitution of India. I am of the view, this submission is untenable inasmuch as Article 311 of the Constitution of India provides a mechanism for redressal of grievances of persons who are members of a Civil Service of Union of India or of civil servant of a State or holds a civil post under the Union or a State. As the petitioner is not holding any of these posts but only has entered into a private contract with the first defendant on certain terms and conditions to play cricket matches for the Indian Team for which certain amount of remuneration per match is paid, the petitioner is not entitled to invoke the provisions of Article 311 of the Constitution of India.'

§4. Players' Obligations

82. The obligations of the player are governed by the contract which player has with the sport federation or association, rules of such bodies and other general rules which may be applicable to professionals. As sportspersons are always in competition with other sportsmen, so they have to adhere to and play their game as per the rules of the game. Perhaps in no other sphere of human activity, decisions and results are as quick as in sporting activity as umpires, referees and judges are available to give on the spot decision.

§5. Transfer of Players

83. The transfer of a sportsman from one club or federation to another sometimes creates acrimony, as these clubs may be competitors like Mohammadan Sporting and Mohun Bagan in Kolkata. The transfer of player also depends on individual contract which a sportsperson has entered into with the club or federation as the case may be and rules of such club or federation. Rules, no doubt may be and remain the same; however, individual contract may vary from case to case.

§6. The Arbitration Clause and Sports Statute

84. The arbitration clause may be a part of the contract which sportsperson enters into with a sporting club, association or federation. The rules of IOA also provide for arbitration in case of disputes between the NSF, associations and State Olympic association affiliated to IOA. An individual player, group of individuals belonging to an association, federation or club taking recourse to Civil Court of law without utilizing the available resources of IOA General Assembly, can be expelled from National Sport Federation, Association or State Olympic Association.

§7. Derogation from the Workers' Statute

85. Clubs, association or federations are required to follow the statutes related to matters affecting the well-being of the sports professionals. As IOA is registered under Societies Registration Act XXI of 1860, therefore, its provisions are also applicable to IOA.

§8. Termination of the Contract

86. The termination of a sportsman's contract may occur because of efflux of time, by mutual consent, or by unilateral action of the sportsperson or entity with which it has employment or sponsorship contract. The termination in case of an employment contract is affected by resignation. Termination can also be brought about by operation of law.

Chapter 3. Tax Law Applied to Sports

87. The general law of taxation is applicable to sports as well, and there is no separate legislation to deal with the taxation in sports. The Income Tax Act provides for taxation of sporting activities and incentives available on donations to sport organizations. Tax deductions are available for the amount donated to club or sporting body. The issue of taxation can be related to taxation on individual sportspersons, on clubs and other sports bodies. The other aspect is taxation and/or duties on sports equipment and other sport goods. The professional clubs and sport federations are generally registered under the Societies Registration Act and function on a no-profit-no-loss basis. The most successful professional sports league of India, The IPL earns hundreds of crores in profit on an annual basis. The success of the IPL has led to a proliferation of interest in the creation of professional sporting leagues and annual events in other sports as well.

§1. Income from Sporting Events

88. Income tax Act, 1961 ('Act') provides for specific provisions for the taxation of incomes earned from sporting pursuits and performances. Sporting events no doubt involve test of skill and strength but it has also become a business and brings significant inflow of capital. As large amount of money is involved in sponsorships, broadcasting, etc. so this generates a significant increase in income which become subject to various types of taxes. Section 115BBA of the Act states that any NRI or non-citizen of India participates in any games or contributes through advertisements, then he will be charged on income above a specified limit. In the case of *Mahalakshmi Cultural Association v. the Commissioner of Police & Ors.* (2016) Supreme Court recognized that skill-based games are to be considered for taxation, and it will also be the duty of the winner to pay the tax.

89. To provide encouragement to sports in India and to promote sporting endeavours, the Act provides that incomes arising from any sporting event held in India to any person or persons can be fully exempted from income tax. This can be accomplished based on approvals by the Central Government using the provisions in section 10(39) of the Act. As per this section, any specific income arising can be exempted provided: such event is sanctioned/approved by the international body regulating such sport. The event has the participation of more than two countries and the event has been notified by the central government in the official gazette for this purpose. This exemption shall extend only to incomes earned specifically from such events and not to any other incomes earned by the organizers of such sporting events. Incomes exempted may include gate revenues, sponsorship money, etc.

Almost all international sporting events organized in India are tax exempt due to this provision. The earnings of sportspersons and the organizers from other revenue sources which are not explicitly covered under the exemption notification follow the general law of taxation and are taxed normally.

I. Media Rights

90. Media or broadcast rights include the right to carry and display the respective sports events on traditional as well as new media such as television, theatres, radio and the Internet. The sale of broadcasting and media rights is now the biggest source of revenue for most sports organizations, generating the funds needed to finance major sporting events, refurbish sports stadia and contribute to the development of sport at grassroots level. In addition, the royalties that broadcasters earn from selling their exclusive footage to other media outlets enable them to invest in the costly organizational and technical undertaking involved in broadcasting sports events to millions of fans all over the world. Television rights pertain to the telecast of shows through terrestrial or satellite television, whether in one country or across different countries. Television rights are often very lucrative, both for the organizers and the telecasters.

Theatrical rights, as well as rights to broadcast sports over radio are some of the other valuable properties in the business of sports. In this internet era, rights to distribute content and images online have also become an additional revenue stream for sports franchises. The importance of these new mediums can be gauged by the fact that even periodic updates and the right to feature live score feeds of cricket matches have become hotly contested properties in India.

§2. Income to Leagues and Organizers

91. Professional sports leagues, such as the IPL and other 'premier' leagues are working for profit and are therefore, quite justifiably, not always accorded exemption by the government. The lack of such recognition from the government often forces such leagues to adopt various complicated structures involving multiple layered entities, both offshore as well as local, this increases the cost of compliance but helps bring down the total tax liability.

92. Other sports bodies such as sports federations work without profit motives, more often than not, and are therefore organized as non-profit entities in the form of trusts that have exempt status in the form of section 12A registration under the income tax act is not taxable.

93. Sponsorships provide a stable source of revenue for the federation, league, franchise and athlete and at the same time provide another avenue for brands to reach out to potential customers and clients.

94. Professional sporting leagues also make money through franchise fee's which are sums paid by interested parties in order to secure rights to operate a franchise in such league, other sanctioned events such as the cricket world cup, Olympic Games earn revenues for the organizers through gate revenues or ticket fee. Other local sources of revenue include concession stands, restaurants operated by teams in their stadiums, merchandise sales and membership's packages offered by them to their patrons.

I. *Commissioner of Income Tax v. Delhi Race Club (1940) Ltd.*

95. In the case of *Commissioner of Income Tax v. Delhi Race Club* (1970, 75 ITR 111, Delhi) High Court of Delhi laid down that subscription received by the club from members is not taxable. Delhi Race Club was established with the object of carrying on racing business and a subscription was payable even if racing stopped or suspended. A question arose as to the amount of subscription received by a club from its members was taxable or not. It was held that the amount of subscription cannot be said to be received by the assessee out of any profit motive. The receipts from members' subscriptions or entrance fees by the assessee cannot form part of its assessable income. Thus, the subscription received by club from its member is not taxable.

96. The details of the case are that the Delhi Race Club (1940) Ltd. (hereinafter referred to as the 'assessee') is an incorporated body and members' club. By Clause 5 of the Memorandum of Association, every member of the club has undertaken to contribute to the assets of the club in the event of the same being wound up during the time that he is a member or within one year afterwards, for payment of the debts and liabilities of the club contracted before the time at which he ceases to be a member, and the costs, charges and expenses of winding up the same, and for the adjustment of the rights of the contributories among themselves, such amounts as may be required, not exceeding INR 100. If upon the winding up of the club or its dissolution, there remains after the satisfaction of all debts and liabilities any property whatsoever, the same shall be paid or distributed among the members of the club in equal shares. 'Regular members of the assessee-club are required to pay an entrance fee and annual subscription, while "life members" pay a life membership subscription. The life members are not required to pay any further subscriptions for the rest of their lives. Each of the above members has a vote on every motion before the assessee-club in general meetings. There are "stand members" also who do not pay any entrance fee, but pay regular periodical subscriptions. "Honorary members" are under no obligation to pay entrance fee or any subscription, but are entitled to all the rights and privileges of a regular member.'

97. The club encourages horse races. The profit and loss account showed that the incomes were mainly from totes, gate-income and bookmakers fees which totalled INR 672,969 out of the total gross receipt of INR 831,062. The items now in dispute are the members' subscriptions consisting of INR 3,500 on account of membership subscription and INR 7,500 on account of life membership subscriptions, totalling INR 11,000. The assessee-company claimed exemption in regard to this item before the Income Tax Officer (ITO) who, in the assessment order, stated:
It is admitted that members are allowed free admission to the club and participants have to pay for the races. The members pay it in lump sum. As such this amount is not of the type which is usually paid to mutual benefit societies. The claim is, therefore, not admitted.

98. The ITO, thus, equating the membership subscription with the gate-money received from the non-members, included the aforesaid sum in the total income. On appeal, the Appellate Assistant Commissioner held against the revenue and the Income Tax Appellate Tribunal concurred with him.

99. The Tribunal, applying the doctrine of mutuality as propounded in the case of *Carlisle Golf Club v. Smith*, ((1912) 6 TC 48) where it was held that in a member's club, the subscriptions by the members are not taxable, held that the receipts are immune from taxation. It was held that the activities of the assessee were mixed; although essentially a member's club offered club facilities to the members, it also carried on the business of horse racing. While the income from the said business was held to be taxable, the member's fees (subscriptions) realized for offering the club facilities were immune from taxation because such receipts fell within the test of mutuality. The observations of Lord Macmillan in the case of *Municipal Mutual Insurance Ltd. v. Hills* ((1952) 16 TC 430, 448) were relied upon.

100. At the instance of the Commissioner of Income Tax (CIT), the Tribunal opined that a question of law does arise out of the order and, on the facts aforesaid; they referred for the opinion of the court the following question:
Whether, on the facts and in the circumstances of the case, the sum of INR 11,000 received by the assessee as subscription from its members is not taxable?

101. The learned counsel for the revenue urged before Delhi High Court that the subscriptions received by the assessee are in the nature of payments for specific services and, therefore, they are taxable. The main reliance of the revenue was upon the case of *Commissioner of Income-Tax v. Royal Western India Turf Club Ltd.*, (1953) 24 ILR 551 (SC) and it was urged that, as held in the said case, the assessee was not a mutual association. The learned counsel submitted that the facts of the case before the Supreme Court (Royal Western, India Turf Club Ltd. case) and the facts of the present case are similar, inasmuch as both allow to members the same or similar amenities as they give to non-members, i.e., the use of a seat in a stand, the facility to watch races and to bet on horses in the races and the use of totalizator in the stand. The charges for admission in the stand are similar from members and non-members alike in the case of Western India Turf Club while, in the present case, the assessee makes no separate charge for such admission, but the members pay it in lump sum under the name of subscriptions. Hence, there is, in reality, no difference between the two. Therefore, it is urged that the principles laid down in that case by the Supreme Court are applicable here and the subscription should be held to be taxable income.

102. It was contended that the principles underlying the assessment of the income of mutual concerns are that the surplus arising from mutual transactions is not assessable where there is complete identity between the contributors and participators, or where the ownership of the surplus is restricted to those who provided it as a class. The surplus arising to the assessee on subscriptions from members in this case shows a complete identity between the contributors and the participators. It was therefore, urged that the members' subscriptions received by the assessee were not taxable income.

103. The subscription paid to the club by its members is paid in order to enjoy the membership of the assessee, entirely for a common cause and mutual benefit. Even if the racing was stopped or suspended, members would have contributed the same subscription according to the Articles of Association of the assessee-company. The receipts as found by the Appellate Tribunal are spent for the common benefit. The club like the Delhi Gymkhana Club offered amenities and facilities offered by a members' club. The payment of subscriptions entitles its members to the right of vote and to participate in the management of the affairs of the assessee-company apart from the right to enjoy other facilities.

104. The privilege in the case of the Royal Western India Turf Club was limited to admission into a separate enclosure where they were not disturbed by the intrusion of non-members. They, like the non-members, however, paid an admission fee in that case. The privilege in the present case is extended further to similar admission in the enclosures for viewing and participating in the races, being free. This extra facility in the present case is incidental to membership and is, therefore, completely immune from every taint of commerciality. The character of the subscription paid by the members in this case cannot be said to undergo a change merely because the facilities or the privileges enjoyed by the members of the assessee are more than the facilities and privileges enjoyed by the members of the Royal Western India Turf Club. These facilities and privileges may be more or less in a given case. The test is whether they are referable to the contributions by members as such and are immune from the taint of commerciality. The entrance fees and periodical subscriptions paid by the members for obtaining membership of the assessee-club in the present case and which remain payable even if the racing is stopped or suspended, cannot be said to be received by the assessee out of any profit motive; and they remain immune from the taint of commerciality even when the members are allowed the privilege of a free admission into stands, where non-members would be required to pay, the said members' privileges being clearly referable to their membership of the club. The receipts from members' subscriptions or entrance fees by the assessee cannot, therefore, form part of its assessable income; and the sum of INR 11,000 received by the assessee as subscription from its members is not taxable.

§3. Winning from Lottery or Cross Word Puzzle

105. Section 194 B of Income Tax Act provides for deduction of tax at source in case an amount exceeding INR 10,000 is being paid to any person including an athlete or a sportsperson, by way of winnings from any lottery or crossword puzzle or card game or any other game of any sort. The rate of deduction shall be as prevailing at the time of making payment which may differ from year to year as per Finance Bill.

The three essential elements to constitute a lottery are:

(1) a prize or some advantage in the nature of prize;
(2) distribution based on and depends on chance; and
(3) consideration paid or promised for purchasing the chance.

The winnings can be in cash or in kind. The tax is to be deducted on both before releasing the payment. For example, if an assessee has won a cash prize of INR 1 lakh along with a car, tax is to be collected both on cash prize and the price of the car. It must be kept in mind that any transaction which requires skill for winning the prize is not a lottery. In the case of *ITO v. Malayala Manorma Co. Ltd.* ((2005) 94 ITD 195 (Cochin Taib)) the company conducted a World Cup Forecast Contest. Out of total entries, twenty-two entries were correct and out of them three entries were selected through lottery. The tribunal held that the company was not liable to deduct tax at source from the prizes given as there was no fees for participation, the scheme required application of skill, choosing a personnel out of skilled persons cannot be termed as pure and simple chance.

§4. Winning from Horse Race

106. Section 194 BB of Income Tax Act deals with deduction of tax at source from winning related to horse races. The section is as under:

> Any person, being a bookmaker or a person to whom a license has been granted by the Government under any law for the time being in force for horse racing in any racecourse or for arranging for wagering or betting in any racecourse, who is responsible for paying to any person any income by way of winning from any horse race in an amount exceeding INR 10,000 shall, at the time of payment thereof, deduct income tax thereon at the rate in force.

Therefore, as per this provision, a person making the payment of income by way of winning from horse race an amount exceeding INR 10,000, is responsible for making the deduction of tax at prevailing rate.

§5. Fees for Commission or Brokerage

107. Section 194 H of Income Tax Act deals with deduction of tax at source when paying any commission or brokerage to any resident sportsperson or athlete. The amount of such payment must be exceeding INR 15,000. In case a person making the payment fails to make deduction, it will have serious consequences.

§6. Fees for Professional or Technical Services

108. In the event of making payment to any person like a chartered accountant or a lawyer a sum of money exceeding INR 35,000, tax is to be deducted at a given rate. This is applicable to sportspersons whose gross receipts exceeds the monetary limit prescribed under section 44 AB of Income Tax Act provided that the sum so paid is being claimed as expense while computing total annual income.

§7. Double Tax Avoidance

109. The Central Government enters into an agreement for avoidance of double taxation of income of an assessee under section 90 of the Income Tax Act, 1961. This facility is available for avoidance of double taxation upon income in one's own country and another where such income is derived. An assessee can choose whatever is more beneficial between the Income Tax Act and the Treaty for taxation purposes. This provision is also applicable to sportsperson when income is earned while interacting with the subjects of another country or while being physically present in such another country. Hence, the income of sportspersons is not taxable in the countries with which India has signed a Double Taxation Avoidance Agreement. An amendment made in 2013 in section 90 of Income Tax Act i.e., 2A lays down that only a resident assessee is entitled for a relief under section 90 or if an assessee obtains a certificate from the government of that country. Also the provisions of Chapter X-A of the Act pertaining to sections 95–102 shall apply to an assessee even if they are not beneficial to him. However this subsection 2A shall be effective from 1 April 2016 only.

§8. Cases on Match-Fixing and Taxation

110. In the case of *Manoj Prabhakar v. Assistant Commissioner of Income Tax* ((2004) 84 TTJ (ITA) 625), the assessee was a prominent cricketer, On the basis of information that some cricket players and other individuals were involved in betting and fixing of matches, a search action was conducted under section 132(1) of the IT Act at the residence of the assessee. The Delhi High Court held in this case that 'after going through the entire material,' we find force in the submissions of the learned counsel for the assessee. In the block assessment, undisclosed income can be worked out on the basis of the material found during the course of search. In the present case, no incriminating document or other evidence was found during the course of search from the possession of the assessee to establish link between bookies and players. Further, the addition has been made on the basis of a statement but neither the copy of his statement was provided to the assessee nor was he confronted against the same and, therefore, the evidence against which the assessee was not confronted cannot be taken into consideration because such procedure is against the settled rules of natural justice. In our view, therefore, the addition made on the basis of a statement of particular person on estimate basis cannot be upheld. Accordingly, ground taken by the assessee is allowed, and the additional amount sustained by the learned CIT (A) is deleted.

I. *Ajay Sharma v. Assistant Commissioner of Income Tax*

111. The main parts of the decision are being given hereunder:

> This appeal filed by the assessee arises out of the block assessment made under section 158BC of the IT Act on 30 July 2002.[6] The assessee is a cricketer who

6. ((2006) 101 TTJ (ITAT) 1065).

represented India both in test cricket and one-day games. There was a search under section 132 of the Act in his residential premises on 20 July 2000, as part of the search on some prominent cricket players and individuals who were suspected to be involved in betting and match-fixing or were considered to be close associates of players indulging in these activities. On the basis of the materials collected during the search and on the basis of the CBI report 30 November 2000, regarding match-fixing allegations and the report 24 November 2000, of the Madhavan Commission, and also relying on the statements made by the assessee during and after the search, the Assessment Officer (AO) completed the block assessment determining the total undisclosed income for the block period at INR 5,301,738. This figure included an addition of INR 2,333,000 as receipts for match-fixing activity and several other additions for investment in properties, unexplained expenditure, unexplained credits and so on and so forth. The assessee's appeal before the CIT (A) being only partly successful, a further appeal was filed to the Tribunal on several grounds which have been dealt with in the following paragraphs.

112. While deciding the various grounds taken in the appeal, the court has taken into consideration, as court is bound to, the orders of the IT authorities, the facts marshalled therein, the rival contentions made elaborately before us, the contents of the paper books filed both by the assessee and the Department and the authorities and precedents to which attention of the court was drawn.

113. The first ground, which is in two parts, is directed against the addition of INR 2,333,000 made on account of receipts from match-fixing. The AO adverted to the reference made by the Ministry of Culture, Youth Affairs and Sports to the CBI to conduct enquiries into the allegations of match-fixing going on regarding test and one-day matches and the role played by cricketers, punters, bookmakers (bookies) and related persons. The CBI prepared a report on 31 October 2000, which was made public the very next day, in which the allegations were confirmed. Prominent among the various names mentioned in the report was the name of a certain bookie, popularly known as 'MK' in cricketing circles. The CBI recorded a statement from MK on 28 June 2000. The statement of the assessee was also recorded by the CBI on 28 July 2000. Both these statements were annexed to the Madhavan Commission's report. On the basis of these reports and statements, the AO concluded that the involvement of the assessee in cricket match-fixing dealings was conclusively proved. The assessee has denied all such receipts contending that there is no evidence in support thereof. He has rejected the contention, referring specifically to the fact that Y, one of the bookies involved, had sponsored the visits of the assessee to the UK and the US which 'clearly establishes beyond doubt his close nexus with the bookies' and that a bill of Muskan Travels, seized during the search of the assessee's residence, and the subsequent enquiries made by him conclusively proved that the assessee and his family undertook the trip in May–June 1999, and that it was sponsored by Y. The AO ultimately held that preponderance of probability is sufficient to establish a finding and strict proof, as required in criminal proceedings, is not required in revenue proceedings and on this basis held that the amount of INR 2,333,000 was to be added as the undisclosed income of the assessee.

114. The details of the amount are given in paragraph 2.4 of the assessment order. In all, seven amounts are mentioned. They are as under:

Sl. No	*Year*	*From*	*Amount (Rs.)*	*Reason*
1.	1995	X	15,000	For purchase of car.
2.	1995	-do-	500,000	For introduction to A.
3.	1996	-do-	300,000	Manipulation of ground at Delhi.
4.	1998	Y	500,000	For introduction to A.
5.	1998	-do-	500,000	Share of C.
6.	1995	A/B	500,000	For helping A in his match-fixing.
7.	1995	Z	18,000	Paid to X for Z.
		Total:	2,333,000	

115. On appeal, the assessee contended before the CIT (A) that the addition is based on mere allegations and there is no evidence unearthed during the search to conclusively prove the receipt of money on account of match-fixing, that no opportunity was given to the assessee to cross-examine persons whose statements were relied on by the CBI and the Madhavan Commission and, therefore, the additions ought to be deleted. The CIT (A) rejected the contention, holding that even in block assessment proceedings, the AO is entitled to act on the basis of 'materials' as contrasted with 'evidence' to produce which is the duty of the assessee, that 'material' is wider than 'evidence', that the only condition is that the 'material' relied on by the AO should be relevant to the addition, that the AO is not bound by technical rules of evidence. Therefore, the AO was perfectly justified in adding the amount of INR 2,333,000 as match-fixing amounts.

116. The assessee is in further appeal. The main contention advanced on his behalf is that no evidence has been found relating to match-fixing allegations against the assessee 'as a result of the search' as required by section 158BC, that the addition is based on the statement of the assessee before CBI which is uncorroborated, that the report of the Madhavan Commission which is only an opinion given by an individual on the basis of some preliminary investigations which can at best be only a starting point for further probe, that the statement made by the assessee before the AO on 12 September 2000, only shows that the assessee may be having links with Y but cannot constitute evidence on the basis of which it can be concluded that the assessee was being remunerated for alleged match-fixing activity, that even the statement dated 6 November 2000, was made before the Investigation Wing of the Department and was not corroborated and that the addition, in these circumstances, was based merely on suspicion which cannot be permitted. It was submitted that the assessee has not admitted any receipt of money for match-fixing. The material referred to by the AO in support of the addition cannot form the basis of a block assessment as it has not been found during the search conducted under section 132.

117. The learned CIT Departmental Representative stoutly defended the assessment and filed a paper book in support of his submissions. He filed a copy of the statement of MK made before the CBI and submitted that the statement contained enough evidence to come to the conclusion that the assessee received monies for match-fixing. He contended that the report of the CBI is a public document on which the AO can rightly place reliance in support of the addition. He pointed out that the assessee was confronted with the contents of the report of the CBI on 6 November 2000, when a statement was recorded from him and thus the assessee has been given an opportunity of knowing and explaining the evidence against him in deference to the rules of natural justice. As regards the assessee's links with Y, it was pointed out that the bill of Muskan Travels, seized during the search, established the links and, therefore, it was permissible to draw the inference that the assessee did receive monies from him for match-fixing. The reports of the CBI and Madhavan Commission were 'material' collected by the AO after the search and is relatable to the evidence gathered during the search within the meaning of section 158BB(1) and, therefore, he was entitled to rely upon them for the purpose of making an assessment of the match-fixing receipts. Reliance was also placed on the statement of the assessee made before the CBI (copy filed) in which the assessee was alleged to have made an admission that he was indulging in match-fixing for monetary consideration.

118. In support of the above submissions, the learned CIT (Departmental Representative) relied on the following judgments:

(a) *Pullangode Rubber & Production Co. Ltd. v. State of Kerala.*[7]
(b) *Thiru John.*[8]

Besides the above arguments, the learned CIT (Departmental Representative) strongly relied on the order of the CIT (A).

We have carefully considered the rival submissions in the light of the material placed on record and contents of the paper books filed by both sides. We have also perused carefully the statements of the assessee given before the CBI as well as before the IT authorities. On considering the above and comparing them with the decision of the Delhi Bench of the Tribunal in the case of Manoj Prabhakar, we find that on the preliminary issue regarding the use of the reports of the CBI and Madhavan Commission and the statements made by the assessee under section 132(4) of the Act for the purpose of making an assessment under section 158BC, the matter rests covered by the above decision of the Tribunal. The relevant portion of the order is from paragraph 10 to paragraph 14. The Tribunal has referred to the fact that the addition for match-fixing receipts has been made, *inter alia*, on the basis of X's statement that Manoj Prabhakar promised him to introduce to other international players and some Ranji Trophy players against a payment of a sum of money. In paragraph 11, the Tribunal has noted that the addition was confirmed by the CIT

7. MANU/SC/0386/1971.
8. MANU/SC/0211/1977.

(A) 'after making reference to the report of CBI and after drawing certain inferences'. In paragraph 12, the Tribunal has noted the submission of the assessee that 'the addition is not based on any evidence or material found as a result of search and, therefore, the additions in the block assessment and particularly in view of provisions of sections 158B(b) and 158BB(1) are not justified' and that 'no question was put to the assessee relating to this issue at the time of search or thereafter'. In the same paragraph, there is reference to the CBI report, dated 31 October 2000 and Madhavan Commission report, dated 24 November 2000, which are the same in the case before us. Having noted the evidence on the basis of which the allegation for match-fixing was made and the arguments of the assessee, the Tribunal held in paragraph 14 as under:

> After going through the entire material, we find force in the submissions of the learned Counsel for the assessee. In the block assessment, undisclosed income can be worked out on the basis of the material found during the course of search. In the present case, no incriminating document or other evidence was found during the course of search from the possession of the assessee to establish link between bookies and players. Further, the allegation has been made on the basis of statement of Mr X, but neither the copy of his statement was provided to the assessee nor was he confronted against the same, and, therefore, the evidence against which the assessee was not confronted cannot be taken into consideration because such procedure is against the settled rules of natural justice. In our view, therefore, the addition made on the basis of statement of Mukesh Kumar Gupta or on estimate basis cannot be upheld. Accordingly, ground taken by the assessee is allowed and the addition of INR 965,000 sustained by the learned CIT (A) is deleted.

119. In the case before us, a perusal of the assessment order shows that no such evidence was collected during the search to show that the assessee was taking money for fixing cricket matches. The AO has almost entirely relied on the reports of the CBI and Madhavan Commission for the purpose of making the addition. He has also referred to the statements of the assessee made before the CBI and the IT authorities during the search. So far as the statements made before the IT authorities are concerned, the decision of the Delhi Bench in the case of Manoj Prabhakar says that they cannot constitute evidence found during the search for the purpose of making the block assessment. The statements made by the assessee and X before the CBI or the Madhavan Commission also stand on the same footing, in our opinion. Those statements only constitute the basis for the reports of the above authorities (CBI and Madhavan Commission). In these circumstances, the ruling of the Delhi Bench of the Tribunal in the case of *Manoj Prabhakar* (*supra*) fully applies to the facts of the present case. We, therefore, hold that the addition for alleged match-fixing receipts cannot be supported. We delete the same.

120. The second ground is directed against the addition of INR 581,607 as amount received from BCCI/Delhi District Cricket Association (DDCA)/Ranji Trophy. During the search, documents showing cricketing receipts from BCCI, etc. were seized. The AO conducted post-search enquiries from DDCA, BCCI, etc. and noted that except for the assessment year 1991–1992 the assessee did not declare any cricketing receipts in his returns. The total amount received from BCCI, DDCA, etc. for playing matches, according to the AO, was INR 819,847. These receipts were not shown in the returns and, therefore, the assessee was asked to clarify. The assessee would seem to have stated that the amounts were in the nature of reimbursement of expenses and fees from BCCI towards representing India in tests and one-day cricket matches in India and abroad. He claimed that they were exempt in terms of a circular issued by the Central Board for Direct Taxes (CBDT) on 26 November 1981. He also stated that some of the amounts received from BCCI were credited to his bank account during the financial years 1993–1994 and 1994–1995. The AO however noted that they were not disclosed in the regular returns. In the assessment year 1991–1992, in which year the assessee declared the receipts in the return, the assessee had claimed deduction of 50% for expenses in terms of the above circular. The AO agreed that the amount received and declared in the return for the assessment year 1991–1992 cannot be considered in the block assessment, but as regards the other receipts relating to the other years, he held that they have to be dealt with in the block assessment.

121. Having held so, he proceeded to examine the question whether the assessee is a professional cricketer and concluded that he was, therefore, not entitled to the benefit of the circular which was applicable only to amateur cricketers. He further noted that the circular issued on 26 November 1981, had been withdrawn by another Instruction No. 1945 issued on 22 September 1997. It would appear that the assessee had claimed that the amounts received represented expenditure reimbursed, but the AO found that the assessee was in receipt of allowances for meeting the expenditure separately and, therefore, concluded that the assessee was not separately entitled to any deduction for expenses against the fee receipts. He, therefore, brought the amount of the receipts to tax in the block assessment.

122. The CIT (A) agreed in principle with the AO, but so far as the amount to be assessed is concerned, excluded an amount of INR 238,240 representing logo money, prize money and bonus, and confirmed the addition of the balance of INR 581,607. He further directed the AO to amend the assessment order to exclude what was declared by the assessee as undisclosed income.

We have considered the matter and we are inclined to agree with the view taken by the IT authorities. It is not denied that the materials seized during the search indicated that the assessee was in receipt of monies from BCCI, DDCA, etc. for playing cricket matches. It is also not the case of the assessee before us that he is not a professional cricketer. The argument advanced was that there is no effective addition and that at any rate disallowance of expenditure is not permissible in a block assessment. If there is no effective addition, then obviously the assessee cannot have any grievance. As regards expenditure, the AO has rightly held that the circular of the Board is not applicable to the assessee's case, he being a professional, and hence not entitled to any deduction against the receipts. We agree with the view taken by the CIT (A) and dismiss the ground.

123. The third ground is directed against the addition of INR 30,000 sustained by the CIT (A) out of the addition of INR 405,000 on account of fees for paying in other cricket matches. The AO jotted down a list of matches played by the assessee as 'unofficial' matches during the block period and asked the assessee to inform how much fees he received for playing such matches. The assessee relied on the Circular No. 1432 issued on 26 November 1981, and also stated that he did not remember the amount of fee or prize money. The AO estimated INR 15,000 for each match and for twenty-seven matches, added INR 405,000. On appeal, the CIT (A) held that the money received up to September 1997, cannot be taxed and only a sum of INR 30,000 for the assessment year 2000–2001 and 2001–2002 can be taxed as undisclosed income.

124. We have considered the matter. The reason why the CIT (A) held that the money received up to September 1997, cannot be taxed is that it was on 22 September 1997, that the earlier Circular No. 1432 issued in 1981 was withdrawn by the CBDT and that in the earlier circular there was no distinction made between professional and non-professional cricketers, with the result that the exemption was available up to September 1997. He has, therefore, held the receipts up to that month cannot be taxed and only INR 30,000 relating to the assessment years 2000–2001 and 2001–2002 can be taxed as undisclosed income. However, the basic question is whether any incriminating material or evidence was seized during the search to show that the assessee was in receipt of such monies. The answer should be in the negative because no such material or evidence is adverted to in the block assessment order. All that the AO has said is that a list of unofficial matches in which the assessee played was given to him by the Investigation Wing on 10 October 2000, which is after the date of search. This information can be used by the AO only if some evidence had been unearthed during the search in this regard, so that it can be related to such evidence within the meaning of the amended section 158BB(1). In the absence of any evidence unearthed during the search, the AO cannot make use of the details given by the Investigation Wing. We, therefore, delete the addition of INR 30,000. The ground is allowed.

125. Ground No. 4 is directed against the addition of INR 105,000 sustained by the CIT (A) out of the addition of INR 210,000 made by the AO on account of receipts from Padiham Cricket Club (PCC) of England. The claim of the assessee, rejected by the AO and the CIT (A), is that the entire amount related to expenditure on account of boarding and lodging and hence not taxable. During the search, a work permit allowing the assessee to play in England for PCC was found and seized. A contract of employment dated 4 February 2000, was also seized. The AO noted there from that the salary of the assessee was GBP 3,500. When the assessee was asked as to the accountability of the receipt, he stated on affidavit that the receipt was in the nature of reimbursement of the expenses on boarding and lodging and did not have any element of income. Another affidavit was also filed stating that the amount was paid to him on weekly basis after deduction of all applicable taxes. The AO was of the view that the two affidavits were contradictory to each other, since if there was no income element in the receipt, there would have been no liability to deduct taxes. He, therefore, held that the amount of GBP 3,500 was taxable in the financial year 2000–2001. In the absence of any proof of payment of taxes in UK by way of deduction at source, he refused to give credit for any TDS. The entire amount, converted into Indian rupees, came to INR 210,000 which was brought to tax.

126. On appeal, the CIT (A) held that that the facts showed that the assessee received monies for the exercise of his profession and so the amount was taxable, but held that the gross amount cannot be taxed and some allowance has to be made for expenses, which he estimated at 50% of the gross receipt and thus sustained an addition of INR 105,000.

The argument of the assessee before us is that the amount was received by way of reimbursement of expenses and hence not income, that even the contract with the PCC confirmed this, that since the assessee was out of India for twenty-two weeks from April 2000 to September 2000, he could not have disclosed the amount as income even assuming that it was his income and that at any rate according to section 158BA(3) the income is assessable only in 2001–2002. The learned CIT (Departmental Representative), on the other hand, placed very strong reliance on the decision of the CIT (A) and his reasoning.

127. On a careful consideration of the rival contentions, we are of the view that the order of the CIT (A) requires no interference. We have seen the work permit which is in the paper book which says that the 'salary/remuneration GBP 3,500 in total'. We have also examined the contract of employment with PCC dated 4 February 2000, which is also compiled in the paper book. In all, there are eight clauses in it, none of which speaks of any payment to the assessee. However, Clause 2 says that the assessee 'is to make his own way from his home to all league and cup fixtures', which suggests that expenditure on conveyance will have to be borne by the assessee himself. But, the expenditure referred to in this clause as well as other incidental expenditure incurred to earn the remuneration have been taken care of by the CIT (A) by estimating 50% of the fees of GBP 3,500. No case has been made out for further relief. We, therefore, uphold the decision of the CIT (A) and dismiss the ground.

128. The fifth ground is directed against the addition of INR 60,000 sustained by the CIT (A). The case of the assessee is that the income belongs to his wife for services rendered by her and has been duly accounted for in her return of income filed for the relevant financial year. In the course of her statement made under section 132(4), the assessee's wife stated that she had received the above amount from a firm by name Video Track, owned by her neighbour for rendering administrative services. But, her neighbour would appear to have stated that it was the assessee who rendered some services to his firm and requested him to pay the remuneration to his (assessee's) wife since he cannot accept any remuneration, being a government employee. The AO, after referring to the statements of the neighbour and the wife of the assessee, came to the conclusion that the amount was due to the assessee for services rendered by him to Video Track and, therefore, the same was includible in the block assessment in two years – INR 40,000 for the assessment year

2000–2001 and INR 20,000 for the assessment year 2001–2002. The CIT (A) having confirmed the same, the assessee is in further appeal before the Tribunal.

129. On a careful consideration of the matter, we are of the view that the addition cannot be made in a block assessment, since no material or evidence has been seized during the search to show that the amount was paid to the assessee for services rendered by him to Video Track. It is only on the basis of statements made by the assessee's wife and Mr Kohli during the search that the AO has come to the conclusion that the amount is taxable in the assessee's hands, disbelieving the claim of the assessee. This is not a matter that can be tackled in a block assessment and is perhaps to be dealt with only in the regular assessment. We, therefore, delete the addition and allow the ground.

130. The sixth ground is directed against the addition of INR 53,000 sustained by the CIT (A) out of an addition of INR 70,000 made by the AO on account of amount spent by the assessee in the purchase of a car. A perusal of the assessment order shows that it was only during the post-search enquiries that it came to light that the assessee had purchased a second-hand Maruti car during the later part of 1991 for INR 70,000 paid in cash. After examining the assessee and seller of car in the course of the assessment proceedings, the AO rejected the assessee's claim and brought the amount to tax for the assessment year 1992–1993. The appeal to the CIT (A) being unsuccessful, the assessee is in further appeal before the Tribunal.

131. This is again a matter for consideration in a regular assessment proceeding and not to be dealt with in a block assessment, as nothing has been found during the search to show that the assessee has paid the amount of INR 70,000 in cash and out of his undisclosed income. Even the AO refers only to 'post-search enquiries' as the basis for the addition. In the absence of any evidence found during the search, the post-search enquiries cannot be acted upon by the AO even as material or information relatable to any evidence found during the search, within the meaning of section 158BB(1). The IT authorities were not, therefore, justified in taxing the amount in the block assessment. We delete the same and allow the ground.

132. The next ground, ground No. 7, is directed against the addition of INR 100,000 received by the assessee on account of sponsorship money received from Sanspareils Green Land Limited (SGL). The amount was paid to the assessee on 1 March 2000, as endorsement money, which he declared in his return for the assessment period 2000–2001 which was filed after the date of search, i.e., on 12 October 2000. The return was due on June 2000. The AO also noted that a sum of INR 100,000 received by the assessee from SGL on 16 August 1995, had not been disclosed in the regular return but was offered for taxation in the block period, for the assessment period 1996–1997. The assessee was, therefore, called upon to explain why the amount of INR 100,000 received during the financial year 1999–2000 shall not be taxed in the block period. The assessee stated that the return for the assessment period 2000–2001 could not be filed within the time prescribed as he was away in UK from April 2000, till September 2000, and that he had no intention of not filing the return. The AO rejected the explanation and invoked section 158BB(1) (ca) and brought the amount to tax in the block assessment. The CIT (A) having upheld the action of the AO, the assessee is in further appeal before the Tribunal.

133. The argument advanced on behalf of the assessee was that the receipt was admitted by the assessee, that tax was deducted at source from the same, that since the assessee was not in India during April to September 2000, he could not file the return, that he filed it immediately on his return to India from UK and that the assessee cannot be said to have concealed the income. Alternately, the learned CIT (Departmental Representative), besides strongly relying on the orders of the IT authorities, relied also on the judgment of the Madras High Court in *B. Noorsingh v. Union of India*[9] and the order of the Mumbai Bench of the Tribunal in *Overseas Chinese Cuisine (India) (P) Ltd. v. Asstt.*[10]

134. On a careful consideration of the matter, we see no reason to interfere. The fact remains that the assessee received the amount of INR 1 lakh in March 2000, and the same has to be included in the return for the assessment year 2000–2001. This return ought to have been filed on or before 30 June 2000. The return was not filed within the due date. It may be that the assessee was away from India, but even so, a return can be filed in India within the due date either by obtaining the assessee's signature by sending the return to him or by getting the return signed by a person duly authorized by him in this behalf under section 140(a)(ii) of the Act. It is not an impossibility. At any rate, section 158BB(1)(ca) is not concerned with the reasons for not filing the return within the due date. It has been rightly invoked, in our opinion. We, therefore, uphold the addition. However, the same amount cannot be taxed twice, once in the block assessment and again in the regular assessment. Apparently, the assessee has included the amount in the regular return filed on 17 October 2000. The IT authorities will have to devise a method by which the double taxation of the same amount is avoided. The addition made in the block assessment is upheld and the ground is rejected.

135. The ground No. 8 is directed against the addition of INR 23,000 on account of alleged receivable amounts. The addition has been made on the basis of a loose sheet found during the search in which the assessee, in his own handwriting, has noted down certain amounts against the names of certain persons as 'lena hai'. These amounts totalled to INR 23,000. In the course of the post-search enquiries, the assessee admitted that these were amounts receivable by him from those persons for playing cricket matches. Later, he contradicted the statement and said that he has to pay the amounts to those persons. The AO rejected the later statement and brought the amount to tax as undisclosed income, which was confirmed by the CIT (A). After going through the facts and the rival arguments, and taking into account that the addition has been made on the basis of evidence found during the search and the fact that the loose sheet is in the handwriting of the assessee, and rejecting his afterthought that the amounts are payable by him, we hold that the addition has been rightly made.

---

9. ((2000) 160 CTR (Mad) 124): ((1999) 105 Taxman 101 (Mad)).
10. *CIT* ((1996) 55 TTJ (Mumbai)(TM) 304): ((1996) 56 ITD 67 (Mumbai) (TM)).

§9. Training Allowance

136. The training allowance is paid to the club or association in which the player carried out his last amateur or junior sporting activity by the club with whom the first professional contract was made.

§10. Regional Tax on Company Income

137. There is no such comparable tax in India; however, there are some regional taxes which may affect sporting activity. Regional or local taxes are also taxes of general application and except some instances are generally applicable to all cases or in other words these are laws of general application.

§11. Amateur Clubs

138. These clubs generally do not carry on any commercial activity and are run on no-profit-no-loss basis. The Bombay High Court has dealt with the matter in a case before it relating to the activities of Gymkhana Club.

I. *Deccan Gymkhana v. Commissioner of Income-Tax*

139. The main portions of the above case are given hereunder with minor modifications.

The Income-tax Appellate Tribunal has referred to the court, the following questions arising out of its order dated 10 February 1988:

(1) Whether, on the facts and in the circumstances of the case, the Tribunal was justified in holding that the assessee-club was not a charitable institution within the meaning of section 2(15) of the Income-tax Act, 1961?
(2) Whether, on the facts and in the circumstances of the case, the income of the assessee was entitled to exemption either under section 11 of the Income-tax Act, 1961 read with section 2(15) of the Income-tax Act, or under the principle of mutuality?

Both the above two references raise a common question of law and, therefore, they were heard together and disposed of by the common judgment.

The basic issue which arises for determination in the above references is: whether the assessee-trust and the activities carried on by it come under the definition of 'charitable purpose' under section 2(15) of the Act and, therefore, whether the assessee-Deccan Gymkhana Trust was entitled to exemption under section 11 of the Income-tax Act.

A. Facts of the Case

140. The assessee is a society registered under the Societies Registration Act, 1860. It was registered on 5 October 1906. It is a public trust. The objects of the society are described in Clause 3 of Part I of the constitution. The main object was to develop and promote gymnastic games (sports) and sportsmanship. The assessee was assessed for the assessment year 1973–1974 by the Income-tax Officer on 20 October 1975, granting exemption under section 11 of the Act. However, the Commissioner of Income-tax initiated proceedings under section 263 of the Act and came to the conclusion that Deccan Gymkhana Trust was not a public charitable institution and was not entitled to exemption under section 11 of the Act. Against the order under section 263, the assessee went in appeal to the Tribunal. By its order dated 20 October 1978, the Tribunal agreed with the Commissioner of Income-tax and dismissed the appeal. The Tribunal disallowed the application of the assessee under section 256(1).

141. The High Court, vide order under section 256(2) of the Act directed the Tribunal to refer the two questions, above quoted, to the High Court and accordingly, by the statement of case dated 18 March 1983, the above two questions were referred to this court by the Tribunal. To complete the chronology of events, it may be mentioned that for the subsequent assessment years 1974–1975, 1976–1977 up to 1979–1980, the Income-tax Officer disallowed the assessee's claim for exemption. However, in appeal, the first appellate authority came to the conclusion that the assessee was entitled to exemption under section 11. Being aggrieved, the Department appealed to the Tribunal. In the Tribunal, there was a difference of opinion between the learned Judicial Member and the Accountant Member. The learned Judicial Member held that the assessee was not a charitable trust, whereas the learned Accountant Member held that the assessee was a public trust and its objects were of a charitable nature. On such difference, the matter was referred by the president under section 255(4) to the Third Member, who opined that the assessee did not fulfil the requirements of section 2(15) and, therefore, disallowed the claim for exemption under section 11. Following the opinion of the majority, the assessee lost the matter. Ultimately, the matter has come to this court by way of reference to answer the above two questions.

142. The entire controversy in this case has taken place in view of Clause 3 of the constitution of Deccan Gymkhana. Clause 3 has sub-clauses A to I. Sub-clauses A to I of Clause 3 are quoted herein below:

(a) to foster and develop (promote) gymnastic (sports) games and sportsmanship;
(b) to make arrangements, as far as possible, for all kinds of Indian and foreign games and systems of sports;
(c) to make efforts in the direction that India should participate in international sports competitions;
(d) to give systematic shape to Indian games and to foster and popularize them;
(e) to publish useful literature on gymnastics, games and sportsmanship and to circulate the same;

(f) to acquire and hold immovable property;
(g) to plan a colony for the members of the society and to make other arrangements ancillary to it;
(h) to raise funds and loan, to invest amounts and advance loans, etc.;
(i) to do all other things helpful in the achievement of the above objects.

143. The issue which arises is in view of sub-clauses F and G quoted above. According to the Department, sub-clauses A to F show that the object of the society was to promote sports, games and sportsmanship, but with the introduction of sub-clauses F, G and H, the assessee cannot claim exemption under section 11 as a charitable trust. Alternately, according to the assessee, sub-clauses A to E constituted the dominant object, whereas sub-clauses F, G and H constituted incidental objects. That, in the alternative, it was contended that in any event, sub-clauses F, G and H were never intended to be implemented; that these sub-clauses were never in fact, implemented. That, subclauses F, G and H was introduced in the light of the situation which prevailed in Pune in 1906. That, after 1923, no colony has been set up by the assessee. That, in 1993, in fact, Subclause G has been deleted and the Department conferred registration under section 12A of the Act for the assessment year 1995–1996.

144. Before considering the legal submissions, the following historical facts are required to be quoted. In 1906, the city of Pune was a cultural and sports centre. Around that period, the city of Pune produced eminent freedom fighters like Chiplunkar, Agarkar and Lokmanya Tilak, who believed that the youth should take part in the freedom movement and for that purpose, the youth required strong physique. They believed that a sports environment was required to be created and with that object in mind, these leaders, fired by idealism, brought into existence an educational society known as Deccan Education Society. This society started its school known as New English School in Pune and, later on, this society set up a college which is Ferguson College. Ferguson College was in the old city of Pune earlier. At that time, in 1906, on the western side of the Mutha river, the area had no inhabitation. Lokmanya Tilak was not only interested in education, but he equally emphasized physical education, gymnastics, sports, games and sportsmanship. Lokmanya Tilak and the band of enthusiastic young men started an institute on 5 October 1906, which was registered as 'Deccan Gymkhana, Pune'. This institute celebrated its diamond jubilee in October 1966. The first general secretary of the institute was N.C. Kelkar. However, Deccan Gymkhana was beyond the city limits. It was on the other side of the river, as stated above. On the western side of the river, there was hardly any inhabitation. The area was quite isolated. To have a Gymkhana in an isolated area having no residential population, would have been a failure. With a view to overcome these difficulties, the persons running the Gymkhana at that time considered a suggestion to have a colony so that sports lovers could reside around the Gymkhana and it was with that object that a housing society was formed and lands were allocated to the members who constructed their own houses on the allocated lands. At that time, the Gymkhana was beyond the municipal limits and under a panchayat. It is in the light of this historical background that one has to read sub-clauses F, G and H.

B. Grounds

145. At the outset, we wish to clarify that we are basing this judgment only to the facts and circumstances of this case. That, we are reading the aforestated sub-clauses F, G and H in the light of the historical facts enumerated above. The counsel for the assessee, submitted that there was a difference between objects of the trust and the powers of the trustees. He contended that sub-clauses A to E indicate the objects of the public trust – Deccan Gymkhana, whereas sub-clauses F, G and H only indicate the power of the trustees to acquire and hold immovable properties, to plan a colony for the members of the society and to raise funds. He contended that the powers of the trustees should not be mixed with the dominant object of the trust as indicated by Clauses 3-A to 3-F. He contended that the Gymkhana was not formed in order to deal in immovable properties. He contended that in the light of the above historical facts, the youth was required to be brought to an area which was a desolate area in 1906, for sports and cultural activities. He contended that in 1906 there were logistical problems. He pointed out from the decision of the Tribunal in the aforestated historical facts to show that in 1906, in this area, there was no electricity. It is in this light that in the objects it was decided to state that a colony would be planned for the members of the society and in the light of those facts, it can never be stated that sub-clauses F, G and H constituted the objects of the trust. He, therefore, submitted that these sub-clauses indicated the powers of the trustees only. In the alternative, he submitted that one has to apply the test of the dominant object.

146. He submitted that the dominant object of Deccan Gymkhana was never to construct houses for the members. That, at the highest, sub-clauses F, G and H refers to incidental objects. He contended that the colony came up only in 1923. That, thereafter, no colony has been put up and in 1993, subclause G has been deleted. He further pointed out that the Tribunal erred in coming to the conclusion that no restriction existed on the trust to apply the income only for sports. Mr Inamdar contended that the majority view of the Tribunal proceeds on the basis that as long as Subclause G existed, nothing prevented the trust from planning one more colony and, in the circumstances the majority view of the Tribunal was that the trust was not entitled to exemption. Mr Inamdar, therefore, contended that keeping in mind the historical facts enumerated above read with the fact that after 1923 till today, no colony has been set up and that in 1993, Subclause G stood deleted, the apprehension in the mind of the Tribunal that the trust would set up one more colony was ill-founded. He further pointed out that the Tribunal has failed to notice a clause under the trust deed dated 4 January 1945, which states as follows:
When the permanent reserve fund has been built to the extent of INR 75,000, the trustees shall hand over surplus to the Gymkhana for being utilized in the cause of sports.

It was, therefore, contended that it was not open to the trust to apply the surplus income for any business and that the trust was duty-bound to apply the income only for the cause of sport and, therefore, the Department was wrong in saying that under the trust deed, there was no restriction to apply the income only to sports. Large numbers of decisions were cited by Mr Inamdar and Mr Desai on behalf of the respective parties.

147. As stated above, we are confining our judgment to the facts of this case. Section 2(15), as it stood at the relevant time, defines the words 'charitable purpose' to include relief of the poor, education, medical relief and the advancement of any other object of general public utility, not involving the carrying on of any activity for profit. In the case of *Thiagarajar Charities v. Add. CIT*[11] it has been held that the correct test to be applied was whether the predominant object of the activity was to subserve the charitable purpose or to earn profit. Where profit making was the predominant object of the activity, the purpose would cease to be a charitable purpose. But, where the predominant object of the activity was to carry out the charitable purpose and not to earn profit, it would not lose the character of a charitable purpose merely because some profit arises from the activity. In that judgment, it has been further laid down that there is a difference between the objects of the trust and the power of the trustees. In that matter, the Supreme Court had to construe two clauses in the constitution of the trust. In that matter, under Clause 1(g) the words were as follows (page 1021):

> To engage in … and assist and promote rural reconstruction work, cottage industry and all other matters incidental thereto … ..

The other clause in the trust deed was Clause 7(e) which reads as follows (page 1021):

> 7(e) To invest in any business undertaking of whatever nature … ..

148. It was held by the Supreme Court that the above Clause 1(g) was an object clause, whereas Clause 7(e), referred to above, indicated the power of the trustees to invest in business. That, the predominant object was in Clause 1(g). In the circumstances, it was held by the Supreme Court, applying the above test, that Clause 1(g) came within the ambit of the words 'relief of the poor, education and medical relief' under section 2(15) of the Income-tax Act, and not to earn profit and, in the circumstances, the fourth limb of section 2(15) stood excluded. According to us, the judgment of the Supreme Court squarely applies to the facts of our case.

149. Basically, one has to read the objects under the constitution in the light of the facts of the case. In this case also, as stated hereinabove, we have to keep in mind, the historical perspective behind the establishment of the institution and if one keeps the historical background in mind, then it is clear that Subclauses A to E constituted the object whereas sub-clauses F, G and H gave power to the trustee to plan a colony for the members so that those members could take part in the promotion of sports, gymnastics and sportsmanship. The colony was set up only in 1923. Once the locality developed, the assessee has not put up any further colonies. In 1993,

11. (MANU/SC/0651/1997).

Subclause G has been deleted. Therefore, keeping in mind the peculiar historical facts of this case, we are of the view that the majority view of the Tribunal was erroneous; that they erred in construing Clause 3G as an object of the trust. We hold that there was no profit motive involved in this case vide the said clause and, therefore, the assessee had fulfilled the requirement of section 2(15) of the Income Tax Act and, consequently, they were entitled to exemption under section 11 for the assessment years 1973–1974, 1974–1975, 1976–1977 up to 1979–1980.

It was held that in the facts and circumstances of the case the Tribunal was not justified in holding that the assessee-club was not a charitable institution within the meaning of section 2(15) of the Income Tax Act, 1961. The income of the assessee was entitled to exemption under section 11 of the Income Tax Act 1961, read with section 2(15) of the Income Tax Act.

§12. Indirect Tax on Sports

150. The indirect tax structure for sports differentiates the sports activity in entrepreneurial or official and for profit/charitable. There is preferential treatment for the officially run or recognized sports activities and for non-profit organizations. Alternately, sports activities by others are taxed. The persons and entities to whom these exemptions are not applicable have to pay Goods and Services Tax (GST) on reverse charge for sponsorships received, on amounts earned for coaching, refereeing or umpiring, for managing a team, or for playing in an event. They have to pay GST on any services provided to anybody, even to a recognized sports body. They have to pay GST on coaching or training provided for recreational sports. The GST for all these is 18% of the amount charged. The GST exemptions are given under items 53, 68 and 80 of notification 12/2017-CT (rate).

I. Sponsorship Services

151. The services provided by way of sponsorship are exempt from GST under following circumstances (Item 53). Services provided:

(a) by a National Sports Federation, or its affiliated federations, where the participating teams or individuals represent any district, State, zone or country;
(b) by Association of Indian Universities, Inter-University Sports Board, School Games Federation of India, All India Sports Council for the Deaf, Paralympic Committee of India or Special Olympics Bharat;
(c) by the Central Civil Services Cultural and Sports Board;
(d) as part of national games, by the IOA; or
(e) under the Panchayat Yuva Kreeda Aur Khel Abhiyaan Scheme.

Services provided to a recognized sports body (Item 68):

(a) by an individual as a player, referee, umpire, coach or team manager for participation in a sporting event organized by a recognized sports body;
(b) by another recognized sports body.

Services by way of training or coaching in recreational activities relating to (80):

(a) arts or culture; or
(b) sports by charitable entities registered under section 12AA of the Income-tax Act.

Thus, sponsorship of sports events organized by certain specified recognized bodies are exempted from GST; coaching, being umpire or referee, managing a team, or playing in an event organized by a recognized sports body; all services provided by a recognized sports body to another recognized sports body;

Coaching or training for recreational sports, by a charitable entity registered under section 12AA of the Income-Tax Act.

152. However, GST is imposed on sports at the local level in the form of an 18% levy on sports coaching and training and all other sports-related services. Earlier, in the service tax regime that prevailed until June 2017, coaching for recreational sports was exempted from tax. This changed with the advent of GST. Now the exemption for such coaching for recreational sports is restricted to charitable entities that are exempted from income tax under section 12AA of the Income-Tax Act. First, it is a rare charitable entity that enters the arena of sports coaching. Second, the player is the person who bears the burden of indirect taxation.

153. A competent coaching business needs to engage skilled coaches and to work on excellence in its methods of coaching. A low turnover does not enable this; usually, the coaching organization will cross the exemption threshold for GST and has to add 18% to its pricing. As the main input for a coaching business is the services of individual coaches, there is hardly any input tax credit to be set off, and therefore the rationale for fixing 18% rather than 12% is not clear: it seems to be an oversight rather than a well-considered decision.

154. As for the equipment used, imports of equipment are taxed at a rate that comes to about 40% of the supplier's price. To this the wholesale and retail margins and taxes are added, making sports goods much more expensive for the 'non-official' trainer, that is, who is not one of the official sports bodies.

155. An eminent sportsperson is also a non-official trainer if he sets up an academy. No tax exemptions are available for such a person, though his contributions in sports training may be immense. Inevitably, part of the cost has to be borne by the trainees. The revenue from GST and customs duties on sports may not be significant at a macro level and the government can reap considerable public good by foregoing it. A blanket exemption for indirect taxes on sports will be a rational approach and would give welcome relief to many struggling sporting aspirants.

§13. CUSTOM DUTIES

156. Sports goods are comprehensively covered under heading 9506 of the Harmonized System of Nomenclature-based customs classification, which covers articles and equipment for general physical exercise, gymnastics, athletics, other sports (including table-tennis) or outdoor games, not specified or included elsewhere; swimming pools and paddling pools. The rate of customs duty for these goods is 20% basic customs duty plus 18% customs Integrated Goods and Services Tax (IGST), which is charged on a value that includes the basic customs duty. Therefore, if the value of an item is 100, the basic customs duty is 20; the value for calculating customs IGST is 120. Thus, the customs IGST will be INR 21.60, rounded off to INR 22. The customs duties on import of sports goods and related items and equipment will therefore come to over 40%. This is the 'tariff rate', which means the rate before applying any exemption that may be notified.

I. Exemption on Custom Duties

157. Exemptions from customs duties are available for import of sports goods. These are as follows.

A. Customs Exemption for Recognized Bodies

158. Customs duty exemptions are available for certain imports for sports under notification 146/1994-Customs. Under the first item of the notification, there is a broad-based exemption for most sports-related goods mentioned below, if imported by certain agencies:

(a) sports goods, sports equipment, sports requisites, including synthetic playing surfaces, fitness equipment, sport's medicine, sport's apparel;
(b) spares, accessories and consumables relating to goods covered by (a) above.

These goods are imported into India by:

(a) SAI or Sports Authority of concerned State, for use in a national or international championship or competition, to be held in India or abroad or for the purposes of training; or
(b) a NSF for its own use or for the use of its State/District Affiliate Associations, in a national or international championship or competition, to be held in India or abroad or for the purposes of training, under a certificate issued by the SAI; or
(c) the Services Sports Control Board (SSCB) in the Ministry of Defence for their own use or for use in a national or international championship or competition, to be held in India or abroad or for the purposes of training, under a certificate issued by the SSCB.

159. The importer, at the time of clearance of the goods, must produce a certificate to the Assistant Commissioner of Customs or Deputy Commissioner of Customs from an officer not below the rank of a Director in the SAI or Secretary, in the SSCB for its own imports or Director of Sports Authority of concerned State indicating:

(i) the name and address of the importer and the description, quantity and value of the said goods; and
(ii) that the said goods are required for specified purpose.

160. Thus, sports goods and requisites are exempted from customs duties if imported by the SAI, sports federations at the national level or their State/district level affiliates, or the SSCB under the Ministry of Defence. The goods must be meant for use in training purposes or competitions at national or international level, and this has to be certified by an officer in the organization, of the specified rank. There is also an exemption for artificial surfaces and synthetic tracks if imported under a specific central scheme for laying these surfaces or tracks.

B. Customs Exemptions for Eminent Sportspersons

161. In addition to the exemptions for imports by recognized sports bodies, the notification 146/1994-Customs also exempts basic customs duty on imports of specified goods by any 'sportsperson of outstanding eminence' for purposes of training. The notification 86/2017-Customs exempts IGST on the same imports. Conditions of both exemptions include a certificate from the Department of Youth Affairs and Sports that the importer is a sportsperson of outstanding eminence and that the items are 'essential for training purposes of the importer'. The items allowed are specified for various sports: for example, shuttlecocks, racquets and racquet strings for badminton; balls and cues for billiards/snooker, and so on. In the case of shooters, the exemption notifications carry a proviso that the importer is to produce a certificate from the National Rifle Association that he is a 'renowned shooter', and the term is defined. This serves instead of the certificate from the Department of Youth Affairs and Sports.

162. In the case of *Nathaniel Karuna Hudson v. G.O.I*, decided by the Madras High Court, the imports made by two shooters who had a record of participation in national and international competitions were denied the exemption under notification 146/1994-Customs at Chennai port for want of a certificate from the Department of Youth Affairs and Sports. The importers approached the High Court for relief. In its judgment on the writ petition filed by the importers, the Madras High Court observed that the proviso in the case of shooters was inserted to forestall such a requirement:

> 'If the interpretation given by the 4th respondent has to be accepted, no eminent sportsman in this particular field would ever be able to import any of the ammunition of arms for the training purpose and he will be languishing in the

corridors of Department of Youth Affairs for years together for obtaining appropriate certification.'[12] Thus, for shooters, a certificate from the National Rifle Association suffices, and the term 'renowned shooter', which is the language that the said association has to use to certify the importer, has been defined in the notification. Further, the exemption is only for imports for the personal use of the eminent sportsperson. If he sets up a training class for other players, customs duty will be payable.

163. The customs exemptions for goods imported for training of aspirants and for use in competitive events are available only to the SAI and recognized sports federations. For eminent sportspersons, the exemption is allowed for goods imported for their personal training only. For others, like neighbourhood sporting clubs, there is no exemption. In GST, the exemption is for recognized sporting bodies and non-profit organizations. There is no exemption from GST for the neighbourhood clubs or coaches or the larger privately run sporting organizations. All these have to pay GST on sponsorship received, and on coaching fees, amounts charged for umpiring, refereeing, managing a team and any other services provided to anybody.

§14. Deduction in Respect of Donations

164. Deduction in tax is available under section 80G of the Income Tax Act, 1961 in respect of donations to sport bodies. The sum on which tax deduction is available can be 'any sum paid by the assessee being a company', in previous year as donation to the IOA or to any other association or institution as notified by the Central Government for:

– the development of infrastructure for sports and games; or
– the sponsorship of sports and games in India.

The explanation 4 to section 80G provides that 'For the purpose of this section, an association or institution having as its objects the control, supervision, regulation or encouragement in India of such games or sports as the Central Government may, by notification in the official Gazette specify on this behalf, shall be deemed to be an institution established in India for a charitable purpose.' The relevant provision is as follows:

Section 80G of the Income Tax Act provides as follows:

(1) In computing the total income of an assessee, there shall be deducted, in accordance with and subject to the provisions of this section.
(2) The sums referred to in subsection (1) shall be the following, namely:
 (a) any sums paid by the assessee in the previous year as donations to;
 (b) the National Sports Fund to be set up by the Central Government;

12. *Nathaniel Karuna Hudson v. G.O.I.*, MF, DR, 2018 (361) ELT 87 (Mad. HC).

(c) any sums paid by the assessee, being a company, in the previous year as donations to the IOA or to any other association or institution established in India, as the Central Government may, having regard to the prescribed guidelines, by notification in the Official Gazette, specify on this behalf for:
 - the development of infrastructure for sports and games; or
 - the sponsorship of sports and games, in India; Explanation 4. – For the purposes of this section, an association or institution having as its object the control, supervision, regulation or encouragement in India of such games or sports as the Central Government may, by notification in the Official Gazette, specify on this behalf, shall be deemed to be an institution established in India for a charitable purpose.

Explanation 5. – For the removal of doubts, it is hereby declared that no deduction shall be allowed under this section in respect of any donation unless such donation is of a sum of money.

§15. Contribution to National Sports Development Fund

165. The National Sports Development Fund (NSDF) was constituted in 1998 under the Charitable Endowment Act, 1890 with initial contribution of the Union Government for promotion of sports and games in the country. All contributions (from within and outside the country) to this fund have been extended to 100% exemption from Income Tax under section 80G. To begin with, the government made a contribution of INR 2 crores as seed money during the period 1998–1999. Further, the contribution of the government is on matching basis to the contributions received from any other source. The fund is managed by a council constituted by the Central Government along with the Union Minister for Youth Affairs and Sports as the chairperson. The day-to-day working of the fund is managed by an Executive Committee headed by a Joint Secretary, Department of Sports, MYAS. The fund helps sportspersons excel by providing them opportunities to train under coaches of international repute with technical, scientific and psychological support and giving them exposure to international competitions. The fund also provides financial assistance for development of infrastructure and other activities for promotion of sports. Contribution can be made for establishment and upgradation of sports infrastructure; for promotion of specific sports disciplines; for training of specific sportspersons; for research projects in sports; for upgradation of SAI centres; and for sports promotion in general. It is permissible for a donor to indicate a project along with any specific location/aspect for funding and also an executing agency for execution of the project, if the amount being contributed is INR 5 lakh (Rupees five lakh) and above. Fund accepts contributions from statutory bodies, international organizations, private and public corporate sectors, trusts, societies and individuals.

§16. Principles for Economic Controls Over Clubs

166. It is binding on all the NSFs, Associations, State Olympic Associations and other units affiliated to the IOA to forward to IOA their annual report and audited statement of account every year. The affiliated units to also conduct their election as and when due or in special circumstances as and when directed by the IOA. However in the elections held by all or any of the unit (s) to reconstitute the Executive Council or to elect new office-bearers, the date and time of the election to be intimated to the IOA and the President of IOA shall nominate an election observer to attend the election meeting and who shall submit his or her report to the President of IOA for appropriate action. The non-compliance of these requirements may result in disaffiliation of the defaulting units by the IOA General Assembly on the recommendations of the Executive Council. All the and State Olympic Associations are required to forward to the IOA a copy of their current and valid Constitution along with amendments if any. Important and significant information and statistics shall also be likewise supplied by them to the IOA from time to time.

There is also a control by taxation of the income of the sporting clubs. For example, the dealing of a club with non-members take place in the ordinary course of business carried on with a view to earning profits as in any other commercial concern. Some of the dealings of the company with its members take place in the ordinary course of business and hence certain receipts are taxable. The club can give its members the same or similar amenities as it gives to non-members. Those facilities are given to members and non-members alike for a price. Thus, the receipts in respect of dealings which disclosed the profit-earning motive and which are tainted with commerciality being in the nature of commercial dealings are subject to taxation.

Chapter 4. Principles of Tort Law

§1. Civil Liability

167. Tort is a civil wrong rather than a criminal wrong which results in some form of injury to person or damage to property giving rise to a claim of compensation. The relationship of sports with tort law is very peculiar as sport activity is generally carried out in the presence of referees or umpires and whose decision on the field is considered as final except to internal appeal procedure. However growing awareness of sportspersons about rights and duties has brought question of compensation for injuries into litigation in the courts.

168. The law of tort is resorted to claim compensation for injuries suffered because of the fault of other players in sporting events. The purpose is that a player at fault must contribute towards the loss of income, pain and suffering of an injured player. The main causes of action which are resorted to are either trespass to person or negligence of the opponent sportsman which is related to and has caused the injury. Other causes can be that match officials losing control of the game or the club which was not able to maintain the playground in safe playing condition or manage the spectators.

169. In *Nawal Kishore v. Rameshwar* (AIR 1955 ALL 954 at p. 585), it was observed that there is no statutory or general law of tort in this country and an Act of England on a specific area of tort may not be applicable. The courts of this country act on the principle of equity, justice and good conscience in matters which are not covered by statute and rely upon the principles of English Law to find out what the rule of justice, equity and good conscience is. Any technical rule or statutory law of England is not as such based on the principles of equity, justice and good conscience, unless it appears to be so to the judge deciding the same. For example, with respect to the concept of apportionment of damages, there is no central legislation corresponding to the Law Reform (Contributory Negligence) Act, 1945 of England but the Kerala Legislature has taken a lead by passing The Kerala Torts (Miscellaneous Provisions) Act, 1976. Thus, with respect to judgment and precedents of English courts, US courts and Australian courts, courts in India have applied the principles based on principles of equity, justice and good conscience. The scope and extent of liability under tort is much wider than criminal liability as tort does not require the existence of intention to cause harm.

§2. Criminal Liability

I. Assaults on Other Players

170. The assault on other players is dealt with under Indian Penal Code (IPC) and under tort by trespass to person or negligence. Section 351 of IPC defines 'assault' as 'whoever makes any gesture or any preparation intending or knowing it to be likely that such gesture or preparation will cause any person present to apprehend that he who makes that gesture or preparation is about to use criminal force to that person, is said to commit assault'. The most common form of trespass in sports and games is battery. In negligence, it is alleged that opponent failed to observe the normal and necessary standard of care owed to the claimant and consequently injuries were caused. To these actions in tort, there are two main defences, namely consent and *volenti non fit injuria*. These defences are based on the principle that if you want something to happen to you, or are prepared to run the risk that it might happen, then you cannot bring an action when it does happen and causes injury to you.

171. Literally *volenti non fit injuria* means no harm is done to one who has assumed the risk of injury. However, it all depends on the facts and circumstances of a case. If injury is caused after disengagement and in the heat of the moment in the game, then even criminal liability may visit on the wrongdoers. The footballer, Duncan Ferguson, head butted an opponent during a game and he was jailed for this offence.

A. *Standard of Care*

172. In the case of *Mark v. Moser*, an attempt was made to clearly define the standard of care one competitor owes to another in a sporting event. The court held 'as a matter of law, participants in sporting events will not be permitted to recover against their co-participants for injuries sustained as a result of the inherent or forcible dangers of sport'.

This proposition has generally been followed but the rationale has been different, sometimes based on 'assumption of risk' and other times on 'absence of legal duty'. The courts have also raised concerns to avoid chilling vigorous participation in recreational and competitive sports.

B. *Liability in Contact Sport*

173. In contact sport where participation is voluntarily, a participant will not be liable for injuries caused by simple or ordinary negligent conduct but will be liable for injuries caused by wilful and wanton conduct. Wilful and wanton conduct means a course of action which shows actual or deliberate intent to harm or which, if the course of action is not intentional, shows an utter indifference to or conscious disregard for one's own safety or the safety or property of others (*Nabozny v. Barnhill*[13]). It was further observed in this case that wilful and wanton conduct is 'a hybrid between acts considered negligent and behaviour found to be intentionally tortuous. Under the facts of one case, wilful and wanton misconduct may be only degrees more than ordinary negligence, while under the facts of another case, wilful and wanton acts may be only a degree less than intentional wrongdoings'.

13. (1975), 31 Ill. App. 3d 212 vide May 1998 NRPA Law Review.

174. In *Pfister v. Shusta* (Ill. 1995), the State Supreme Court, in determining the applicability and operation of the exception of contact sport found 'the relevant enquiry is whether the participants were involved in a contact sport, not whether the sport was formally organized or coached'. The practical reasoning given by the court for applying wilful and wanton standard was as described in the following paragraphs.

175. In cases where rules govern the permissible degree of physical contact among participants of a game, it is generally difficult to determine what may be an acceptable degree of physical contact allowed or permissible under the rules. In games where physical contact is inherent, rule infraction, deliberate or unintentional are inevitable and justify a different standard of care. In common understanding, football, wrestling and boxing among others, are clearly recognized as contact sport. Basketball, hockey and soccer all permit some degree of bodily contact and, in actual practice, more contact is permitted than reading of the rules would indicate. In all these sports, players regularly commit contact beyond that which is permitted by the rules even as applied. In basketball, such an illegal contact is described as a foul for which a sanction is imposed. But there will be a limit for imposing a sanction.

So compensation can be claimed for injuries resulting from wilful and wanton intentional misconduct where participation is voluntary, physical contact is anticipated and risk of injury caused by the contact is inherent. For example: in team sports like hockey, football, volleyball, baseball, etc. there can be close physical contact and a participant assumes all of the obvious and foreseeable risks which are incidental to that particular sports activity. However, participation does not assume the risk of injury from fellow players who act in an unexpected or unsportsmanlike manner with a reckless lack of concern for other participants.

II. Organizers of Sports Events

176. An organizer of the sport event owes a duty of care not only towards competitors but also with respect to spectators. In a hockey match, a spectator was injured as a result of fight between two players. The spectator established liability and recovered damages (*Payne v. Maple Leaf Gardens Ltd.* (1949) IDLR 369 Ont. CA). The organizing and conducting of a sport event requires and includes a large number of individuals and bodies like tour operators, ticket selling agents, persons or bodies responsible for maintaining and securing the stadia and equipment and items required for playing sports.

177. If somebody enters the sporting arena without a valid ticket, he will be considered as a trespasser and can be ousted by use of reasonable force. In *Pratap Daji v. BB & CI Railway* ((1875) 1 Bomb. 52), the plaintiff entered a carriage on the defendants' railway but by oversight failed to purchase a ticket for his travel. At one station, he asked for a ticket but it was refused. At another station, he was asked to get out of the carriage since he did not have a ticket. On his refusal to get out, force was used to make him get out of the carriage. In the action by the plaintiff for his forcible removal, it was held that the use of force was justified as he, being without a ticket, was a trespasser. The defendants were, therefore not liable. However, use of excessive force would not be justified. These principles will be equally applicable to a spectator without a ticket in sport arena.

178. A similar type of situation arose in *Cricket Association of West Bengal and Others v. State of West Bengal and Others* (AIR 1971 SC 1925), but it could not lead to conviction as case was preceded under certain sections of the IPC. A complaint was filed on 3 January 1967 before the Court of the Chief Presidency Magistrate, Calcutta, in respect of the incident which took place on the second day (1 January 1967) of the Second Cricket Test Match between India and the West Indies at Eden Gardens. The test match was to be played under the control, management and supervision of the Cricket Association of Bengal, which had sold tickets of various denominations for the game. There were tickets sold for all days of the match, and there were arrangements made for the sale of daily tickets. The game started as scheduled on 31 December 1966. The play was interrupted by a number of spectators scaling the fencing erected around the field of play and entering the cricket field. However, nothing untoward happened on that day.

According to the prosecution, the first appellant started selling tickets announcing that arrangements had been made for the accommodation of about 60,000 spectators, while as a matter of fact nearly a lakh of spectators were admitted into the enclosure. The sitting arrangement was most inconvenient and highly unsatisfactory. The arrangements made by the first appellant for accommodating the persons inside the enclosure were so grossly inadequate that it tended to endanger the personal safety of the spectators.

179. On the day in question, the complainant, who was a holder of a season ticket for INR 45 went to attend the game and found all the stands jam-packed. Notwithstanding this the people with tickets were being pushed into different enclosures with the result that the spectators within the enclosures started jumping over the fence and occupied the space between the lines of the field and the fencing. The police, unable to control the rush and confusion caused by the behaviour of the crowd, suddenly started a lathi-charge followed by the bursting of tear gas shells, which resulted in causing injuries to various persons. This infuriated the crowd, which retaliated with acts of arson. The arrangements for going out of the enclosures were also grossly inadequate with the result that some of the spectators who wanted to clear out quickly in panic sustained injuries. The match had to be abandoned for the day.

From these facts, it was alleged that 'the first appellant who acted most rashly and negligently in over-selling the tickets and admitting a large number of people than could be conveniently accommodated inside the ground and thereby endangered human life and the personal safety of thousands of spectators. It was further alleged that as a matter of fact the rash and negligent act of the first appellant also resulted in hurt being caused to a number of persons, who had come to witness the match. Apart from the Cricket Association of Bengal, which was the first accused, he also accused thirty-three others in his complaint petition. Those persons were the President, the Vice President and other office-bearers and Members of the Working

Committee of the Cricket Association of Bengal. The complainant prayed for issuing summons against the thirty-four accused persons under sections 337 and 338 read with section 114 of the IPC and to proceed against them according to law'.

§3. Public Health and Safety

I. Sports Doctors

180. Doctors play a vital role in the field of sports by keeping the sportsman physically and mentally fit and in fighting condition and also attending to their injuries and other ailments which may sometimes be peculiar to sporting activity. Besides, sport doctors have to be extra careful in prescribing medicines for any ailment so that these may not contain prohibited drugs.

181. Based on the physical condition of the sportsperson, doctors may allow or disallow the continuation of an event, as we see in boxing matches. In case a doctor fails to properly diagnose and prescribe proper medicines, he can be charged with culpable homicide. In the cases of games involving high physical risk, the responsibility and consequently the liability of a doctor is much more than in a game where there is no or less physical contact. For example, based on the physical condition, and nature and extent of injuries sustained by a boxer, a doctor can stop a fight.

182. In *Dr Lakshman Balkrishna Joshi v. Trimbak Bapu Godbole* (AIR 1969 SC 128 at 131–132) explaining the nature of duty of care in medical profession, the Supreme Court observed:
The petitioner must bring to his task a reasonable degree of skill and knowledge and must exercise a reasonable degree of care. Neither the very highest nor is a very low degree of care and competence judged in the light of the particular circumstances of each case what the law requires. The doctor, no doubt, has discretion in choosing the treatment which he proposes to give to the patient and such discretion is relatively greater in cases of emergency.

183. In *Medical Association v. V.P. Samantha* (AIR 1996 SC 550), the Supreme Court recognized the liability of medical practitioners for their negligence and held that the liability to pay damages for such negligence was not affected by the fact that the medical practitioners are professionals, and are subject to disciplinary control of Medical Council. It held that the service rendered by the medical practitioner was covered by section 2(o) of the Consumer Protection Act, 1986, and the same was actionable in the forums established under the Consumer Protection Act, 1986.

In sport arenas, the doctors have to deal with the emergencies like a fatal blow to a competitor and a doctor has to choose the best-suited treatment which can be given first hand before taking the competitor to the hospital.

II. Hooliganism

184. Hooliganism is a big challenge for sporting clubs and other sport organizing bodies that organize sporting events. As maintenance of law and order is the primary duty of police forces, so it is also a challenge to law enforcing agencies. Hooliganism can occur at any time. It can be before an event when sport lovers do not get tickets or entry is denied because of overcrowding resulting in gate crashes. In some instances, it may be the result of mismanagement and improper regulation of entry and exit points. It may be the result of clashes between sports fans of different clubs. Digging up the pitch in a cricket field is another problem which is sometimes faced by the organizers.

During a match, the spectators may throw bottles or crackers on to the field. There can be abusive comments and remarks by spectators or sportspersons which may lead to clashes and ugly situations in a match.

185. Football is one of the games which in international arena is associated with large numbers of hooliganism cases, and efforts are made to segregate the rival club fans in the stadia. In India, the club rivalries are confined to only some cities like Calcutta where there are strong football clubs. In India, main problems of hooliganism emanate from large turnout and mismanagement of the sport venue. Sometimes, security concerns and consequent restrictions create the problem of hooliganism.

III. Crowd Behaviour and Club Liability

186. The sport venues may be owned by the organizers of an event or might have been hired for organizing an event. Since an organizer is the occupier and responsible for managing the event, therefore, he is liable for any damage to third parties caused at the sporting event because of and related to the crowd gathered to see the match. Hence, there is transfer of liability from owner to occupier or organizer. But one thing is to be kept in mind that crowd behaviour and resultant damage is also a law and order problem and to be dealt with by the police authorities who are generally informed of an event and in certain cases their permission is sought before organizing an event.

187. In *Shayamal Baran Saha v. State of West Bengal* (AIR 1998 Cal. 203), the facts were that a cricket match was to be played at Eden Garden Grounds in Calcutta. There was a long queue of ticket seekers since morning and later on it became uncontrollable. There was a stampede and a young boy of 16 years standing in the queue was seriously injured. The concerned Cricket Association did not ask for security from the government. The State had also failed to control the crowd and provide even the basic facilities like drinking water and medical help to those who were in the queue. The State pleaded and took the defence of delegated sovereign power. But, it was rejected by the court as it was a case of failure of police to perform its duties rather than a case of brutality. Both Cricket Association and the State government were held liable for negligence.

IV. Vandalism and Public Order

188. The individuals and fans that have a record of vandalism may be prevented or prohibited from having access to sporting events and venues. In India, there is no specific legislation to deal with sport vandalism, but general laws which are applicable for keeping public order are applied to maintain law and order and to prevent vandalism in sporting venues as well.

V. Security in Sports Venues

189. The occupier of a sport facility has a duty to all users to ensure that it is safe to be used for sports played there, which includes playing surfaces and equipment necessary for each individual sport. While selecting sports venues its connectivity with road, rail and air links, total space available for spectators inside the stadium and other facilities required for a large number of people are to be seen and taken care of. If one allows or gathers a large number of people or spectators to a sport venue which does not have adequate facilities then one is compromising the safety and security of the spectators and he can be held responsible for that. The security of sports venues also requires that there must be proper manning and management so that entry and exit of spectators is regulated and they are not left to fend for themselves.

In sports like cricket, baseball, hockey, the game involves high velocity hard projectiles, i.e., balls, and it is required that some of the available seats be protected by screening or a net and the spectators be given an opportunity to select the safer seats.

Chapter 5. Sporting Fraud

§1. Match-Fixing and Spot-Fixing

190. The sport is corrupted by match-fixing and illegal betting which jeopardize the integrity of the competitions, damage the social, educational and cultural values reflected by sports, and threaten the economic role of sports. The phenomenon of match-fixing brings to the surface its links to other criminal activities such as corruption, organized crime and money-laundering. In fact, a criminal justice response against match-fixing would demonstrate that sporting manipulation is not a 'simple' breach of sporting rules, but also an offence against the public in a broader sense. Legislation to establish criminal offences against match-fixing is therefore needed as a complement to independent sporting sanction systems, which include bans, relegations and penalties. The lack of criminalization measures and legislative approaches calls for more streamlined action to develop standard-setting model instruments.

191. Betting falls under Entry 34 of the State List of the Constitution of India, thereby giving exclusive powers to the State legislatures to make laws. Therefore, different States have enacted their own legislations. While gambling is not allowed but a game of skill is legal. The judiciary has differentiated between a game of skill and a game of chance or gambling in its pronouncements. A game of skill is played using a substantial quantum of skills. Individual expertise and capabilities determine the success of a game of skill. In a game of skill, players know the rules and execute several strategies while playing to win like chess, carrom and rummy. A game of chance does not involve any skill and the victory is based on luck or any other random factor.

I. The Sports (Online Gaming and Prevention of Fraud) Bill, 2018

192. The Sports (Online Gaming and Prevention of Fraud) Bill, 2018 (Bill) was introduced in the Lok Sabha in 2018. However, the Bill has not been passed but shows the thinking on this issue. The intent behind introducing the Bill was to regulate the largely unorganized online gaming sector that includes online gambling at the central level.

193. Section 3 of the Bill provided different kinds of actions that would amount to sports fraud such as manipulation of sports result, irregular alteration of field of play, misapplying the rules of the sport deliberately, etc. The appropriate authority as designated by the Central Government, investigates on such matters. Section 6(2) imposed a fine of five times the reward earned through malpractice, along with imprisonment. Section 8(1) states that if activity is performed by a company, then the company shall be held guilty. Section 14(1) states that a licence is required to operate an online gaming website and no online sports happens except through such a website. The Bill also provided for constitution of an Online Sports Gaming Commission (Commission) to regulate the online gaming sector. The Commission was to grant licence to applicants for running an online gaming server.

194. The Bill also mandated the maintenance of accounts relating to online sports gaming by the licensee. If for any reason, the online gambling platform were to shut down, the customers will be able to recover their funds. The maintaining of accounts and auditing shall ensure fairness. The Bill also permitted Foreign Direct Investment (FDI) in the online gaming industry. The online gaming industry is flourishing in India and FDI would definitely boost growth.

195. In the absence of laws to deal with match-fixing and its variants, no court can convict any player who might be involved in fixing. For want of an adequate law, a player was tried under the Maharashtra Control of Organized Crime Act. It was nobody's case that the player was a terrorist or involved in organized crime. It was like using a road roller to trap a fly. The BCCI has concluded that a number of players, from internationals to local stars have been guilty of match-fixing, spot-fixing, or not reporting knowledge of these 'crimes' to the authorities. Yet, so long as there is a reluctance to pass a law, there cannot be a fair trial for those who are hauled up for these activities. In view of the huge vacuum of law in this regard in the realm of law, the courts are helpless to proceed further under any of the penal statutes.

II. Rules of Sport Governing Bodies

196. There have been many charges of match-fixing which involved not only the bookies but also allegedly the players and after investigations ban was imposed on some players. The Kerala High Court upheld the claim of a cricketer under Article 226 of the Constitution against excessive punishment of lifelong ban for match-fixing. The lifelong ban imposed by BCCI was lifted on the ground that cricketer has already suffered it for four years. Therefore the continuation of punishment will be unreasonable and unjust. Earlier the Delhi High Court had acquitted the cricketer from all charges except knowledge of cricket (*Economic Times*, 7 August 2017). It is very difficult to find a definition of match-fixing. The match-fixing and its punishment is generally dealt with in the rules of sports governing bodies. The instances which may amount to match-fixing have been enumerated in the CBI Report on Match-Fixing Allegations as follows:[14]

- instances where an individual player or group of players received money individually/collectively to underplay;
- instances where a player placed bets in matches in which he played that would naturally undermine the performance;

14. www.legalserviceindia.com/articles/social.htm 'Match Fixing as a Crime: An Analysis' by Sumit Agarwal.

- instances where players passed on information to a betting syndicate about team composition;
- instances where grounds men were given money to prepare a pitch in a way which suited the betting syndicate;
- instances of current and ex-players being used by bookies to gain access to Indian and foreign players to lower performance for a monetary consideration.

The contract law prohibits agreement by way of wager. Section 30 of the Contract Act 1872 provides that, 'Agreements by way of wager are void; and no suit shall be brought for recovering anything alleged to be won on any wager, or entrusted to any person to abide by the results of any game or other uncertain event on which wager is made.' However, prizes and competitions which are games of skill like picture puzzles, athletic competitions, etc. are not considered as wagers.

197. In *Board of Control for Cricket in India v. Cricket Association of Bihar & Ors.* (2015 STPL (web) 131 SC (DB); 2015 AIR (SCW) 2258, Dated 22 January 2015), the issue of match-fixing and spot-fixing came up and was dealt with in detail. The facts as given in the judgment of the Supreme Court are that allegations of sporting frauds like match-fixing and betting have for the past few years cast a cloud over the working of the Board of Cricket Control in India (BCCI). Cricket being more than just a sport for millions in this part of the world, accusations of malpractices and conflict of interests against those who not only hold positions of influence in the BCCI but also own franchises and teams competing in the IPL format have left many a cricketing enthusiasts and followers of the game worried and deeply suspicious about what goes on in the name of the game. There is no denying the fact that lower the threshold of tolerance for any wrongdoing higher is the expectation of the people, from the system. And cricket being not only a passion but also a great unifying force in this country, a zero tolerance approach towards any wrongdoing alone can satisfy the cry for cleansing.

The appeals arise out of two successive writ petitions filed in public interest by the appellant-Cricket Association of Bihar before the High Court of Bombay for several reliefs including a writ in the nature of mandamus directing BCCI to recall its order constituting a probe panel comprising two retired Judges of Madras High Court to enquire into the allegations of betting and spot-fixing in the IPL made among others against one Gurunath Meiyappan. The High Court has by its order dated 30 July 2013 passed in PIL No. 55 of 2013 granted that relief but declined a possible reconstitution of the panel. Aggrieved, BCCI has assailed the order passed by the High Court in Civil Appeal No. 4235 of 2014. In the connected Civil Appeal No. 4236 of 2014, Cricket Association of Bihar has prayed for further and consequential orders *inter alia*, for removal of respondent No. 2 namely Srinivasan from the post of President of BCCI and cancellation of the franchise favouring Chennai Super Kings and Rajasthan Royals for the IPL matches to be conducted in future. In Civil appeal arising out of SLP (C) No. 34228 of 2014, the association challenges the validity of Regulation 6.2.4 of the BCCI Regulations for Players, Team Officials, Managers, Umpires & Administrators (for short 'BCCI Regulations') and the order passed by the High Court dismissing PIL No. 107 of 2013.

198. Cricket Association of Bihar is a society registered under the Societies Registration Act, 1860 just as respondent – BCCI is a society registered under the provisions of Tamil Nadu Registration of Societies Act 1975. Mr N. Srinivasan – respondent No. 2 in Civil Appeal No. 4236 of 2014 is the President of the Board besides being the Vice Chairman and Managing Director of respondent No. 3 – India Cements Limited, a Public Limited Company. In a meeting held on 13 September 2007, the working committee of the respondent-Board appears to have taken a decision to launch IPL to be run by a committee constituted by general body of the BCCI to be called IPL Governing Council. In December 2007, the IPL Governing Council invited tenders for grant of IPL franchises on open competitive bidding basis, in which only corporate bodies were allowed to participate. India Cements Ltd. was one of those who participated in the auction for the Chennai franchise and emerged successful in the same. The team it assembled was named as Chennai Super Kings. Jaipur IPL Cricket Private Limited partly owned and promoted by respondent No. 5 similarly emerged successful for the Jaipur Franchise and assembled a team called Rajasthan Royals. Franchise agreements were, pursuant to the auction, signed by BCCI with the franchisees concerned.

199. On 27 September 2008, Mr N. Srinivasan was elected as the Secretary of the BCCI in a General Body Meeting. In the same meeting Regulation 6.2.4 of the IPL Regulations was amended to exclude from its operation events like IPL and Champions' League Twenty20. In April 2013, Special Cell, Delhi Police, Lodhi Colony, New Delhi, is said to have received secret information that certain members of the underworld were involved in fixing of matches in the recently concluded edition of the IPL. FIR was registered by the Special Cell, Delhi Police, under sections 420 and 120B of the IPC and Mr S. Sreesanth, Mr Ajit Chandila and Mr Ankit Chavan of the Rajasthan Royals along with seven bookies detained for allegations of spot-fixing. Shortly, thereafter, Mr. Gurunathan Meiyappan (GM), son-in-law of Mr N. Srinivasan was also arrested by the Mumbai Police on 25 May 2013 in a spot-fixing/betting case. Soon after the arrest on 26 May 2013 came an announcement that a Commission comprising two members of the BCCI and one independent member would be constituted to enquire into allegations of betting and spot-fixing. This was followed by nomination of two former Judges of the High Court of Madras and Shri Sanjay Jagdale as members of a Probe Commission to enquire into the allegations of betting and spot-fixing. Shri Sanjay Jagdale, however, resigned as member of the Probe Commission leaving the two former judges to complete the probe. Mr N. Srinivasan announced that he was stepping aside from the post of President of the BCCI until the probe was completed ostensibly because of the alleged involvement of his son-in-law in the betting and spot-fixing racket.

200. The appellant-association filed W.P. No. 55 of 2013 before the High Court of Judicature at Bombay, *inter alia*, for a declaration that appointment of the two-member Probe Commission was ultra vires of the Rules and Regulations of the BCCI and for a mandamus directing constitution of a panel comprising retired judges to hold an enquiry against among others Mr Gurunath Meiyappan (GM) for his involvement in betting and spot-fixing. The petitioner also prayed for termination of the franchise agreement entered into between the BCCI, on the one hand,

and Chennai Super Kings and Rajasthan Royals on the other. A mandamus directing institution of disciplinary proceedings against Mr N. Srinivasan was also prayed for, besides a prayer for his suspension pending the probe and other proceedings. The appellant-association in addition prayed for a prohibition against Mr N. Srinavisan restraining him from contesting the election for the post of President of BCCI in future and representing the BCCI in the ICC.

201. By its order dated 30 July 2013, a Division Bench of the High Court of Bombay held that the Probe Commission set up by the BCCI was not validly constituted being in violation of the provisions of Rules 2.2 and 3 of section 6 of the IPL Operational Rules. The High Court, however, declined to grant any further relief by way of constituting a panel to conduct an enquiry under the supervision of the High Court. The High Court was of the view that constitution of a Probe Committee under section 6 of the IPL Operational Rules was the prerogative of the BCCI. Civil Appeal No. 4235 of 2014 preferred by the BCCI assails the said order of the High Court to the extent it declares the constitution of the Probe Commission to be illegal and ultra vires of the relevant rules and regulations. The Cricket Association of Bihar has also assailed the same order in Civil Appeal No. 4236 of 2014 to the extent it has declined to grant further and consequential relief to the appellant. The matter came up for hearing on 27 September 2013 before a Division Bench, which permitted the Annual General Meeting of the BCCI to be held on 29 September 2013 as scheduled and so also election to the post of president, subject to the condition that in case respondent No. 2Mr N. Srinivasan got elected, he will not take charge until further orders. When the matter came up again on 8 October 2013, the court noted that although Mr N. Srinivasan had been elected as the President of the Board yet a probe into the allegations of betting and spot-fixing was necessary. A reading of order dated 8 October 2013 passed by this court would show that the constitution of the Probe Committee comprising Mr Justice Mukul Mudgal, retired Chief Justice of Punjab and Haryana High Court as Chairman, Mr L. Nageshwar Rao, Additional Solicitor General and Mr Nilay Dutt, Senior Advocate, Guwahati High Court, was passed with the consent of the parties.

202. The Probe Committee started its proceedings and invited persons who have any information in their possession regarding the Terms of Reference to furnish such information to the Committee. Based on the enquiries made by it, a report dated 9 February 2014 was submitted, in which the committee arrived to the following conclusions:

- That GM formed an integral part of Chennai Super Kings (CSK) and most persons viewed him as the face of the team, though de jure ownership vested in India Cements Ltd.
- That GM was a team official within the meaning of IPL Operational Rules if not de facto owner of CSK.
- That GM had knowledge of or was in a position to easily access sensitive team information, team strategies, knowledge about match conditions, etc. which knowledge was outside the purview of an ordinary person following the game of cricket.

- That, GM was also a participant under IPL Anti-corruption Code, hence IPL Rules and Regulations were squarely applicable to him.
- That GM was in regular touch with bookies and punters.
- That several calls were traced between GM and Vindoo Dara Singh (VDS) who was himself a punter in close proximity with several other bookies, evident from the telephonic transcripts produced by the Bombay Police.
- That Mr Ramesh Vyas (RV) and Jupiter were acting for VDS who was also placing bets for certain IPL stakeholders and actors including Mr GM who was in close contact with Mr Vikram Agarwal (VA) who is a hotelier and alleged punter operating from Chennai as revealed by call record details produced by the Chennai Police in Crime No. 1 of 2013 registered by the CBCID Branch.
- That Mr GM would regularly place bets in IPL matches both in favour of his team (i.e., CSK) and against his team – a fact established from call records produced by the Mumbai Police.
- That Mr GM would place bets through VDS and such bets were even placed during the course of IPL match as revealed by transcripts produced by Mumbai Police.
- That in one instance Mr GM made certain predictions to Mr VDS regarding the runs that would be scored in a match between CSK and Rajasthan Royals held on 12 May 2013 at Jaipur. According to Mr GM's prediction that CSK would score 130–140 runs came true as CSK actually scored 141 runs only.

203. The Probe Committee on the basis of above findings held Mr GM guilty of betting which in its opinion was accentuated by his position in the CSK. What is important is that the Probe Committee held that Mr GM had, in his acts of betting, the implicit approval of the franchisee owner India Cements, thereby bringing the team to disrepute and violating sections 2.2.1 and 2.14 of the IPL Operational Rules besides Articles 2.2.1, 2.2.2, 2.2.3 of the IPL Anti-Corruption Code and Article 2.4.4 of the IPL Code of Conduct for Players and Team Officials.

204. The committee also held that franchisee owner of CSK was responsible for its failure to ensure that Mr GM complied with BCCI Anti-Corruption Code, IPL Operational Rules and IPL Regulations. The franchisee's actions were on that basis held to be in violation of section 4.4.1 of the IPL Operational Rules and Clause 11.3 of the franchise's agreement. The committee summed up its conclusion regarding the investigation against Mr GM and India Cements Ltd. the owner of ICL as follows:

> Thus, the Committee is of the view that for the acts of betting by Mr. Meiyappan, which is further accentuated by the position he held in CSK, which was held by Mr. Meiyappan with the implicit approval of the franchisee owner India Cements, Mr. Meiyappan is in violation of Sections 2.2.1 and 2.14 the IPL Operational Rules for bringing the game in disrepute, Articles 2.2.1, 2.2.2 and 2.2.3 of the IPL Anti-corruption Code for his acts of betting and Articles 2.4.4 of the IPL Code of Conduct for Players and Team Officials, for bring disrepute to the game of cricket. The said illegal acts further stand accentuated in light of his position/role in CSK. The Committee is also of the opinion that the

franchisee owner of CSK is responsible for failing to ensure Mr. Meiyappan (Team Officials) had complied with the BCCI Anti-Corruption Code, IPL Operational rules, IPL Regulations and hence the franchisee's actions are in violation of Section 4.4.1 of the IPL Operational Rules and Clause 11.3 of the franchises agreement.

205. As regards the allegations of betting and spot-fixing in IPL made against Mr Raj Kundra (RJ), the committee concluded that further and serious investigation was required to be conducted into the said allegations of betting if proved against RJ and his wife, would constitute a serious infraction of the provisions of IPL Operational Rules, the Anti-Corruption Code and the Code of Conduct for Players and Team Officials. The committee also examined the allegations of match/spot-fixing made against several players and noticed that the BCCI had conducted an inquiry into the allegations and found the same to be proved. The committee was, however, of the view that the disciplinary action taken by BCCI against the delinquent players was adequate and satisfactory, the Honourable Court observed.

206. The committee referred to allegations of sporting frauds made before it during its interaction with several persons connected with the game. The committee placed before the Supreme Court the names of persons against whom such allegations were made in a sealed envelope. The committee also mentioned other issues including the issue of 'conflict of interest' between Mr N. Srinivasan as the BCCI President on the one hand and CEO of India Cements Ltd. on the other. The committee concluded its report by making certain recommendations that would, in its opinion, help remove the malaise of spot/match-fixing and detect sporting frauds by BCCI's Investigation Wing.

207. The report submitted by the Probe Committee was then considered by the Supreme Court in order dated 16 May 2014 by which the Probe Committee was permitted to enquire into the allegations made against those named in the sealed cover filed before the court by the committee including Mr N. Srinivasan. The committee filed an interim report dated 1 September 2014, and wound up its proceedings by its third and final report dated 1 November 2014 in which it took note of the scientific evaluation of GM's recorded voice which revealed that the recorded voice was indeed that of Mr GM. In a separate report submitted by Mr Nilay Dutta, the third member of the Probe Committee, Shri Dutta had observed that for the committee to arrive at a conclusive finding as regards the voice alleged to be that of Mr GM, a scientific evaluation was necessary. The Committee's final report took note of the scientific evaluation and recorded a unanimous conclusion that Mr GM had actually indulged in betting in IPL matches. It, however, found no material to show that GM was involved in match-fixing. As regards Mr R K, the committee came to the conclusion that Mr R K had indulged in betting in violation of BCCI Regulations and IPL Anti-Corruption Code. The committee further came to the conclusion that N. Srinivasan was neither involved in match-fixing activity nor was he involved in preventing investigation into match-fixing. The committee held that although Mr N. Srinivasan was aware of the violation of the players' code, yet no action was taken against him by Mr Srinivasan or any other official who was aware of the infraction.

208. The Probe Committee, on an interpretation of the provisions of the relevant rules and the material placed before it, recorded a specific finding that Gurunath Meiyappan (GM) was working/associated with the IPL as team official of the Chennai Super Kings. The committee further held that for the operation of the relevant rules and regulations it made no difference whether Gurunath Meiyappan was the owner or simply a team official of CSK. That is because so long as Gurunath Meiyappan was a team official, which the committee found he was, the consequences of his acts of betting would flow even when he was not the owner, or the perceived owner of the CSK. That, Gurunath Meiyappan was a team official of CSK which was owned by India Cements Ltd. and was not disputed by either India Cements Ltd. or any other party appearing before us. The learned senior counsel appearing for Mr Gurunath Meiyappan, however, declined to commit himself to any stand on that aspect. When asked if his client was a team official of CSK, Mr Luthra claimed the right to remain silent as his client was being prosecuted in a Court at Mumbai for betting. The court conceded to Mr Gurunath Meiyappan the right to silence in view of the pendency of the prosecution launched against him. That does not, however, prevent the court from examining whether Gurunath Meiyappan was a team official for purposes of disciplinary action permissible under the relevant rules and regulations. We may hasten to add that our examination of that issue will be without prejudice to Mr Gurunath Meiyappan's right to claim that he was neither a team official if at all the said question arises for consideration in the criminal trial pending against him, nor shall opinion of the court on the subject be taken as binding upon the criminal court where the question can be examined independently.

209. The Supreme Court found that the Probe Committee has correctly appreciated the facts as emerging from the documents and the depositions of witnesses recorded by it and rightly come to the conclusion that Gurunath Meiyappan was a team official of CSK. That is so especially when India Cements Ltd. owners of the team made admission before the court that Gurunath Meiyappan was indeed a team official within the meaning of that expression under the rules. Thus there is no real, much less compelling reason, to disagree or reverse the finding recorded by the Probe Committee on that aspect.

The Probe Committee has on the basis of the material available to it further held that Gurunath Meiyappan was indulging in betting and that finding was not seriously assailed by learned Senior Counsel appearing on his behalf. The counsel's concern was that since Mr Gurunath Meiyappan was being prosecuted, any specific stance that he may take is likely to prejudice him at the trial in the criminal case. However, it has been made clear that any finding as to the involvement of Mr Gurunath Meiyappan in betting activities recorded by the Probe Committee or by the court shall remain confined to the present proceedings which are addressing the limited question whether any administrative/disciplinary action needs to be taken against those accused of such activities. Having said so, we must make it clear that given the nature of the proceedings entrusted to the Probe Committee and the standard of proof applicable to the same, we see no reason to disagree with the conclusion of the Probe Committee that Gurunath Meiyappan was indeed indulging in betting. The material assembled in the course of the investigation by the Probe Committee provides a reasonably safe basis for holding that the accusations made against Gurunath Meiyappan stood established on a preponderance of probabilities. The finding is by no means without basis or perverse to call for our interference with the same. That brings to the findings recorded against Mr Raj Kundra, whose part ownership and accreditation, as a team official of Rajasthan Royal was not disputed. In its report dated 9 February 2014, the Probe Committee had referred to the statement of Mr Umesh Goenka, recorded under section 164 of the Criminal Procedure Code (Cr.P.C.) by a Delhi Court in which the said Mr Goenka had stated that Mr Raj Kundra used to indulge in betting in IPL matches through him. The Probe Committee opined that the allegations levelled against Mr Raj Kundra and his wife required to be investigated further. The committee held that if the allegations of betting were found proved against Mr Raj Kundra and his wife the same would constitute serious infraction of the IPL Operational Rules, the IPL Anti-Corruption Code and the IPL Code of Conduct for Players and Team Official. The committee observed:

> The Committee is thus of the view that if the allegations of betting against Mr. Raj Kundra and Ms. Shetty who are part of Rajasthan Royals, stand proved the same would constitute a serious infraction of Sections 2.2.1 and 2.14 of the IPL Operational Rules for bringing the game in disrepute, Articles 2.2.1, 2.2.2 and 2.2.3 of the IPL Anti-corruption Code for acts of betting and Articles 2.4.4 of the IPL Code of Conduct for Players and Team Officials, for bring disrepute to the game of cricket.

210. The committee understands that the suspension imposed on Mr Raj Kundra by the BCCI is still in force. The BCCI must take a zero tolerance position as regards corruption in cricket and any possible violation of the BCCI Anti-Corruption Code and the Operational Rules by any person. It goes without saying that Mr Raj Kundra and his wife were owners as per the franchise agreement and accredited as such under the IPL Operational Rules. They are team officials within the meaning of the said rules. Being team officials, they are subject to the Code of conduct for Players and Team Officials prohibiting betting in course of IPL matches and would face appropriate sanctions under the Operational Rules. It would be in fitness of things that pending final determination of the culpability of the Kundras, they be kept suspended from participating in any activity of the BCCI including the IPL matches in view of the materials on record.

The Supreme Court taking note of the observations made by the Probe Committee not only directed further investigation into the allegations against Mr Raj Kundra but also provided necessary support to the Probe Committee to do so effectively. The committee has on the basis of the said further investigation and enquiry come to the conclusion that Mr Raj Kundra was a 'team official', a 'player support personnel' and 'participant' within the meaning of the relevant rules and that he had indulged in betting.

211. The committee has, while dealing with the case of Mr Raj Kundra, referred to as Individual No. 11 in the said report observed:

Individual 11: This individual was in touch with the bookies about betting and thus by not reporting contact with the bookie has violated BCCI/IPL Anti-Corruption

Code. The Committee also found that the investigation against this individual was abruptly and without reason stopped by the Rajasthan Police upon receiving the case papers from Delhi Police. The Committee found that a friend of individual 11 was a known punter. The said punter has given a section 164 statement to the effect that he was placing bets on behalf of individual 11. Individual 11 had introduced him (punter) to another bookie who dealt with larger stakes. Section 161 statement made by another player confirmed that individual 11 introduced him to a bookie. Materials on record indicate that individual 11 was placing bets or was at the minimum standing guarantee for his punter friend. These infractions also violate BCCI/ IPL Anti-Corruption Code.

Appearing for Mr Raj Kundra, the learned senior counsel, argued that the report submitted by the Probe Committee could at best be taken as a preliminary report. A proper enquiry into the allegations made against Mr Raj Kundra shall have to be separately conducted in terms of the relevant rules and regulations. In support of that contention, he placed reliance upon the disciplinary procedure prescribed under Rule 6.2.2 of the IPL Operational Rules, which postulates establishment of a 'Disciplinary Procedure Commission' to hear and adjudicate upon any complaint alleging any breach or misconduct under the regulations. In terms of Rule 6.2.2, the Commission has to comprise three members of IPL Code of Behaviour Committee selected by BCCI. The Commission is in terms of Rule 6.2.4 empowered to investigate any breach of the regulations or any player contract by any person subject to the Operational Rules. Rule 6.3.1 prescribes the complaint procedure which is according to the learned counsel mandatory especially when Rule 6.3.8 requires the hearing to be conducted in a fair manner and in consonance with the principles of natural justice including the right to call and to question and examine witnesses in person or by telephone or video conference where necessary. Reliance was placed upon Rule 6.3.19 to argue that standard of proof in support of the complaint shall be whether 'the Commission is comfortably satisfied' bearing in mind the seriousness of the allegations made regarding the 'commission of the offence' and that the standard of proof in all cases shall be considered on a sliding scale from, at a minimum, a mere balance of probability up to proof beyond a reasonable doubt from the least serious to the most serious offences. It was contended that the person found guilty is then entitled to file an appeal before the Appeal Commission established under section 6.5.4 consisting up to three members to hear and decide the appeal. This procedure, it was argued, could not be deviated from as the rules were binding upon the parties concerned. Reliance in support was placed on the decisions in *T.P. Daver v. Lodge Victoria* No. 363 S.C. Belgaum and Ors. (AIR 1963 SC 1144), *Ambalal Sarabhai and Ors. v. Phiroz H. Anita* (AIR 1939 Bombay 35) and *Lennox Arthur Patrick O' Reilly and Ors. v. Cyril Cuthbert Gittens* (AIR 1949 PC 313).

212. On behalf of Jaipur IPL Cricket Private Ltd., it was argued by the learned senior counsel that there was no direct allegation against the said company and that the findings recorded by the Probe Committee that Mr Raj Kundra was the owner of Rajasthan Royals was not wholly correct inasmuch as Raj Kundra and his family own just about 11% equity in the holding company of respondent No. 4-Jaipur IPL Cricket Private Ltd. Having said that Mr Desai fairly conceded that Raj Kundra was duly accredited and doubtless a 'team official' in terms of IPL Operational Rules and also 'Player Support Personnel' and participant in terms of the IPL Anti-Corruption Code. Mr Desai, however, assailed the findings recorded by Justice Mudgal Committee that Mr Raj Kundra had indulged in betting in IPL matches and argued that the report was vague and unsustainable against Mr Raj Kundra more so against Rajasthan Royals. It was argued by him that Mr Raj Kundra was never a part of the management directly or indirectly and had never participated in the management decisions including decisions regarding the purchase of players or the strategy adopted by the franchisee or its team. No notice was, according to Mr Desai, served upon respondent No. 4 the company although Mr Raj Kundra was summoned and examined by the Probe Committee. According to the learned counsel, Justice Mudgal Committee had only completed the first-stage process of investigation leaving the second-stage 'fact finding' and the third-stage 'adjudication' issues open. It was contended that even if Mr Raj Kundra was held to be guilty of betting, the question whether any punishment/sanctions could be imposed upon a franchisee will have to be considered in the totality of the circumstances having regard to the fact that other promoters of the company that owns Rajasthan Royals need not be punished for the misconduct of one of the promoters holding only 11% equity. The question of proportionality of the sanction/punishment shall also have to be kept in mind.

213. The IPL Operational Rules provide for what is described as 'disciplinary and complaint procedure' to be followed in regard to the complaints and/or breaches of the regulations and/or charges of misconduct levelled against anyone connected with the IPL. This procedure includes establishment of a 'Disciplinary Procedure Commission' to hear and decide such matters. The Commission is in terms of Rule 6.2.2 to comprise three members of the IPL Code of Behaviour Committee to be selected by the BCCI. It is also clear from Rules 6.3.1 to 6.3.21 that the Commission is required to follow a fair and reasonable procedure consistent with the principles of natural justice. In terms of Rule 6.3.19, standard of proof can vary between balance of probability and proof beyond a reasonable doubt depending upon the seriousness of the allegations being examined by the Commission. Two distinct aspects all the same need be kept in mind in the case at hand. The first is that even the BCCI had not adhered to the prescribed procedure in the present case. Instead of constituting a 'Disciplinary Procedure Commission' comprising three members of IPL Code of Behaviour Committee, the BCCI had appointed a three-member committee comprising two former Judges of the High Court of Madras with Mr Jagdale as the third member. The departure came ostensibly because of a public hue and cry over betting by those owning the participating teams. The situation was in that view extraordinary which called for an extraordinary approach. A committee comprising two former Judges of the High Court of Madras was BCCI's response to the extraordinary situation with Mr Jagdale as the third member. The Probe Committee was reduced to two members after Mr Jagdale decided to resign, but the committee was asked by the Board to continue and complete the probe even with its reduced strength. This was a conscious departure by the BCCI from the procedure laid down by the IPL Operational Rules which was faulted by the High Court of Bombay in the writ petition filed by the appellant-association. When the matter travelled to this Court, the seriousness of the allegations and the ramifications involved led to the setting up of a High Powered Probe Committee in place of the Disciplinary Procedure Commission contemplated by the IPL Operational Rules and Regulations. The whole purpose behind setting up of the Probe Committee was to make the entire process of investigation and enquiry into the allegations credible. The Probe Committee headed by a former Chief Justice of the High Court of Punjab and Haryana was never intended to conduct a preliminary investigation as was suggested by the learned counsels. It was on the contrary understood by all concerned to be a substitute for the Disciplinary Procedure Commission under the rules empowered to examine the allegations and record findings. It is wholly wrong to suggest that the report of such a High Powered Probe Committee could be trivialized by treating it as a preliminary investigation that could lead to no more than initiation of proceedings before the Disciplinary Procedure Commission envisaged by Rule 6.2.2 of the rules mentioned above. The second aspect is that the Probe Committee set up by the BCCI had expressed its inability to do anything in the matter on account of absence of any material to support the allegations appearing in the press. The BCCI had, for all intents and purposes, treated that finding to be conclusive giving a quietus to the controversy. It was not as though the finding of the committee comprising two former Judges of the Madras High Court was meant to be some kind of a preliminary report, which would require scrutiny or examination by the Disciplinary Procedure Commission before a clean chit was given to the individuals concerned. If that be so, it is difficult to countenance the argument that IPL Operational Rules had any further role to play in the matter of an enquiry into the allegations levelled against the persons concerned. It is equally difficult to appreciate how the significance of the reports submitted by the Probe Committee set up by this Court could be undermined simply because the IPL Operational Rules provide for a Disciplinary Procedure Commission with a particular composition. We have in that view no hesitation in rejecting the contention that the procedure prescribed by the IPL Operational Rules must be followed despite all that has transpired till now or that the report submitted by Justice Mudgal Committee was of no value except that it could be provided a basis for setting the Disciplinary Procedure into motion. It is to be remembered that the direction for appointment of a Probe Committee was issued in exercise of appellate powers vested in Supreme Court in proceedings arising out of Article 226 of the Constitution as also those vested under Article 142 thereof.

214. Further, the directions came in a public interest petition with a view to finding out whether there was any truth in the allegations that owners of IPL teams and franchisees were in a big way indulging in sporting frauds thereby discrediting the game and cheating the public of their confidence in its purity. That being the object, it is futile to set up the 'disciplinary procedure' under the rules against the exercise of such plenary powers as are vested in the Supreme Court under the constitutional provisions mentioned above. As a matter of fact, like the Disciplinary Procedure Commission even the Probe Committee set up by the court was bound to observe the principles of natural justice in the matter of conducting the probe entrusted to it. That is because of the consequences that would flow from any finding, which the Probe Committee would record against those accused of wrongdoings. As seen earlier, Raj Kundra has been found to be a team official of Rajasthan Royals by the

Probe Committee. Even according to the learned counsel appearing for Mr Raj Kundra Jaipur IPL Cricket Private Ltd., he was a duly accredited team official. Such being the position a notice was required to go only to Mr Raj Kundra for it was he alone who was alleged to have indulged in betting. The contention that since the committee did not issue any notice to Jaipur IPL Cricket Private Ltd. the owner of Rajasthan Royals, the finding recorded by the Probe Committee holding Mr Raj Kundra guilty of betting was vitiated does not appear to be sound. Whether or not Mr Raj Kundra's misconduct can and should result in loss of franchise granted to Rajasthan Royals is a matter which may concern Jaipur IPL cricket Private Ltd. but that is a different matter altogether. The question is whether Mr Raj Kundra was heard by the Justice Mudgal Committee, before holding him guilty of betting. Our answer to that question is in the affirmative. Admittedly, Mr Raj Kundra was heard by the committee before concluding that he had indulged in betting. Absence of any notice to anyone else was of little consequence so long as the person concerned was duly notified and afforded a fair opportunity.

215. There was no serious challenge to the findings recorded by the Probe Committee on the merits of the findings against Mr Raj Kundra. Jaipur IPL Cricket Private Ltd., contended that the finding was based on certain assumptions, but there is no merit in those contentions. Even otherwise strict rules of evidence do not have any application to an enquiry like the one entrusted to the Probe Committee or contemplated by IPL Operational Rules. The essence of the rules applicable even to the Disciplinary Commission is that it ought to adopt a fair and reasonable procedure while enquiring into the allegations of misconduct. Rule 6.3.19 of the Operational Rules specifically states that the standard of proof in respect of all complaints shall be 'whether the Commission is comfortably satisfied' with the allegations that the offence has been committed. Such satisfaction could on a sliding scale vary from a mere balance of probability up to proof beyond a reasonable doubt. Rules of evidence are made specifically inapplicable to the disciplinary proceedings in terms of Rule 6.3.20 of the IPL Operational Rules. The Probe Committee's findings comply with all the basic requirements of fairness and reasonableness and, therefore, call for no interference from us particularly when we are neither sitting in appeal over the said findings nor are we required to substitute our own conclusion based on a reappraisal of the material that was available before the Probe Committee for those of the Committee.

216. The following principles may be gathered from the above discussion:

(1) A member of an organization is bound to abide by its rules; and if the rules provide for expulsion, he shall be expelled only in the manner provided by the rules.
(2) The organization is bound to act strictly according to the rules whether a particular rule is mandatory or directory falls to be decided in each case, having regard to the well-settled rules of construction in that regard.
(3) The jurisdiction of a Civil Court is rather limited; it cannot obviously sit as a Court of Appeal from decisions of such a body; it can set aside the order of

such a body, if the said body acts without jurisdiction or does not act in good faith or acts in violation of the principles of natural justice.

217. At any rate, the domestic Tribunal under the rules in the instant case was substituted by a Tribunal constituted under the orders of the court and with the consent of the parties, to serve a larger public good, namely to find out the veracity of the serious allegations of sporting frauds like spot-fixing, match-fixing and betting by those who were not only participants in the tournaments played but also managing the affairs of the BCCI giving rise to serious issues of conflict of interest adversely affecting the game so popular in this country that any fraud as suggested was bound to shake the confidence of the public in general and those who love it in particular. Same is the position with the decision of the *Bombay High Court in Ambalal Sarabhai and Ors. v. Phiris H. Antia* (AIR 1939 Bom. 35). That was also a case where a member of a social club was expelled from the club and the expulsion challenged in the Court. A Single Judge of the High Court of Bombay in second appeal held that the club had not followed the elementary principles of natural justice which gave enough room to the Civil Court to interfere. The position in the case at hand is in no way analogous to the fact situation of that case. So long as Mudgal Committee has conducted the proceedings in consonance with the principles of natural justice, the Committee's finding that Raj Kundra was a team official of Rajasthan Royals and that he had indulged in betting cannot be faulted. Therefore Gurunath Meiyappan and Raj Kundra were 'team officials' of their respective IPL teams – Chennai Super Kings and Rajasthan Royals and allegations of betting levelled against them stand proved.

What possible action is permissible against Mr Gurunath Meiyappan and Mr Raj Kundra and their teams and franchisees is what logically falls for our consideration. There is no gainsaying that the question shall have to be answered by reference to the set of rules applicable. It is common ground that there are different sets of rules and regulations applicable to the fact situation at hand. It is also not in dispute that even the franchise agreement between the BCCI and the franchisees contain provisions that provide for action in situations like the one at hand.

A. Permissible Action in Terms of the IPL Operational Rules

218. Section I of the IPL Operational Rules define different expressions used in these rules. Sections 2 and 4 stipulate obligations of the franchisees and team/players while section 6 thereof prescribes regulations and disciplinary procedure which, *inter alia*, includes under section 6.1 sanctions that can be imposed for acts of misconduct if any committed. A careful reading of the Operational Rules show that every franchisee, player, team official and/or match official is subject to the said rules. In terms of Rule 2.1, participation or other involvement with the league is deemed to constitute an acceptance by each person subject to these operational rules of an agreement with an obligation owed to BCCI to be bound by the regulations, the laws of cricket, the terms of the player contract and the jurisdiction of the BCCI in connection therewith. In terms of Rule 2.1.4, each person subject to these rules is restrained from acting or omitting to act in any way that would or might reasonably be anticipated to have an adverse effect on the match and/or reputation of such person, any team, any player, any team official, the BCCI, the league and/or the game or which would otherwise bring any of the foregoing into disrepute. More importantly, each franchisee is in terms of Rule 4.1.1 under an obligation to ensure that each of its team official complies with the regulations, and in particular Article 2 of the BCCI and Anti-Corruption Code. The rule, however, provides that all those persons who are accredited for the league by BCCI either centrally or locally, shall be deemed to be team officials for the purposes of those regulations. In terms of Regulation 6.4, BCCI can impose any one of the sanctions which includes suspension of the player or other person subject to the Operational Rules from playing or involving in matches for a specified period and suspension of the team or franchisee from the league. Payment of money from a person subject to these Operational Rules either to BCCI or to any other person subject to those rules is also provided as one of the permissible sanctions.

Therefore, once Mr Gurunath Meiyappan and Mr Raj Kundra are accepted as team officials, their misconduct which has adversely affected the image of the BCCI and the league as also the game and brought each one of them to disrepute can result in imposition of one or more of the sanctions stipulated under Rule 6.4. The sanctions are not limited to Gurunath Meiyappan and Raj Kundra alone but may extend to suspension of the team or the franchisee from the league also.

B. Permissible Action under the Anti-corruption Code for Participants

219. The BCCI claims to have adopted the Anti-corruption Code for achieving, what it describes as certain 'fundamental sporting imperatives'. The fundamental sporting imperatives highlight that the BCCI is, by the standards set by it, duty-bound to ensure that the game of cricket is played in accordance with those sporting imperatives not only because the game itself is described as a gentleman's game but also because adherence to sporting imperatives alone can maintain the public confidence in its purity. The BCCI has, as will appear from a plain reading of the imperatives set out in the rules, committed itself in no uncertain terms to maintaining public confidence in the game. The BCCI stands firmly committed to the following fundamental sporting imperatives:

1.1.1 All cricket matches are to be contested on a level playing-field, with the outcome to be determined solely by the respective merits of the competing teams and to remain uncertain until the cricket match is completed. This is the essential characteristic that gives sport its unique appeal.

1.1.2 Public confidence in the authenticity and integrity of the sporting contest is therefore vital. If that confidence is undermined, then the very essence of cricket will be shaken to the core. It is the determination to protect that essence of cricket that has led the Board of Control for Cricket in India to adopt this Anti-Corruption Code.

1.1.3 Advancing technology and increasing popularity have led to a substantial increase in the amount, and the sophistication, of betting on cricket matches.

The development of new betting products, including spread-betting and betting exchanges, as well as internet and phone accounts that allow people to place a bet at any time and from any place, even after a cricket match has started, have all increased the potential for the development of corrupt betting practices. That, in turn, increases the risk that attempts will be made to involve participants in such practices. Even where that risk is more theoretical than practical, its consequence is to create a perception that the integrity of the sport is under threat.

1.1.4 Furthermore, the nature of this type of misconduct is such that it is carried out under cover and in secret, thereby creating significant challenges for the BCCI in the enforcement of rules of conduct. As a consequence, the BCCI needs to be empowered to seek information from and share information with competent authorities and other relevant third parties, and to require Participants to cooperate fully with all investigations and requests for information.

1.1.5 The BCCI is committed to taking every step in its power to prevent corrupt betting practices undermining the integrity of the sport of cricket, including any efforts to influence improperly the outcome or any other aspect of any Match or Event.

220. In Appendix 1 to the Anti-Corruption Code for Participants are given definitions for different terms appearing in the said code including a definition for expressions like, bet, corrupt conduct, domestic match, event, ineligibility, inside information, match, participant, player, player support personnel, etc. The relevant part of the Appendix dealt with the definition may also be extracted for the sake of clarity:

DEFINITIONS:

Anti-Corruption Code: This Anti-Corruption Code promulgated by the BCCI on the Effective date.

Bet: Any wager, bet or other form of financial speculation, and Betting is the carrying out of such activity.

Corrupt Conduct: Any act or omission that would amount to an offence under Article 2 of this Anti-Corruption Code or the equivalent provisions of anti-corruption rules of any other National Cricket Federation or the ICC Anti-Corruption Code.

Domestic Match: Any 'First-Class Match', 'List A Limited Overs Match' or 'List A Twenty20 Match', as those terms are defined in the ICC Classification of Official Cricket (as amended from time to time) including all matches organized by the BCCI.

Event: Any competition, tournament, tour, event or equivalent that involves one or more Matches.

Ineligibility: Means the Participant is barred for a specified period of time from participation in the sport of cricket, as set out more specifically in Article 6.5.

Inside Information: Any information relating to any Match or Event that a Participant possesses by virtue of his/her position within the sport. Such information includes, but is not limited to, factual information regarding the competitors in the Match or Event, the conditions, tactical considerations or any other aspect of the

Match or Event, but does not include such information that is already published or a matter of public record, readily acquired by an interested member of the public, or disclosed according to the rules and regulations governing the relevant Match or Event.

Match: A cricket match of any format and duration in length in which two cricket teams compete against each other.

Participant: Any Player, Player Support Personnel, Umpire, Match Referee or Umpire Support Personnel.

Player: Any cricketer who is selected (or who has been selected in the preceding twelve months) in any playing or touring team or squad that is chosen to represent the BCCI or any of its affiliate and associate bodies in any International Match or Domestic Match.

Player Support Personnel: Any coach, trainer, manager, selector, team official, doctor, physiotherapist or any other person employed by, representing or otherwise affiliated to a playing/touring team or squad that is chosen to represent a National Cricket Federation in any Domestic Match or International Match or series of such Matches.

Suspension: Means the Participant is temporarily barred from participating in the sport of cricket pending a decision on the allegation that he/she has committed an offence under this Anti-Corruption Code, as set out more specifically in Article 4.6.

221. In terms of Article 2 appearing in the Code of Anti-corruption, betting, misuse of inside information are some of the actionable wrongs under the Code. Article 2 reads:

Article 2: Offences Under This Anti-corruption Code

2.1 CORRUPTION

2.1.1 Fixing or contriving in any way or otherwise influencing improperly, or being a part to any effort to fix or contrive in any way or otherwise influence improperly, the result, progress, conduct or any other aspect of any Match or Event.

2.1.2 Seeking, accepting, offering or agreeing to accept any bribe or other Reward to fix or to contrive in any bribe or other Reward to fix or to contrive in any way or otherwise to influence improperly to result, progress, conduct or any other aspect of any Match or Event.

2.1.3 Soliciting, including, enticing, instructing, persuading, encouraging or facilitating (a) any Participant to commit an offence under any of the foregoing provisions of this Article 2.1 and/or (b) any other person to do any act that would be an offence if that person were a Participant

2.2 BETTING

2.2.1 Placing, accepting, laying or otherwise entering into any Bet with any other party (whether individual, company or otherwise) in relation to the result, progress, conduct or any other aspect of any Match or Event.

2.2.2 Soliciting, including, enticing, instructing, persuading, encouraging, facilitating or authorizing any other party to enter into a Bet for the direct or indirect benefit of the Participant in relation to the result, progress, conduct or any other aspect of any Match or Event.

2.3 MISUSE OF INSIDE INFORMATION:

2.3.1 Using, for Betting purposes, any inside information

2.3.2 Disclosing inside information to any person (with or without Reward) before or during any Match or Event where the participant might reasonably be expected to know that disclosure of such information in such circumstances could be used in relation to Betting.

NOTE: Any potential offence under this Article will be considered on its own set of facts and the particular circumstances surrounding any relevant disclosure. For example, it may be an offence under this clause to disclose inside information: (a) to journalists or other members of the media; and/or (b) on social networking websites where the Participant might reasonably be expected to know that disclosure of such information in such circumstances could be used in relation to Betting. However, nothing in this Article is intended to prohibit any such disclosure made within a personal relationship (such as to a member of the Participant's family) where it is reasonable for the Participant to expect that such information can be disclosed in confidence and without being subsequently used for Betting.

2.3.3 Soliciting, inducing, enticing persuading, encouraging or facilitation (a) any Participant to commit an offence under any of the foregoing provisions of this Article 2.3 and/or (b) any other person to do any act that would be an offence if that person were a Participant.

2.4 GENERAL

2.4.1 Providing or receiving any gift, payment or other benefit (whether of a monetary value or otherwise) in circumstances that the Participant might reasonably have expected could bring him/her or the sport of cricket into disrepute.

NOTE: This Article is only intended to catch 'disrepute' that, when considered in all of the relevant circumstances, relates (directly or indirectly) to any of the underlying imperatives of and conduct prohibited by this Anti-Corruption Code (including as described in Article 1.1.)

Where any substantial gift, payment or other benefit is received by any Participant from an unknown person or organization and/or for no apparent reason, such Participant is advised to report such receipt to the Designated Anti-Corruption Official (or his/her designee). Where such Participant does not make such a report, then that is likely to constitute strong evidence of the commission of this offence.

2.4.2 Failing or refusing to disclose to the ACU BCCI (without undue delay) full details of any approaches or invitations received by the Participant to engage in conduct that would amount to a breach of this Anti-Corruption Code.

2.4.3 Failing or refusing to disclose to the ACU BCCI (without undue delay) full details of any incident, fact or matter that comes to the attention of a Participant that may evidence an offence under this

Anti-Corruption Code by a third party, including (without limitation) approaches or invitations that have been received by any other party to engage in conduct that would amount to a breach of this Anti-Corruption Code.

NOTE: All Participants shall have continuing obligation to report any new incident, fact, or matter that may evidence an offence under this Anti-Corruption Code to the ACU-BCCI, even if the Participants' prior knowledge has already been reported.

2.4.4 Failing or refusing, without compelling justification, to cooperate with any reasonable investigation carried out by the Designated Anti-Corruption Official (or his/her designee) in relation to possible offences under this Anti-Corruption Code, including failure to provide any information and/or documentation requested by the Designated Anti-Corruption Official (or his/her designee) (whether as part of a formal Demand pursuant to Article 4.3 or otherwise) that may be relevant to such investigation.

2.5.1 Any attempt by a Participant, or any agreement between (a) a Participant and (b) any other person, to act in a manner that would culminate in the commission of an offence under this Anti-Corruption Code, shall be treated as if an offence had been committed, whether or not such attempt or agreement in fact resulted in the commission of such offence. However, there shall be no offence under this Anti-Corruption Code where the Participant renounces the attempt or agreement prior to it being discovered by a third party not involved in the attempt or agreement.

2.5.2 A participant who authorizes, causes, knowingly assists, encourages, aids, abets, covers up or is otherwise complicit in any acts or omissions of the type described in Article 2.1–2.4 committed by his/her coach, trainer, manager, agent, family member, guest or other affiliate or associate shall be treated as having committed such acts or omissions himself and shall be liable accordingly under this Anti-Corruption Code.

222. Sanctions prescribed under Article 6 of the Code include suspension ranging from six months to a lifetime depending upon the nature and gravity of the offence/misconduct proved against the person concerned. Article 6 runs as under:

6.1 Where it is determined that an offence under this Anti-Corruption Code has been committed, the BCCI Disciplinary Committee will be required to impose an appropriate sanction upon the Participant from the range of permissible sanctions described in Article 6.2. In order to determine the appropriate sanction that is to be imposed in each case, the BCCI Disciplinary Committee must first determine the relative seriousness of the offence, including identifying all relevant factors that it deems to:

6.1.1 aggravate the nature of the offence under this Anti-Corruption Code, namely:

6.1.1.4 where the offence substantially damaged (or had the potential to damage substantially) the commercial value and/or the public interest in the relevant Match(es) or Event(s);

6.1.1.5 where the offence affected (or had the potential to affect) the result of the relevant Match(es) or Event(s);

6.1.1.6 where the welfare of a Participant or any other person has been endangered as a result of the offence;

6.1.1.7 where the offence involved more than one Participant or other persons; and/or

6.1.1.8 any other aggravating factor(s) that the BCCI Disciplinary Committee considers relevant and appropriate.

6.1.2 mitigate the nature of the offence under the Anti-Corruption Code, namely:

6.1.2.2 the Participant's good previous disciplinary record;

6.1.2.3 the young age and/or lack of experience of the Participant;

6.1.2.4 where the Participant has cooperated with the Designated Anti-Corruption Official (or his/her designee) and any investigation or Demand carried out by him/her;

6.1.2.5 where the offence did not substantially damage (or have the potential to substantially damage) the commercial value and/or the public interest in the relevant Match(s) or Event(s);

6.1.2.6 where the offence did not affect (or have the potential to affect) the result of the relevant Match(s) or Event(s);

6.1.2.8 where the Participant has already suffered penalties under other laws and/or regulations for the same offence; and/or

6.1.2.9 any other mitigating factor(s) that the BCCI Disciplinary Committee considers relevant and appropriate.

6.2 Having considered all of the factors described in Articles 6.1.1 and 6.1.2, the BCCI Disciplinary Committee shall then determine, in accordance with the following table, what the appropriate sanction(s) should be:

ANTI-CORRUPTION CODE OFFENCE
RANGE OF PERMISSIBLE PERIOD OF INELIGIBILITY
ADDITIONAL DISCRETION TO IMPOSE A FINE
Articles 2.1.1, 2.1.2, 2.1.3 and 2.1.4 (Corruption)
A minimum of five (5) years and a maximum of a lifetime.
AND (in all cases) the Anti-Corruption Tribunal shall have the discretion to impose a fine on the Player or Player Support Personnel up to a maximum of the value of any Reward received by the Player or Player Support Personnel directly or indirectly, out of, or in relation to, the offence committed under the Anti-Corruption Code.
Articles 2.2.1, 2.2.2 and 2.2.3 (Betting)
A minimum of two (2) years and a maximum of five (5) years.
Articles 2.3.1 and 2.3.3 (as it relates to an offence under Article 2.3.1) (Misuse of inside information)
A minimum of two (2) years and a maximum of five (5) years.

Articles 2.3.2 and 2.3.3 (as it relates to an offence under Article 2.3.2) (Misuse of inside information)
A minimum of six (6) months and a maximum of five (5) years.
Articles 2.4.1 and 2.4.2
(General) A minimum of one (1) year and a maximum of five (5) years).
Articles 2.4.3 and 2.4.4
(General) A minimum of six (6) months and a maximum of two (2) years.
Article 2.2.1 treats betting as one of the actionable wrongs under the Code. In terms of Article 2.5.2 the participant who authorizes, causes, knowingly assists, encourages, aids, abets, covers up or is otherwise complicit in any act or omission of the types described in Articles 2.1 to 2.4 committed by his/her coach, trainer, manager, agent, family member, guest or other associate shall be treated as having committed such an act or omission himself and shall be liable accordingly under the Anti-Corruption Code.
The expression 'participant' has been defined to include any player, player support personnel, Umpire, match Referee or Umpire Support Personnel. The expression 'player support personnel' means any coach trainer, manager, selector, team official, doctor, etc. Mr GM having been found to be a team official of Chennai Super Kings is a 'player support personnel' hence a participant within the meaning of the Anti-Corruption Code. What is important is that apart from GM in his capacity as the team official if any participant connected with CSK, authorizes, causes, knowingly assists, encourages, aids, abets, covers up or is otherwise complicit in any act or omission he/she will also be liable to action under the Anti-Corruption Code as if he/she had himself/herself committed the act of misconduct.
In terms of Article 6 of the Code, upon consideration of relevant factors the disciplinary committee of the BCCI is empowered to impose an appropriate sanction upon the delinquent having regard to the provisions of Article 6.2 and the table appearing thereunder. There is, therefore, no manner of doubt that even under the Anti-Corruption Code for participants any act like betting can attract sanctions not only for the person who indulges in such conduct but also for all those who authorize, cause, knowingly assist, encourage, aid, abet, cover up or are otherwise complicit in any act of omission or commission relating to such activity.
(iii) Permissible action under the 'Code of Conduct for Players and the Team Official':
Code of Conduct for Players and Team Officials also prescribes punishment/sanctions for players or team officials found guilty of different levels of offences stipulated in the said code. Articles 2.1–2.5 stipulate different levels of offences which, if committed by the players or team officials, can lead to imposition of sanctions against them. Article 2.4.4 is, however, a catch-all provision to cover all types of conduct which are not covered by specific offences set out in the Code. It reads:
'2.4.4. Where the facts of the alleged incident are not adequately or clearly covered by any of the above offences, conduct that either; (a) is contrary to the spirit of the game; or (b) brings the game into disrepute.

> Note: Article 2.4.4 is intended to be a "catch-all" provision of cover all types of conduct of an overwhelmingly serious nature that are not (and, because of their nature, cannot be) adequately covered by the specific offences set out elsewhere in the Code of Conduct.
>
> The guidance notes to Article 2.1.8 may be referred for examples of conduct that may (depending upon the seriousness and context of the breach) be prohibited under Article 2.4.4.'
>
> The team official who is found guilty of betting is certainly acting against the spirit of the game and bringing disrepute to it. Article 7 of the Code empowers the match Referee or the Commissioner to impose suitable sanction upon the person concerned depending upon the level of the offence which is committed. The punishment can range between warning to suspension for a lifetime depending upon the nature and the gravity of the offence committed.
>
> We may, before parting with the discussion on this question, refer to the franchise agreement executed between BCCI on the one hand and the franchisees on the other. Clause 11.3 of the said agreement reads:
>
> 11.3 BCCI-IPL may terminate this Agreement with immediate effect by written notice if:
>
> a. there is a Change of Control of the Franchise (whether direct or indirect) and/or a Listing which in each case does not occur strictly in accordance with Clause 10;
> b. the Franchisee transfers any material part of its business or assets to any other person other than in accordance with Clause 10;
> c. the Franchisee, any Franchisee Group Company and/or any Owner acts in any way which has a material adverse effect upon the reputation or standing of the League, BCCI-IPL, BCCI, the Franchisee, the Team (or any other team in the League) and/or the game of cricket.

In terms of Clause 11.3(c) if the franchisee, any franchisee group company and/or any owner acts in a manner that has a material adverse effect upon the reputation or standing of the league, BCCI-IPL, BCCI, the franchisee, the team or any other team and/or the game of cricket, the BCCI-IPL is empowered to terminate the agreement. The expression 'owner' has been defined in Clause 1.1 as under:

> 'Owner shall mean any person who is the ultimate Controller of the Franchisee;'

It is evident from the above provisions that the BCCI-IPL is in situations stipulated under Clause 11.3 competent to direct the termination of the agreement. What would constitute 'material adverse effect' upon reputation or standing of the league or BCCI-IPL, BCCI, the franchisee, the team or game of cricket shall, however, depend upon the facts and circumstances of each case. What cannot be disputed is that the right to terminate the agreement is available to the BCCI-IPL even in accordance with the provisions of the franchise agreements.

§2. National Code Against Age Fraud

223. The purpose of the Code is to eliminate age fraud in sports so as to ensure fair play and put in place an effective regulatory mechanism so that suitable action can be taken against athletes found guilty of committing age fraud. This Code forms part of the sport rules governing the conditions under which sport is played. This Code has become operational from 1 April 2010. SAI implements this Code for its various sports promotional schemes for various age groups and for holding national coaching camps. This Code now finds place in National Sports Development Bill, 2013 and deemed to have been notified under it (section 20.1). National Olympic Committee, NSFs, National or Regional Sports Organization and the SAI are bound by the Code (section 20.2).

SAI, at the time of admitting an athlete into its Sports Promotion Schemes and NSFs at the time of registering or allowing a new athlete to participate in an event, will get all the players in age level competitions medically examined and as per medical report will issue an identity card to the athletes. The athletes who are playing in age level competitions either with SAI or NSF, as the case may be, are also subjected to medical examination and will also be issued identity card. If any existing athletes is found overage even after going through the appeal process, will be subjected to performance review before readjusting in the appropriate age group as part of the normal weeding out process.

I. Prevention of Sporting Fraud Bill, 2013

224. The purpose of the 'Prevention of Sporting Fraud Bill, 2013' (the 'Bill') is to prevent and combat sporting fraud affecting the integrity of sports and fair play in relations to national and international sporting events and for connected or incidental matters. The Bill defines sporting frauds in sporting events that can be domestic, national or international in section 3 as any direct or indirect activity of a person which:

(i) manipulates the sports result (even if the final outcome is actually altered or not) or arranges an irregular alteration of the field of play or the result of a sporting event including its incidental results or deliberately misapplies the rules of the sport in order to obtain any economic or other advantage or benefit for his own self or for any other person so that the uncertainty normally associated with the result of a sports event is removed or reduced;

(ii) wilfully fails to perform to his/her full potential for an economic or any other advantage or benefit of his own self or any other person except if such underperformance can be attributed to a strategic or tactical reason deployed in the interest of that sport or team;

(iii) possesses insider information (any information which is not in the public domain and is not published or exists only as a matter of record or is specifically within the knowledge of a member due to his position, participation or such involvement in the sporting event) being a member but discloses such information to any person before or during any sporting event with the knowledge that such disclosure shall likely lead to financial gain or to be used in relation to betting or manipulation of a sporting event;

(iv) omits to perform the duty imposed under section 4 i.e., any person who gets an information as to the commission of any of the above acts shall give such information to the appropriate authority, i.e., any person designated by the Central Government including the State government and its nominees or the team management or the NSF in writing and therefore has a duty to inform.

225. Any person held liable for committing sports fraud relating to (i) and (ii) above shall face an imprisonment up to five years and a fine of INR 10 lakhs or five times the economic benefit derived from such sporting fraud, whichever is greater whereas, a person liable under (iii) and (iv) above will face an imprisonment up to three years and fine of INR 5 lakhs or three times the economic benefit derived from such sporting fraud, whichever is greater.

Attempting to commit an offence of sporting fraud or the abetment of the same is punishable with the same punishment as is provided for the offence.

If a sporting offence is committed by a company, then the liability, as per section 8, falls on the company as well as on every person who at the time of committal of offence was in charge of and responsible for the conduct of the business unless the person can prove that such offence was committed without his knowledge or that he exercised complete possible due diligence towards preventing it.

As per section 9, only a court not inferior to that of a Metropolitan Magistrate or Judicial Magistrate of the first class can try the offences punishable under this Bill. Suo Moto cognizance powers are not given under this Bill, so a court shall only take cognizance of a sporting fraud if a complaint is made by either the appropriate authority or by a person from the National Sport Federation who is in charge of implementing its anti-corruption code or rule or by a person who has given a prior notice of at least sixty days to the appropriate authority of the alleged offence and of his intention to make a complaint to the court.

The Central Government has the power to make rules for this Act. Every such rule once made shall be laid before each house of the Parliament, in its session for a total period of thirty days. Before the expiry of such session if both houses agree in making modification in the rule or regulation or agree that it should not be made, the rule or regulation shall have effect only in such modified form or be of no effect, however, any such modification or annulment shall be without prejudice to the validity of anything previously done under that rule or regulation.

Chapter 6. Relationship Between Ordinary Justice and Sport Justice

226. There can be various types of sport disputes like administrative, disciplinary, procedural, technical, financial and commercial or contractual. There can be issues of interpretation of rules of a sporting body or club or their jurisdiction. So far as various parties are concerned, disputes can be between sportsperson and umpire, referees, team, clubs or with third parties. The sport disputes may arise out of selection procedure of athletes for representation at national and international forums, disciplinary issues against the athletes, bans imposed due to age fraud, gender inequality, maintenance and submission of medical records and issues regarding financial support.

§1. Internal Mechanism

227. The concept of sport being autonomous gives rise to thinking that disputes should be resolved through internal mechanism within a suitable forum established by the relevant NSF. Sport disputes are resolved either through internal systems for settlement of disputes or through arbitration and conciliation. The last resort is no doubt filing a case in the court and resolving it through litigation. There is another dimension to the freedom of getting the matters resolved through courts; the rules of IOA provide that a member of IOA will not seek redress in any court of law. The NSFs, Associations or State Olympic Associations affiliated to IOA include in their Constitution a provision that the federations or associations would have all unresolved disputes settled by the IOA and their members voluntarily surrender their right of seeking redress in any court of law. Further, every member is deemed to continue its membership of the IOA on the specific condition that it voluntarily surrenders its right of seeking redress in any court of law. The courts on their own refrain from interfering in internal dispute resolution mechanism of sports bodies. In *Shyam Babu Verma v. Union of India* ((1994) 2 SCC 521), the Supreme Court of India observed that 'the court should refrain from interfering in the decision of the expert body, tribunal or a specially constituted body unless the decision of such body is unreasonable, arbitrary, illegal and infringes the fundamental right or constitutional right of a citizen of India'.

I. Indian Court of Arbitration for Sports

228. In 2011, a governing body to set up the Indian Court of Arbitration for Sports, was constituted consisting of Chairman and seven other members. This was one of the first efforts made in India to set up a uniform and effective dispute redressal mechanism keeping in mind the complex issues involved in Sports. This Court was set up for speedy and effective redressal of disputes. However steps taken to establish an efficient dispute resolution mechanism have not resulted in resolving disputes efficiently. The Commission set up in 2011 was not very successful in setting up a Court of Arbitration for Sports (CASs). Hence, there is lack of effective dispute resolution mechanism for sportspersons in India. Arbitration is preferred in many foreign countries and they have submitted to the jurisdiction of the CASs.

The NSFs also have failed to establish satisfactory internal mechanisms and forums for redressal of grievances and dispute resolution. This problem is compounded by their failure to incorporate an arbitration clause within their regulations entitling athletes final recourse to the CAS. As a result, athletes are left with only remedy to approach the courts to resolve their grievances.

229. The failure of NSFs to provide adequate internal dispute resolution mechanisms received national attention by two recent cases. The first concerned the female boxer Sarita Devi, which led to filing of a Public Interest Litigation (PIL) (*Rajiv Dutta v. Union of India & Ors.*, W.P.(C) No. 8734/2014).[15] The PIL challenged the decision of International Boxing Association ('AIBA') which suspended Devi for refusing to accept a bronze medal at the Asian Games. It was argued that these federations should take note of the rules and regulations of CAS.

230. The second case concerned former Olympic wrestler, Sushil Kumar (*Sushil Kumar v. Union of India* W.P.(C) 4514/2016),[16] who filed a writ petition against the arbitrary selection procedure adopted by the Wrestling Federation of India (WFI) for India's representation at the 2016 Olympics, and made 'MYAS' a party to the dispute. On 17 June 2016, as a response to the case filed by Sushil Kumar, the MYAS issued a new set of guidelines titled: 'Safeguarding the Interests of Sportspersons and Provision of Effective Grievance Redressal System in the Constitution of National Sports Federations'.[17] The Guidelines direct all NSFs to ensure that they:

(i) establish an effective, transparent and fair 'Grievance Redressal System' (i.e., dispute resolution system) to safeguard the interests of sportspersons; and
(ii) include within their constitution the right for aggrieved sportspersons to appeal their case to CAS.

§2. Problems Faced by Athletes

231. Prior to the publication of the guidelines, the remedies available to sportspersons against most NSFs have been twofold:

(i) informally plead to their respective NSF to reconsider any decision; and/or
(ii) file a suit in the courts to override such decision pronounced by the NSF.

Both these remedies have proven to be for all practical purposes, futile. NSFs usually decline to reconsider their decisions. And the courts have either taken too

15. https://lobis.nic.in/ddir/gro/judgement/15-01-2016/ GRO15012016CW87342014.pdf.
16. https://lobis.nic.in/ddir/dhc/MMH/judgement/06-06-2016/MMH06062016CW45142016.pdf.
17. Ministry of Youth Affairs and Sports, Safeguarding the Interests of Sportspersons and Provision of Effective Grievance Redressal System in the Constitution of National Sports Federations published on 17 Jun. 2016 (Guidelines).

long to settle the dispute, where the action became infructuous (fruitless) as the event in contention was already over, or refused to interfere with decisions of the NSF.

232. The Honourable Delhi High Court in Sushil Kumar observed:
41. Keeping in view the aforesaid, this Court is of the view that a writ Court will not interfere in the exercise of discretion of the National Sports Federation and substitute its own judgment except where the discretion is shown to have been exercised in an arbitrary or capricious or perverse manner or contrary to settled principles or practices.

233. Despite being mandated by the NSDC, 2011 most of India's NSFs still do not have written rules, which make it difficult for the courts to determine what may be termed as arbitrary, capricious or perverse. For example, WFI's Olympic selection procedure, which was at the centre of Sushil Kumar's case, operates largely by tradition or precedents. The guidelines clearly establish that it is the responsibility of the NSFs to incorporate into their constitution or by-laws appropriate and coherent internal mechanisms to resolve all grievances. The guidelines mandate all NSFs to create rules to address this.

§3. Taking Grievances to CAS

234. CAS is an independent arbitral body whose jurisdiction is based upon contractual consent. Thus it is a prerequisite for a matter to be heard by CAS is a relevant contractual provision included within the NSFs regulations or by-laws. NSDC 2011 (section 6.1(b)11) implicitly recognizes the jurisdiction of CAS by stating that NSFs must comply with the principles laid down in the Olympic Charter. Section 15.1 of the NSDC, 2011 further provides for a grievance redressal mechanism.

235. Devi was banned by the AIBA for breaching the AIBA Disciplinary Code by refusing to accept the bronze medal at the Asian Games. However, she was unable to file an appeal against the ban with CAS as the relevant NSF, being Boxing India, failed to provide for such a right within its regulations. The court in its judgment stated:
It is apparent from the material placed on record that no remedy is available as of today to appeal to CAS against the decision of the International Sports Bodies like AIBA. The fact that CAS is the final authority for settlement of disputes arising out of the decisions of International Sports Bodies has not been disputed by the Respondent No. 1 [MYAS]. It also appears that the National Sports Code of 2011 contains a provision of appeal to CAS against any decision of Sports Federations in India.

236. It is important to note that while the courts have refused on several occasions to interfere with the internal functioning of the NSFs, the court in this case acknowledged the importance of the right for athletes to appeal to CAS:
It also appears that the National Sports Code of 2011 contains a provision of appeal to CAS against any decision of Sports Federations in India …

… we deem it appropriate to direct the Respondent No. 1 to consider the contents of this petition as a representation and take an appropriate decision in accordance with law after giving an opportunity of personal hearing to – petitioner herein to substantiate his plea that it is essential to ensure incorporation of a specific provision for dispute settlement with International sports bodies.

237. With respect to the publication of the guidelines, the court in Devi's case directed the MYAS to ensure that all NSFs incorporate the CAS clause within three months from the date of the judgment i.e., 16 January 2016. As there was no punitive measure attached for non-compliance, the MYAS did not adhere to this deadline, and it took the latter case of Sushil Kumar for them to finally capture the direction in clause (ii) of the guidelines.

§4. The Guidelines and Dispute Resolution

238. As per guidelines, the NSFs must establish appropriate internal mechanisms to resolve disputes in a coherent manner based on the written guidelines in their constitution. The guidelines mandate all NSFs to create rules addressing the said issue. Furthermore, they have brought to the fore pertinent issues in the current operations of NSFs and the contrasting nature in which they function. The guidelines have reaffirmed the jurisdiction of CAS and the MYAS has advised all NSFs to add it in their respective constitutions/by-laws, it unfortunately does not specify a time period within which NSFs must incorporate the guidelines. The guidelines are not the government's only effort to improve sports regulation and fight injustice. The National Sports Ethics Commission Bill 2016, aiming to improve the integrity of sports in India, was tabled in Parliament. The Bill aims to provide for the constitution of a National Sports Ethics Commission to ensure ethical practices and fair play in sports including elimination of doping practices, match-fixing, fraud of age and sexual harassment of women in sports and for matters connected therewith or incidental thereto. The Bill also proposes that the National Commission which is established to oversee the matters of ethics, be made a quasi-judicial adjudicatory body for all the disputes in which the NSFs are impleaded.

§5. Classification of Sports Disputes

239. As evident the sport disputes cannot and are not confined to the sporting community inter se. It can be between sporting body and a supplier of the sport equipment or a general supplier. Hence settlement of a sporting dispute is not exclusive domain of the sporting club or other sports associations but can be the subject matter of general administrative and judicial settlement process and machinery.

I. Technical Disputes

240. These disputes pertain to application of rules of a particular sport to an individual sportsperson or a team. These arise during sporting event and are settled in accordance with technical rules applicable to a particular sport by referees, umpires or judges. The decision or ruling on such disputes is revised or appealed against in accordance with and before the authorities as provided in the rules of such sporting body.

II. Administrative Disputes

241. This type of dispute covers the areas where disputes are related to applicability of rules or measures adopted by the governing sports body. For example disputes pertaining to eligibility of an individual player or a club in a tournament.

III. Disciplinary Disputes

242. This includes disputes relating to disciplinary proceedings started against a player. It may be related to the behaviour of the player in a sporting event or misconduct or negligence as an employee of a club or body. For example, age fraud or use of doping by a player will give rise to disciplinary dispute and action.

A. Disciplinary Actions

243. The IOA member units are liable to the following disciplinary actions:

(a) Caution.
(b) Warning.
(c) Suspension for a specified period of time.
(d) Expulsion from IOA.

244. The following conditions are to be satisfied:

(a) No penalty can be imposed before the unit at fault has been heard at the enquiry specially conducted for this purpose; that is, application of *audi alteram partem* rule.
(b) Should an affiliate Unit fail to present itself through its accredited office-bearer at the enquiry, it shall be considered as having been interrogated.
(c) As a general rule, except in special circumstances duly appreciated, suspension shall be applied as a temporary measure.

Disciplinary sanction will not be taken unless supported by two-thirds of the General Assembly Members present and voting.

B. Appeal

245. All NSFs/State Olympic Associations affiliated to the IOA commit themselves to appeal only to the President of the IOA in the event of any differences which may arise with regard to the functioning of the NSFs/Associations/State Olympic Associations within its laid down statutes and regulations. NSFs/Associations are not allowed to appeal to any other jurisdiction. This situation will change after coming into force of the National Sports Development Bill, 2013.

C. Unsportsmanlike Behaviour and Acts of Violence

246. During the Olympic, Commonwealth Games, Asian Games, SAF Games and national games, or any other international competitions, any unsportsmanlike behaviour on the part of a sportsman or sportswoman, official or coach, which includes insulting, making undesirable gestures, abusing the decision of the judges or referees and provoking the opponents or spectators, etc., in a word, committing any act not in keeping with the propriety of sports, or any act of violence can be punished as follows:

(a) Disqualification for the duration of the activity of that sporting activity.
(b) Disqualification for the entire duration of competition.
(c) Prohibition from participation in competitions for a fixed period of time.

D. Residual Powers

247. In the event of disagreements concerning the above Disciplinary Rules, the interpretation of these regulations falls within the competence of IOA Executive Council, which is the final authority.

E. Officiating Arrangements

248. The President of IOA is authorized to make officiating arrangements for office-bearers, including the office of president, Secretary General, Joint Secretaries and Treasurers as and when considered necessary by him, or when an office-bearer is away from his office on leave, other duties, sickness, etc.

F. Disaffiliation or Suspension

249. The following actions can be taken against sports associations or federations:

(a) The IOA General Assembly, on the recommendation of the President of IOA, either directly or through the IOA Executive Council, based on his discretion, is entitled to consider disaffiliation, de-recognition or suspension of the NSFs, Associations or State Olympic Association on one or more of the undermentioned grounds, after ensuring that a show-cause notice has been served and an explanation has been obtained and considered from the organization recommended for disaffiliation, de-recognition or suspension:
   - Non-observance of directives issued by the IOA from time to time.
   - Not holding elections after the completion of the normal tenure for which the office-bearers are elected. Any extension of the tenure of the office-bearers will be subject to obtaining prior written permission from the IOA.
   - Not submitting annual audited statement of accounts, annual report and list of current office-bearers within the stipulated time period.

(b) The decision of the IOA General Assembly must be supported by two-thirds majority votes of the members present and voting.

250. If the IOA General Assembly takes a decision to disaffiliate an NSF, Association or State Olympic Association, the President of IOA has the authority to constitute an ad-hoc body, preferably from among the Members of the IOA General Assembly, to look after the work done by the disaffiliated NSF, Association, State Olympic Association till such time that the President, IOA arranges for fresh elections to be held in the concerned NSF, Association or State Olympic Association which would then start functioning in the normal manner.

G. *Expulsion*

251. From time to time, cases of an individual, or group of individuals, belonging to, or associated with, an NSF, Association or State Olympic Association indulging in activities, including taking recourse to a Civil Court of law come up, which are prejudicial to the promotion of sports, including the efficient functioning of the concerned NSF, Association or State Olympic Association without utilizing the available resources of the IOA General Assembly either directly or through the IOA Executive Council, to issue a directive in consultation with the concerned NSF, Association or State Olympic Association, to take necessary action in the matter. A decision on this matter is required to be supported in the General Assembly by two-thirds majority of votes of the members present and voting. The IOA General Assembly is to ensure that before taking a decision, a show-cause notice has been served and an explanation to be obtained and considered from the individual, or group of individuals, recommended for disciplinary action. The decision for expulsion of an individual or group of individuals by the IOA General Assembly must be supported by a two-thirds majority of votes of the members present and voting.

252. A classic example of a disciplinary dispute is the ban imposed on a famous cricketer by the BCCI acting under its rules. *Md. Azharuddin v. Dr A. Muthaiiah and Others* (AIR 2002 AP 409) threw light on the disciplinary action of banning taken by BCCI. In this case, action was taken under Clause 38(ii) of the Rules of

BCCI. And after disciplinary proceedings dated 5 December 2000 punishment was given and a life ban was imposed thereunder, was challenged as being null and void contrary to the rules and regulations of BCCI, in violation of the principles of natural justice and Articles 14, 16, 19(1)(e), (g), 20(3) and 21 of the Constitution of India. The plaintiff also claimed that it is also further just and necessary to declare that the plaintiff be permitted to play cricket during his lifetime for the Indian National Team and such other teams during his lifetime and shall be entitled to all retirement benefits as an international cricketer in India and to permit him to hold any such position as may be available as may be considered by the BCCI or ICC.

253. The facts of the case were that the plaintiff, who was a former captain of the Indian cricket team instituted the said suit against three defendants, namely: (1) The BCCI; (2) K. Madhavan, Commissioner appointed by the defendant No. 1; and (3) Dr A.C. Muthiah, the then President of the defendant No. 1. The plaintiff claimed that because of his excellent performance in cricket, he was selected to represent India in cricket tests against England in India during 1984–1985. As he is a prolific batsman and player of high calibre, he was selected as Captain of Indian cricket team. He represented Indian cricket team not only in this country but also outside the country and had brought laurels not only to the Indian cricket team but also to the nation in the field of cricket.

254. The plaintiff instituted the suit mainly questioning the order dated 5 December 2000 communicated to him on 11 December 2000 imposing a life ban on the cricketing career of the plaintiff by the first defendant – BCCI. In the plea set out in several paragraphs, the plaintiff has taken pains to narrate the instances of irregularities committed by the BCCI and the biased attitude of the third defendant against the plaintiff and also the manner in which the second defendant was appointed as enquiry officer by the third defendant and the manner in which the proceedings dated 5 December 2000 imposing a life ban on his cricketing career were issued.

255. According to the principle averments in the plaint, the first defendant is a society registered under the provisions of Indian Societies Registration Act at Madras on 28 November 1940. The power duties and control over the affairs and conduct of players, enquiry, working committee, etc., are all governed by the memorandum of rules and regulations of the first defendant, as amended from time to time. The plaintiff claimed that the relationship between himself and the first defendant is in the nature of a service contract. In the plaint averments, the plaintiff alleged that there have been serious allegations of mismanagement, corruption against the first defendant. The second defendant at the instance of the first defendant who was appointed as Commissioner to go into the allegations against the plaintiff, is the handpicked person of the third defendant and had made a preliminary enquiry against the plaintiff and on the basis of the preliminary enquiry, the first defendant imposed a punishment of life ban on the cricketing career of the plaintiff by proceedings dated 5 December 2000 on account of which the plaintiff is prevented from playing first-class cricket. The plaintiff in his averments narrated the instances and the manner in which the enquiry was conducted and the deficiencies therein and the bias shown towards him, apart from pleading that the principles of natural justice have been violated by these defendants while imposing the penalty of life ban on his cricketing career and contended that such action of the first defendant is volatile of Articles 14, 16, 19(1)(e), (g), 20(3) and 21 of the Constitution of India.

IV. Financial and/or Commercial Disputes

256. These disputes include claims for the breach of a contractual provision or other breaches for which compensation is claimed. It may be related to default in payment or non-payment to a player by a club or sponsor under a contract, relating to sponsorship, sale of telecasting rights, etc.

§6. Dispute Settlement Proposed under National Sports Development Bill, 2013

257. Section 10(d) of the Bill lays down that, every accredited NSF shall provide for a free, fair, expeditious and transparent in-house mechanism for redressal of grievances. Similarly, National Olympic Committee shall provide for in-house mechanism for redressal of grievances.[18] The Bill provides for constitution of Sports Appellant Tribunal and Athlete Commission for the purpose of dispute resolution. The Athlete Commission will advise the NSF and National Olympic Committee on the need of the athletes *inter alia* on athlete's grievances.[19] The decision given by Sports ombudsman on Sports Appellant Tribunal shall be final and enforceable under Arbitration and Conciliation Act, 1996 and shall be binding upon the parties.

I. Sports Appellate Tribunal

A. Procedure for Appointment

258. Section 27 provides for establishment of Appellate Sports Tribunal by the Central Government. The selection of the Tribunal shall be made on the recommendation of selection committee consisting of Chief Justice of India or his nominee judge – chairperson, Secretary Department of Sports President National Olympic Committee or his nominee (section 28).

B. Jurisdiction

259. The jurisdiction of the Civil Courts has been ousted with respect to matters pending before the Sports Appellate Tribunal. Further, no injunction can be granted

18. Section 7(2)(d).
19. Section 42(2)(3).

by any court or any other authority, in respect of an action in pursuance of power conferred by or under the Sports Development Act (section 32). An appeal against the order of the Tribunal shall lie only to the Supreme Court of India (section 34). The Tribunal shall have for the purpose of discharging its functions the powers of a Civil Court with respect to specified matters.

260. The orders passed by the Tribunal shall be treated as a decree of the Civil Court, and for this purpose, Tribunal shall have all the powers.[20] Tribunal can also transfer any order made to a Civil Court having jurisdiction, and such Civil Court shall execute the order as if it were a decree made by that court.[21] Section 29(a) provides that Tribunal shall not adjudicate *inter alia*, any matter or dispute or conflict arising during the Olympic Games, Commonwealth Games, Asian Games or during other similar events organized by the international federations in respect of which the CASs established in Lausanne has the exclusive jurisdiction.

§7. Court of Arbitration for Sports

261. Arbitration in India is governed by the Arbitration and Conciliation Act 1996 ('Indian Arbitration Act'), which is based on the UNCITRAL Model Law. The Indian Arbitration Act is broadly divided into two parts. Part I applies to arbitrations held in India, whether domestic or international, and Part II applies to arbitrations held outside India. Part II, incorporates the rules related to international arbitrations governed by the New York or Geneva Conventions. In sports, the disputes are first referred to the federations that govern a particular sport and subsequently to the international forums that is CAS in Switzerland.

I. Creation and Scope of CAS

262. The CAS was created by IOC in 1984 and is placed under the administrative and financial authority of the International Council of Arbitration for Sport (ICAS). It evolved from pressure to find solution to disputes among athletes, IOC and NSFs, National Olympic Committees and other game organizers. The CAS has a large number of arbitrators from countries throughout the world, chosen for their specialist knowledge of arbitration and sports law. A dispute can be referred to CAS only if there is arbitration agreement between the parties. The CAS is independent of any sports organization, which provides for services in order to facilitate the settlement of sports-related disputes through arbitration or mediation by means of procedural rules adapted to the specific needs of the sports world. All international disputes relating to sports are referred to it. The CAS has its headquarters in Lausanne, Switzerland. It also has two permanent outposts in Sydney, Australia and New York, USA.

20. Section 35(1).
21. Section 35(2).

263. The body was originally conceived by IOC President Juan Antonio Samaranch to deal with disputes arising during the Olympics. It was established as part of the IOC in 1984. However in a case decided by the CAS, an appeal was made to the Federal Supreme Court of Switzerland, challenging CAS impartiality. The Swiss court ruled that the CAS was a true court of arbitration, but drew attention to the numerous links which existed between the CAS and the IOC. The biggest change resulting from this reform was the creation of an 'ICAS' to look after the running and financing of the CAS, thereby taking the place of the IOC. CAS is placed under the administrative and financial authority of the ICAS.

264. Almost all international sports federations or associations which are part of the Olympic Games require sports disputes arising between themselves and sportspersons to be decided by the CAS. Sporting federations whose sports are not part of the Olympics such as Formula I where the FIA which is the governing body of motor sports has its own dispute settlement tribunal. Even some sports which are included in the Olympics have their tribunals like football where its governing body FIFA has its own tribunal.

II. Applicable Law

265. In the context of ordinary arbitration, the parties are free to agree on the law applicable to the merits of the dispute. Failing such agreement, Swiss law applies. In the context of the appeals procedure, the arbitrators rule on the basis of the regulations of the body concerned by the appeal and, subsidiary, the law of the country in which the body is domiciled. The procedure itself is governed by the Code of Sports Related Arbitration. Judicial recourse to the Swiss Federal Tribunal is allowed on a very limited number of grounds, such as lack of jurisdiction, violation of elementary procedural rules like violation of the right to a fair hearing or incompatibility with public policy.

III. Arbitration Agreement

266. A dispute may be submitted to the CAS only if there is an arbitration agreement between the parties which specifies recourse to the CAS. The language for the CAS is either French or English. In principle, two types of dispute may be submitted to the CAS:

(i) commercial nature; and
(ii) disciplinary nature.

A. Commercial

267. The first category essentially involves disputes relating to the execution of contracts, such as those relating to sponsorship, the sale of television rights, the staging of sports events, player transfers and relations between players or coaches and clubs and/or agents (employment contracts and agency contracts). Disputes relating to civil liability issues also come under this category (e.g., an accident to an athlete during a sports competition). These so-called commercial disputes are handled by the CAS acting as a court of sole instance.

B. Disciplinary

268. Disciplinary cases represent the second group of disputes submitted to the CAS, of which a large number are doping-related. In addition to doping cases, the CAS is called upon to rule on various disciplinary cases (violence on the field of play, abuse of a referee). Such disciplinary cases are generally dealt with in the first instance by the competent sports authorities, and subsequently become the subject of an appeal to the CAS, which then acts as a court of last instance.

IV. Rules of Procedure

269. The CAS is governed by its own statutes and rules of procedure namely the Statutes of the Bodies Working for the Settlement of Sports Related Disputes, Code of Sports Related Arbitration and Mediation Rules. According to Articles S12, S20, R27 and R47 of the Code, the Appeals Arbitration Procedure is open for the appeal against every decision rendered by a federation or club and not limited to disciplinary matters, especially doping cases. In addition, Article R57 empowers the CAS Panels not only to annul a certain decision, but also to replace a decision by a decision by a decision of the arbitrators, or to refer the case back to the issuing body. Moreover, Article R58 authorizes the panel to apply the 'rule of law' it deems most appropriate for the case. Thus the panels may deviate from the laws of the country in which the federation is domiciled and reach a decision on the basis of laws of another country or other rules of law, such as general principles of law.

V. Jurisdiction

270. The CAS acquires its jurisdiction in a particular case only through the mutual consent of the parties involved. The Olympic International Federations and many National Olympic Committees have recognized the jurisdiction of the CAS and included in their statutes an arbitration clause referring disputes to it. The CAS hears approximately 200 cases per year. While it was the international response to the rise in the use of performance-enhancing drugs and the resulting doping cases that fuelled the creation of the CAS, the court is called upon to assist in a wide range of sport conflicts, including sponsorship disputes, the eligibility of a particular athlete in accordance with a sport's constitution, as well as the resolution of disagreements concerning competition results. The determination of issues arising in doping cases remains a significant portion of the CAS caseload.

VI. Important CAS Rulings

271. In 2003, Canadian cross-country skier Becky Scott successfully appealed to the CAS with respect to her claim that she be awarded the 2002 Olympic gold medal in the 5 km pursuit event. Russian skiers Olga Danilova and Larissa Lazutina finished first and second respectively in the competition, with Scott in third place, and each athlete passed their post-event doping test. Danilova and Lazutina each failed a subsequent doping test administered in relation to another Olympic cross-country event, when the presence of a prohibited blood doping agent, darbepoetin, was detected in each skier's sample. Scott appealed her 5 km race result on the basis that both Russian skiers were engaged in ongoing doping practices. The Scott ruling was the first time in Olympic history that a gold medal had been awarded to an athlete as a result of a CAS ruling.

272. In 2005, the CAS arbitration panel ruled that American sprinter Tim Montgomery be banned from international competition for two years as a result of doping, in spite of the fact that Montgomery had never failed a doping test. The CAS ruled that it could find a doping violation on the basis of the third party evidence called against Montgomery, most of which connected Montgomery to the Bay Area Laboratory Cooperative (BALCO) athlete steroid scandal that had arisen in the US in 2003.

273. In February 2010 Five-time Olympic speed-skating champion Claudia Pechstein lost her appeal against a two-year ban for blood doping. CAS dismissed the German's appeal against a ban imposed by the International Skating Union. Setting aside proceedings against CAS arbitral awards may only be filed with the Swiss Supreme Court due to the seat of CAS tribunals being in Lausanne.

VII. Mediation and Conciliation

274. Mediation and conciliation are also very important alternative modes for settlement of disputes. Conciliation is a legally recognized mode for settlement of disputes in India. There may be one conciliator appointed by mutual consent of the disputing parties, or each party may appoint its own conciliator and the two conciliators so appointed shall appoint the third conciliator. In case of three conciliators, the decision can be taken by majority. The decision of conciliator(s) is not binding unless parties consent to the same. As per Arbitration and Conciliation Act, 1996 once parties consent then the decision of the conciliator is treated and implemented as an arbitration award and can be enforced through the court.

275. The ICASs pursuant to the Code of Sports Related Arbitration has adopted the Mediation Rules. These rules provide that this mediation is a non-binding and informal procedure, based on a mediation agreement in which each party undertakes to attempt in good faith to negotiate with the other party and with the assistance of a mediator, with a view to settling a sport-related dispute. The disputes related to disciplinary matters and doping issues are expressly excluded from mediation.

276. CAS offers mediation services to any requesting parties of a sports dispute. Unlike arbitration, the mediation process by CAS is not binding – the mediator will provide recommendations, with solutions suggested, but these are not imposed without consent. Mediations are designed to permit the adverse parties an opportunity to air their grievances in an atmosphere aimed at conciliation of the dispute. CAS is a private procedure and therefore is conducted without the public or media interference. The arbitrators and CAS staff are obligated not to disclose any information connected with the dispute.

Part II. Sports Organizations and Their Regulations

Chapter 1. Government Institutions and Bodies

277. There are a large number of government and private institutions and bodies which deal with sports and games in the country. At the top of the government set-up, is the MYAS. This ministry was initially set up as the Department of Sports in 1982 at the time when the IX Asian Games were organized in New Delhi. Its name was changed to the Department of Youth Affairs and Sports during celebration of the International Youth Year in 1985. It became a full-fledged ministry on 17 May 2000.

§1. Ministry of Youth Affairs and Sports

278. The specific subjects relating to sports being dealt with by the Ministry are contained in the Order of the Government of India (Allocation of Business) Rules, 1961, the Second Schedule of which specifies the following subjects:

(1) Sports Policy.
(2) Sports and Games.
(3) National Welfare Fund for Sportsmen.
(4) Netaji Subhas National Institute of Sports.
(5) SAI.
(6) Matters relating to the International Olympic Association (IOA) and NSF.
(7) Participation of Indian sports teams in tournaments abroad and participation of foreign sports teams in international tournaments in India.
(8) National Sports Awards, including Arjuna Award.
(9) Sports Scholarships.
(10) Exchange of sportspersons, youth delegations, experts and teams with foreign countries.
(11) Sports infrastructure, including financial assistance for creation and development of such infrastructure.
(12) Financial assistance for coaching, tournaments, equipment, etc.
(13) Sports matters relating to Union Territories (UT).
(14) Physical Education.

All attached or subordinate offices and autonomous bodies set up by the Ministry concerning any of the subjects specified above.

279. The Ministry is headed by the Cabinet Minister of Youth Affairs and Sports, and also has a Minister of State for Youth Affairs and Sports. In April 2008, the Ministry was bifurcated into the Department of Youth Affairs and Department of Sports, each under the charge of a Secretary. Besides, there are three Joint Secretaries in the Ministry, namely Joint Secretary (Sports), Joint Secretary (Youth Affairs) and Joint Secretary (International Sports Division).

280. Sports promotion and governance is the responsibility of the various NSFs, which are autonomous bodies. The role of the government is to create the infrastructure and promote capacity building for broad basing sports as well as for achieving excellence in various competitive events at the national and international levels. The Ministry's schemes are geared towards achieving these objectives.

§2. Subordinate Offices and Autonomous Organizations

281. Following autonomous organizations function under the administrative control of the Ministry:

- National Anti-Doping Agency (NADA).
- National Dope Testing Laboratory (NDTL).
- Sports Authority of India (SAI), New Delhi.
- Lakshmibai National University of Physical Education, Gwalior, Madhya Pradesh.
- National Playing Field Association of India (NPFAI).

I. Vigilance and Public Grievances

282. Vigilance and Public Grievance Cell in the MYAS works under the overall supervision of the Chief Vigilance Officer (CVO). Each autonomous organization and subordinate offices of the Ministry have their independent CVOs to deal with vigilance and public grievances.

283. The Ministry takes a keen interest in redressing public grievances. A vigilance awareness week is observed in the Ministry as well as in all the field organizations of the Ministry. During this week, various activities like debates, essay competitions, displays of banners and films on the menaces of corruption in society are undertaken.

II. Library

284. The Ministry has a departmental Library where publications of interest on subjects like sports and games, yoga, physical education, youth programmes, literature, law, rules, etc. are preserved for reference. There are also a large number of other publications of importance, like sports and youth magazines, annual and other reports of various ministries, departments, audio and video cassettes and thousands of photographs, etc.

III. Vision of the Ministry

285. The vision of the Ministry is to provide opportunities for developing the personality of youth so that they may achieve their full potential and involving them in various nation-building activities on the one side, and, 'broad basing' of sports and 'achieving excellence' at national and international levels on the other.

IV. Mission of the Ministry

286. The following have been described as the Mission of the Ministry:

- To formulate policies aimed at promotion and development of Youth and Sports.
- To formulate and implement policies and programmes aimed at facilitating the all-round development of the personality of youth through sports and community services.
- To formulate and implement policies and programmes aimed at involving the youth in various nation-building activities.
- To formulate and implement policies and programmes for broad basing sports.
- To formulate and implement policies and programmes, encouraging and popularizing indigenous sports, designed to achieve excellence in competitive sports and to establish India as a leading country in sports in Asia and the World.

V. Commitment

287. The Ministry is committed to the following:

- To provide impartial, sympathetic and prompt services to the public in matters related to youth affairs and sports.
- To process the proposals received expeditiously and efficiently.
- To take steps to speedily redress the grievances received either from the public or from staff.
- To formulate policies and initiate consultations with all concerned parties and to amend them whenever required.

VI. The Clients

288. The following can be considered as clients of the Ministry:

- Youth and adolescents, Non-Governmental Organizations (NGOs); Voluntary Organizations; Associations.
- Nehru Yuva Kendra Sangthan (NYKS) and the youth clubs and Mahila Mandals affiliated there under, National Service Scheme volunteers and its various regional centres.
- State and UT Governments.
- Sportspersons, their coaches and supporting personnel.
- NSFs, Regional Sports Associations, Bodies, International Sports Bodies.
- SAI and IOA.
- Various Ministries, Departments of Central, State and UT Governments.
- Sports Goods Industries.

There are certain schemes in the Ministry like Promotion of Adventure which are implemented by the Ministry through NGOs.

§3. Sport Bodies

I. The Sports Authority of India

289. The Government of India is making all efforts to develop a sports culture in the country and make the sporting scene as attractive as possible. Sports have been accorded a very high priority in the National Youth Policy as well. In practical terms, the policy of sports promotion is directly linked to generating employment in government and public sector undertakings. The steps taken in the direction of sports promotion consisted of formulation of a draft Comprehensive National Sports Policy 2007, the creation of a full-fledged Department of Youth Affairs and Sports in the Ministry of Human Resource Development and the setting up the country's apex body for sports promotion namely SAI. SAI, set up in 1984, conducts various training programmes at its institutes in Patiala, Calcutta, Rohtak, Bengaluru Gandhinagar, Gwalior, Guwahati and Thiruvananthapuram.

A. Establishment of SAI

290. SAI was established by the government in January 1984 as a registered society with the aim to ensure effective maintenance and optimum utilization of the various sports infrastructure that were built in Delhi during Asiad, 1982. It is now the nodal agency in the country for broadbasing sports and for training of sportspersons to achieve excellence in national and international sports arena. SAI provides support to NSFs for holding camps and performance of other activities and their monitoring.

In order to have only one government agency at the apex for the promotion of sports, the Society for National Institute of Physical Education and Sports (SNIPES) was merged with SAI on 1 May 1987. Subsequently, Netaji Subhas National Institute of Sports (NSNIS), Patiala and its allied centres at Bangalore, Calcutta and Gandhinagar and Lakshmibai National College of Physical Education at Thiruvananthapuram were also brought under the SAI.

291. SAI now has twelve regional centres at Patiala, Thiruvananthapuram, Bengaluru, Sonepat, Guwahati, Mumbai, Bhopal, Lucknow, Gandhinagar, Kolkata, Chandigarh and Imphal. Its regional centre at Bengaluru has been developed as a 'Centre of Excellence'. It has two sub-centres at Guwahati under the north-eastern centre and at Aurangabad under the western centre. SAI maintains and utilizes five stadia in Delhi namely Jawaharlal Nehru Stadium, Indira Gandhi Stadium, Major Dhyan Chand National Stadium, Dr Shyama Prasad Mukherjee Swimming Pool Complex and Dr Karni Singh Shooting Ranges.

B. Sport Schemes and Programmes of SAI

292. The SAI offers a number of sports schemes and programmes. Under the spotting and nurturing of talent project, SAI has National Sports Talent Contest, adoption of akharas for promotion of wrestling and Army Boys Sports Company scheme to scout talent in the age group of 8–14 years to provide them with systematic training with scientific backup. The scheme has been extended to the talent scouting to Kendriya Vidyalayas, Navodaya Vidalayas, large-sized residential schools and public sector townships. SAI also has a scheme for the promotion of sports in special areas, national coaching scheme. SAI also implements a number of central schemes. Steps have been taken for setting up regional and national academics for different sports disciplines with a number of public and private sector undertakings.

293. SAI is in the serious business of coaching and training in sports. It has qualified trainers from the National Institute of Sports, Patiala. The students practice for long hours which prove their dedication. A very nominal fee is charged to let them take advantage of the facilities provided at SAI. SAI has different departments, each taking care of specific areas of action. The academic wing deals with training of coaches, physical education and research and development in sports. The operational wing is meant for promotion of sports. The team's wing, on the contrary, has a special function of training elite athletes and providing management support.

294. The government-sponsored sports institutions have officials to manage the work at various levels. Senior officials, usually, are sports teachers and coaches who have managed sports activities at lower levels. Planning and managing sports activities through these organizations are their responsibilities. It is also one of the responsibilities of the SAI, both at the central and State levels, to manage certain programmes.

II. National Playing Field Association of India

295. Concerned at the shortage of open spaces and playing fields and diversion to other activities, the Ministry set up the NPFAI in 2009. The association is registered under the Societies Registration Act, 1860 with the Union Minister as the Chairperson and eminent personalities as members of the society. The main focus of NPFAI has been in making efforts to protect, preserve, promote, develop and improve playfields, open spaces and other facilities for sports and games by evolving a national policy on playing fields, playgrounds, play pitches, parks and open spaces and granting affiliations to State Playing Field Associations. NPFAI has developed basic playfields model of different sizes providing minimum facilities which include levelled grounds, kids play area with swings/slides, etc., play facility for one or two disciplines, toilet facility, etc. General guidelines for development of playfields have been finalized and circulated to all States and UT for adoption of these guidelines with suitable modifications according to the local conditions. Playfields facilities have been developed in two welfare organizations for government employees, thirteen colleges and five schools in Delhi under the Commonwealth Legacy Plan with Central Government's assistance. The facilities created include construction of synthetic courts for basketball, table tennis, shooting range, fitness centre, etc.

III. Sport Institutes

296. Two very prominent schools of sports in India are Netaji Subhas National Institute of Sports, Moti Bagh, Patiala and Motilal Nehru School of Sports. The diploma in coaching admits graduates who are proficient in some form of sport and have played either at the national or international level. Patiala is the only institute of its kind in the country for training of sportspersons in becoming coaches. The Bachelor of Physical Education is a three-year course having an admission test for senior secondary students. The Master in Physical Education, on the contrary, is a two-year course which can be pursued after BA (Physical Education).

297. There are many other institutes for training in sports and physical education. For instance, the Government College of Physical Education, Kandivali, Mumbai offers Bachelors in Physical education, for which the eligibility requirement is Higher Secondary School (HSC)/plus two or equivalent.

Other prominent institutes for courses in various sports activities/physical education are:

- SAI National Sports South Centre, University Campus, Bangalore.
- SAI National sports East Centre, Salt Lake City, Sector III, Calcutta.
- SAI National Sports West Centre, Sports Complex, Sector 15, Gandhinagar, Gujarat.
- SAI Lakshmibai National University of Physical Education, Gwalior-474002.
- SAI Lakshmibai National College of Physical Education, Thiruvananthapuram.

– Indira Gandhi Institute of Physical Education and Sports, B Block, Vikaspuri, New Delhi-110018.
– The Naval Tata Centre of Excellence in Sports Management.

A. Courses Offered at Delhi University

298. The University of Delhi offers a variety of sports-related courses that include BSc in Physical Education, Health Education and Sports. The duration of these courses is three years each. The other course, a PG Diploma in Physical Education, is of one-year's duration. Aspirants need to have studied BSc, BA, B Com or B Physical Education and participated in inter-university tournaments and have at least had a second position in inter-collegiate tournaments to be eligible for this course.

299. The Master of Sports Sciences is a two-year course. The PG Diploma in Health Education, PG Diploma in Physical Fitness and Adventurous Sports and PG Diploma in Officiating and Coaching are all of one-year duration each. DU offers a few short-term courses also; the Master of Physical Education is a summer course of three-semester duration whereas the diploma in Sports Management and Protocol is just a three-month programme.

B. Netaji Subhas National Institute of Sports, Patiala

300. Housed in the erstwhile Palace of Maharaja (King) of Patiala in the State of Punjab, National Institute of Sports was established on 7 May 1961 with the objective of developing sports in the country on scientific lines and training the coaches in different sports disciplines. After the merger of SAI and SNIPES in 1987, the Institute became the Academic Wing of the SAI. The Institute was renamed as Netaji Subhas National Institute of Sports (NSNIS) on 23 January 1973. The Institute is housed in an area of 268 acres and is Asia's largest Sports Institute. The Institute has enormous facilities for academic programmes and sports training and hostels for the comfortable stay of the students, national players and coaches. Department of Sports Medicine provides all medical assistance to the players, students and staff. The sports training facilities of international standard are available comprising of gymnasium, swimming pool, indoor halls, cycling velodrome, squash courts, conditioning units, hockey fields (grass and synthetic), athletics track (cinder and synthetic) and outdoor courts. For the recovery of players, well-maintained sauna bath, steam bath and hydrotherapy facilities are also available.

1. Activities

301. Academic courses and the holding of national coaching camps were started at the Institute from its inception. The Institute is producing high-calibre coaches in sports disciplines through its Diploma Course and Master Course in Sports Coaching. The Institute holds the key to sports development in India. The abundant talent in the country is well looked after by its field-wing coaches, working in the regional and district centres all over the country.

302. In its aim to promote sports in the country, the Institute is engaged in multifarious activities, producing coaches of high calibre, organizing IOC solidarity courses, international clinics, congresses, seminars, workshops, conferences, etc. Moreover, despite its preoccupation with such diverse activities, the task of training national teams for prestigious events like the Olympic Games, Commonwealth Games, Asian Games and so forth, is entrusted to the Institute by the NSFs for proper scientific coaching.

2. Faculty of Sport Sciences

303. Since all training programmes at the Institute are geared for scientific requirements, a faculty of Sports Sciences has been established comprising various departments like Department of Sports Medicine, Department of Sports Biochemistry, Department of Sports Psychology, Department of Sports Nutrition, Department of Biomechanics, etc. Audio video aids, publications and library have been provided to scientists, research fellows, coaches, teachers and students to keep themselves abreast of the latest trends in sports development.

3. Training and Hostel Facilities

304. A large number of facilities have been developed for training like gymnasium cum swimming pool complex; volleyball, handball and judo; hockey fields; synthetic surfaces; football ground; tennis; cricket ground (turf wicket); archery. Hostel facilities for both boys and girls accommodating approximately 700 persons have been developed. Other facilities like the Faculty of Sport Sciences, Sports Medicine Hospital, Sports Library, National Sports Museum and State Sports Academy have also been developed.

C. Naval Tata Centre of Excellence in Sports Management

305. The Naval Tata Centre of Excellence in Sports Management of the Indian Institute of Social Welfare and Business Management, Calcutta conducts a one-year full-time Postgraduate Diploma in Sports Management (PGDSM). The programme assists the students to gain a thorough understanding of the multidimensional importance and the value of sport. The candidates also acquire business skills relating to public relations, marketing and entrepreneurship, which assist them in the administration of institutions engaged in various sporting activities.

306. The programme exposes students to the tools and techniques of sports administration including those of event management as well as acquaints them with contemporary trends and issues in sport. The sports science section covers sports medicine, sports psychology, sports physiology, sports therapy and health promotion. The course has dedicated modules to cater to the emerging needs of the sports industry, modules on sponsorship, broadcasting, celebrity management, research methods, media management, crowd management and infrastructure management.

Sports law is growing to be an important aspect of the sports industry. The knowledge of the legal aspects of sports business is a tool, which each manager must possess. The course has a subject dedicated to the legal aspects of sports.

307. Throughout the world, much research has gone into studying the humanitarian aspects of sport. Theoretical sports studies have delved deeply into understanding the nature of effects, which sports have on society. The Centre of Excellence considers that sport has a major role to play in the society, for nation-building and for solving societal problems. The course recognizes the impact of sport in society and provides insights and modules on various aspects of sociological, philosophical and theoretical aspects of sports studies.

308. Each sport is unique and has its own nuances. Organization and structures of team games are different from individual games. A special series of lectures has been devoted to understanding the nuances of these individual games. Students are exposed to games like cricket, football, tennis, rugby, horse racing, golf and Formula 1.

309. The role of fitness and leisure in today's lifestyle is known to one and all. The fitness industry is fast growing in India and that too at an amazing pace. The course incorporates a series of lectures concerning this part of the industry, including fitness, leisure and country club management. The programme has been designed and developed for the benefit of candidates, particularly those with a passion for sport, who wish to make a career in the sports and entertainment industry. The orbit of the programme would assist even those who are at present actively connected with sport in an administrative capacity to develop their sport-oriented job skills.

D. National Sports University, Manipur

310. The National Sports University Act, 2018 has replaced the National Sports University Ordinance, 2018 that was promulgated on 31 May 2018. The Act has established a National Sports University in Manipur. The Act deemed to have come in to force on 31 May 2018. It may establish outlying campuses (within or outside India), colleges, or regional centres. The University will: (i) undertake research on physical education, (ii) strengthen sports training programmes, and (iii) collaborate internationally in the field of physical education, among others.

311. Key powers and functions of the University include: (i) prescribing courses of study and conducting training programmes; (ii) granting degrees, diplomas and certificates; (iii) providing facilities through a distance education system; and (iv) conferring autonomous status on a college or an institution.

312. The University has: (i) a Court, which will review the policies of the University and suggest measures for its development; (ii) an Executive Council, which is the principal executive body; (iii) an Academic and Activity Council supervise academic policies; (iv) a Board of Sports Studies approves the subjects for research and recommend measures to improve standards of teaching; and (v) a Finance Committee, examines proposals related to creation of posts and recommend limits on the expenditure of the University. Further, additional authorities may be declared through statutes.

313. The Executive Council is responsible for all administrative affairs of the University. Members of the Council are nominated by the central government and will hold office for two years. The members include: (i) the Vice Chancellor (appointed by the central government), (ii) the Joint Secretary, MYAS, and (iii) four persons from among eminent sportspersons and distinguished coaches. Key functions of the Council include: (i) creating academic posts and their appointment, (ii) managing the revenue and property of the University, (iii) managing and regulating the finances of the University, and (iv) partnering with industry and non-government agencies to advance knowledge.

314. The Schedule to the Act contains statutes which specify the establishment, composition, and powers of various authorities such as the Chancellor, Vice Chancellor, and Dean of Schools. The Executive Council may make additional statutes, amend specified statutes, or repeal these statutes. Any such action will require the approval of the central government.

315. The central government reviews the functioning of the University. The Executive Council may take action based on the findings of the inspection. If no action is taken within a reasonable time period, the central government may issue binding directions to the Council. In addition, the central government may annul any proceeding of the University which is not in conformity with the Bill.

316. The University will maintain a fund and the following amounts will be credited to the fund: (i) contributions by the central government, State governments, or the University Grants Commission; (ii) loans, gifts and donations; (iii) income from fees; and (iv) amounts received from any other source. Funds will be invested based on the recommendations of the Finance Committee.

317. Any student or candidate whose name has been removed from the rolls of the University and who has been barred from appearing for examinations may appeal to the Executive Council for review of the decision. Any dispute arising out the disciplinary action taken by the University against a student may be referred to a Tribunal of Arbitration (at the request of the student). Disputes arising out of the contract between an employee and the University may also be referred to a Tribunal of Arbitration.

IV. Establishment of Sports Academies

318. The growing role of sports in society, media attention, national honour and international prestige, have made participation and winning of medals in competitive sports a matter of great significance and prestige. In recognition of this fact, need has been felt to set up national training academies and specialized centres of sports excellence which offer an opportunity for exceptionally talented young children to train under experts for long duration with modern training aids and in a better overall environment.

319. The success of any scheme depends on varied inputs from many quarters. Expertise in the field of finance, marketing and sports coaching, etc. are also essential inputs for the success of the scheme. Keeping this in view, the concept of Sports Academy has been developed both to be set up by the government and also as a co-operative venture between the Central Government, State government and sponsors from public and private sectors. The State government and the corporate sector are encouraged to set sports academies in association with the Central Government, SAI and the NSFs.

320. The National Sports Academies (NSA) Scheme functions under Sports Promotional Schemes of SAI with a view to promote sports on single discipline basis. Sports Academies are therefore being set up by SAI, in collaboration with the NSFs to attract sports talent in the respective sports discipline in the age group of 12–25 years. The Academy Scheme envisages modern training centres having state of the art sports facilities, equipment, requisite sports science infrastructure as well as qualified personnel to meet the daily requirement of the trainees. The Sports Academies will have both residential and non-residential trainees.

321. Some academies have been set up through private institutions like Prakash Padukone Badminton Academy in Bangalore, Gopichand Badminton Academy in Hyderabad, St John's Sports Coaching Foundation (cricket) in Hyderabad, Dr Dy. Patel Sports Academy (cricket) in Navi Mumbai, SOL Sports (Tennis) in Bangalore, etc. Besides, coaching camps are mushrooming and they are thriving even in suburban areas. With the amount of money involved in this game, more and more parents are admitting their children in cricket academies. With the advent of IPL and ICL tournaments, there is no limit on earning not only from the matches but also from endorsements and now players are being taken through auction or bidding. Another game, which has wide following and acceptance is, football but it is restricted to certain parts of the country like West Bengal. A number of public and private sector undertakings have contributed in the setting up of regional and national academia for different sports disciplines. MRF, for instance, has been promoting promising cricketers through its Pace Foundation. Hinduja Foundation offers scholarships for sportspersons from a variety of fields. Similar efforts are being made by Oil and Natural Gas Corporation Limited (ONGC), Steel Authority of India Limited (SAIL), etc. There are certain private companies which do not only sponsor players, but also have their own full-fledged teams. Nationwide, these companies hunt for talented young boys and girls.

322. Ministry of Corporate Affairs has notified the Corporate Social Responsibility Rules on 27 February 2014 wherein new activities related to sports like training to promote rural sports, nationally recognized sports, paralympic sports have been included in Schedule VII of the Companies Act, 2013. It will give a boost to the promotion and development of sports as much needed funds will flow in the sports sector.

Chapter 2. National Olympic Committee

323. The management and development of Sports in India are the function of the International Olympic Association (IOA) and the NSFs, which are autonomous bodies and which, in turn, have affiliated State level and District level associations. Though this situation may change after coming into force of the National Sports Development Bill, 2013. The government and other concerned agencies and the federations and associations have to work together harmoniously and in a coordinated manner to fulfil the objectives of the national sports promotion. At the same time, the IOA and the various Sports federations and associations are required to demonstrate orientation towards the achievement of results and ensure tangible progress in the field of sports, keeping which in view, model by-laws and organizational structures have been formulated for the NSFs, in consultation with them, and with due regard to the Olympic Charter.

324. As per National Sports Development Bill, 2013, the sports federations must ensure that its constitution incorporates all standard of good governance and ethics in accordance with its principles enshrined in the Code of Ethics and make such amendments in its rules and by-laws as may be required. The National Sports Development Bill, 2013 also envisages constitution of an Athlete Commission by the National Olympic Committee,[22] which is to function as institutionalized mechanism for cooperation and development between the government, NSF and other stakeholders. The Commission shall advise the NSF and National Olympic Committee on development, training and competition schedules, Athletes grievances, selection and technical criteria, logistical and administrative support and athlete support beyond sports career.[23]

Acknowledging the importance of National Championships for developing competitive spirit and for talent scouting, it is incumbent on the federations and associations to hold Annual Championships in various disciplines in all categories, i.e., seniors, juniors and sub-juniors at the district, State and national levels. Each National Federation draws the Annual National Calendar of these events sufficiently in advance, every year, which would be compiled and published by the IOA. Greater emphasis will be placed on promoting the development of Sports among the juniors and sub-juniors and the more talented among them identified for Special Training and Support.

325. The national federations of various sports are registered as societies and are autonomous in character. These federations are affiliated directly with concerned International Federation, and the government has a role as accreditation is provided by it. So, government can indirectly influence their working by not according accreditation for which federations have to fulfil certain criteria and submit required documents every year. The office-bearers of all these federations and associations are elected functionaries. Like the NSF, all the States and UT have their separate

---

22. Section 7(2)(f).
23. Section 42(1).

State Associations or Federations. These are also independent in character and are affiliated to the respective NSF and Association.

§1. The IOA

326. Towards the end of 1919, Sir Dorabji Tata first sowed the seeds of the future IOA which was later on established, though no Olympic body had yet been formed in India. Sir Tata managed to send a token team of four athletes and two wrestlers to the 1920 Olympic Games in Antwerp. Sir Tata, with the help of Dr A.G. Noehren, then Director of the Young Men's Christian Association (YMCA) in India, began to search throughout India for new talent in athletics. This aroused national interest in athletics and helped to promote, control and further the organization of athletic meetings in all States and provinces in India.

327. In February 1924, an interstate athletics meet was organized in Delhi with the result that an eight-member team was sent to participate in the Olympic Games in Paris later the same year. In 1927, the IOA was formed with Sir Dorabji Tata as its First President and Dr Noehren as Secretary. They held these two offices until 1928 when they were replaced by Maharaja Bhupinder Singh of Patiala (1928–1938), and Professor Guru Dutt Sondhi (1928–1952) respectively. Sir Dorabji Tata continued as IOC member in India until his death in 1931. In 1932, after the demise of Sir Dorabji Tata, Professor Guru Dutt Sondhi, who was also the Indian representative within the International Amateur Athletic Federation, assumed his responsibilities.

328. It would be pertinent to mention here that the name and emblem of the IOC consisting of five interlaced rings are protected from improper use under sections 2(a) and 3 of the Emblems and Names (Prevention of Improper Use) Act, 1950. Section 2(a) defines 'Emblem' as any emblem, seal, flag, insignia, coat of arms or pictorial representation specified in the schedule. The schedule in paragraph 21 includes 'The name and emblem of the IOC consisting of five interlaced rings.' Section 2 prohibits improper use of emblems and names as follows:

> Prohibition of improper use of certain emblems and names-Notwithstanding anything contrary contained in any law for the time being in force, no person shall, except in such cases and under such conditions as may be prescribed by the Central Government use, or continue to use, for the purpose of any trade, business, calling or profession, or in the title of any patent, or in any trademark or design any name or emblem specified in the schedule or any colourable imitation thereof without the previous permission of the Central Government or of such officer of Government as may be authorized in this behalf by the Central Government.

I. Governance

329. There is a General Assembly of IOA (Association) which means and includes the representatives deputed by the members in accordance with rules and Indian citizens holding Membership of International Olympic Association. The management of the association entrusted and vests in the Executive Council.

II. Membership of Association

330. The membership of the association is open subject to recognition by the General Assembly to the following:

(a) NSF or associations, whose sport is included in the Olympic or Asian or Commonwealth Games.
(b) NSFs or Associations, which represent widely, played Indian sports recognized by IOA.
(c) Olympic Association of States, as well as the Centrally Administered UT (the geographical boundaries of a State, Centrally Administered UT shall be the same as recognized by the Constitution of India).
(d) Services Sports Control Board (SSCB).
(e) Indian citizens who are members of the IOC other than honorary member or member expelled from the IOC.

III. Functions, Powers and Duties of General Assembly

331. Some of the important functions, powers and duties of General Assembly are as follows:

(a) To formulate and enforce the policy of association.
(b) To carry out the objects of the association.
(c) To hold and control the funds and other properties of the association.
(d) To appoint committees and subcommittees, as and when necessary.
(e) To enforce all the rules and regulations of the IOC.
(f) To enforce and defend the exclusive right of the association to the use of the Olympic flag and Olympic Insignia, confining their use and, as far as possible, that of the words 'Olympic Games'.
(g) To be the official organization in complete and sole charge of all Olympic, Commonwealth and Asian Games matters in the country.
(h) In cooperation with NSF or associations to guard and enforce amateur rules.
(i) To have full and complete jurisdiction over all matters pertaining to the participation of India in the Olympic Games and other games under the parentage of the IOC, Commonwealth Games Federation, Olympic Council of India and or IOA.

(j) To assist in cooperation with NSF/associations to arrange the selection, training and coaching of the teams that will represent India in Olympic, Commonwealth and Asian Games and other international competitions/tournaments.
(k) To act as channel of communication between the NSFs/Associations and the Government of India for financial and other assistance to the federation.
(l) To take disciplinary action against any NSF/association for misbehaviour or any other undesirable activity bringing discredit to the country.
(m) To grant recognition to such NSFs/Associations, the games of which are duly recognized by the IOC. Under special circumstances, the indigenous games can also be given recognition.

IV. Constitution of the Executive Council

332. The Executive Council consists of one president, twelve vice presidents, a Secretary General, six Joint Secretaries, a Treasurer, ten members elected from among the representatives of the NSFs and associations/SSCB. The tenure of the office-bearers and members of the Executive Council is four years each. There are one or more paid assistant secretaries for the association to look after the day-to-day administration of IOA Secretariat under the guidance and supervision of the Secretary General.

V. Secretary General

333. The Secretary General is the in charge of day-to-day administration of the association and shall transact all official business in accordance with the decision of President, IOA, General Assembly and Executive Council. He carries on all the correspondence in the name of association, save as otherwise directed by the president. He keeps and maintains the minutes of all the meetings of the IOA General Assembly and Executive Council of the association; the register of the members and all such records as may be necessary for the smooth and efficient working of the association. He is also responsible for the maintenance of the properties of the association.

VI. Functions, Powers and Duties of Executive Council

334. The functions, powers and duties of the Executive Council are as follows:

(a) To conduct the business of the association during the interval between meeting of the General Assembly and duly report all the decisions and the actions to the General Assembly for its information.
(b) To be responsible for the proper supervision of the Indian teams for the Olympic Games, Commonwealth Games and Asian Games during the period of the games and their trip from and to the games.

(c) To initiate and recommend to the General Assembly schemes and proposals for the promotion and development of sports and games in the country.
(d) To consider and, if feasible, recommend to the General Assembly schemes and proposals for the grant of financial assistance to State Olympic Associations and NSFs or Associations for development of sports and games with special reference to those that are not developed or in areas that are underdeveloped.
(e) To consider the Annual General Meeting of the Secretary General and submit it to the General Assembly with their recommendations.

335. The association is responsible for the preparation and participation of competitors in the Olympic Games as well as in regional events like Commonwealth and Asian Games. There is a separate federation at national level in each game/sport which assists the IOA and preparation of sportsmen. The selection of sportsmen is generally carried out on the basis of performance at national level. However, at times, special selection trials are also held to choose the competitors for participation in the Olympic Games and other international events. After initial selection, the competitors are required to attend training camps. The national federations are assisted by the Netaji Subhas National Institute of Sports, situated at Patiala, Punjab which provides intensive training for athletes. The selected competitors are then recommended by the national federations to the IOA for official sponsorship for participation in the Olympic Games.

336. A special feature of the IOA is that, in addition to the national federation for each sport, there are State Olympic Associations in various States. The State bodies controlling the different sports are affiliated to the national federations and to the State Olympic Associations. The aim of the State Olympic Associations is to ensure the promotion of sports in their respective States, in conjunction with the State bodies for the different games and sports.

VII. Bodies and Functions

337. The IOA is recognized by IOC and the government as the National Olympic Committee of India. The overall responsibility for participation in the Olympic Games rests with the IOA. The other responsibilities undertaken by the IOA are as follows:

(1) Deciding the organization of national games.
(2) Maintaining liaison between the Government of India and member federations or associations.
(3) Protecting the amateur status of sportsmen.
(4) Promoting and developing the Olympic Movement.

The 'IOA' is also called as 'Bharatiya Olympic Sangh' and its registered office is situated in the National Capital Territory of Delhi.

338. The main objectives of the IOA are as follows:

(1) To develop and promote Olympic movement and amateur sport.
(2) To promote and encourage the physical, moral and cultural education for the development of character, good health and good citizenship.
(3) To enforce all rules and regulations of the IOC and the IOA.
(4) To enforce and defend the exclusive right of the association to the use of the Olympic insignia, confining their use and, as far as possible, that of the words 'Olympic' and 'Olympiad' to activities concerning the Olympic Games.
(5) To be the official organization in complete and sole charge of all Olympic matters in the country.
(6) To educate the public of the country as to the value of amateurism in sports.
(7) In cooperation with NSFs or Associations to guard and enforce amateur rules.
(8) To maintain the highest ideals of amateurism and to promote interest therein, particularly in connection with the Olympic Games and other games under the patronage of the IOC, as well as the IOA.
(9) To have full and complete jurisdiction over all matters pertaining to the participation of India in the Olympic Games and other games under the patronage of the IOC as well as the IOA.
(10) To assist in cooperation with NSFs/Associations the selection, training and coaching of the teams that will represent India in the Asian. Commonwealth, Olympic and other international competitions and tournaments, under the patronage of the IOC as well as the IOA. After selection of the team, to supervise and control the participation of the team in the said competition and tournaments.
(11) To undertake with the assistance of NSFs/Associations the financing, management, transportation, maintenance and welfare of teams from India taking part in the Olympic Games and other games under the patronage of the IOC as well as IOA.
(12) To certify the amateur status of competitors from India for such international competition as requiring such certification.
(13) To stimulate the interest of the people of the country in the promotion of the sports and game in the Olympic Programme, and to that end the formation of State Olympic Associations of the development of sports and games within a State and NSFs for games and sports in Olympic Programme.
(14) To act as the channel of communication between NSFs and the Government of India for financial or other assistance to the federations.
(15) To admit the membership of State Olympic Associations and NSFs which shall be required to submit their annual reports and audited statement of accounts to the IOA for information.
(16) To take disciplinary action against any federation for misbehaviour or any other undesirable activity bringing discredit to the country and sport.
(17) To do all other things that may be necessary or expedient to promote the development of amateur sports and games in the country and for the conduct of its business.
(18) To resist in the realm of sports all pressures of any kind, whether of a political, racial, religious or economic nature.

VIII. General Disciplinary Regulations

339. The general disciplinary regulations are as follows:

- Violation of the rules cannot be excused on the grounds of ignorance of the said rules.
- Whoever incites a member unit to commit an infraction or aids and abets the said unit infraction, shall be sanctioned in the same manner as the unit which commits the infraction.
- All units of the IOA shall undertake to supply to the IOA, copy of their respective statutes, Constitution and Rules and Regulations, a list of their respective accredited member units and their office-bearers and members, a copy of annual report, annual balance sheet and audited statement of accounts and a report of their activities, duly approved by their general body, within six months of the closing of the financial year, along with a calendar of sports for the ensuing year. Failure to supply this information within the stipulated period will constitute a breach of this rule and may render the defaulting unit to disciplinary action under these rules.

The President, IOA has the power to call for explanation from its member units regarding the issue where a sportsperson has been found guilty of use of dope or consumption of IOC prohibited substances, but no action has been taken by the concerned member unit. The recommendations of the IOA President shall be placed before the general body for appropriate disciplinary action.

340. The IOA is to ensure *inter alia* that:

- Each NSF/association in the particular field of specialization has appointed, or would appoint, a National Coach who possesses a valid coaching diploma. Prior approval of the IOA would be necessary if the person already appointed, or proposed to be appointed, as National Coach, does not possess the requisite coaching qualifications.
- The NSFs, in their respective field of specialization, must hold not less than one competition annually each for specified age groups for senior, junior and sub-junior level. These competitions should be organized through Inter-Block and Inter-District competitions in each State, leading to the competition at the National level.
- For any one game, only one sports association is permitted in one State. It implies, therefore, that in the field of sports, it will be 'One State, One Unit'.

341. No NSF or Association shall affiliate a sports unit of any State or department not affiliated or recognized by the State Olympic Association which is affiliated to the IOA:

(a) The association may sue or be sued in the name of Secretary General, IOA.
(b) A lawsuit can only be filed at New Delhi, the headquarters of the IOA and the Delhi Courts alone shall have the exclusive jurisdiction in all the legal disputes wherein the legality, correctness and propriety or otherwise the action of the IOA has been challenged.
(c) The provisions of the Societies Registration Act XXI of 1860 will apply to the association.
(d) In all matters relating to the interpretation and application of the Constitution, as well as in matters not specifically provided for herein, the decision of the Executive Council shall be final and binding on all concerned.
(e) The Executive Council may, at its discretion, frame by-laws not inconsistent with or contrary to this Constitution, for the proper and efficient administration of the association.
(f) The IOA shall be guided by the statutes, rules, regulations by-laws, directions and instructions issued from time to time by the IOC.
(g) In case of interpretation difficulties of the articles mentioned in this Constitution or in the eventuality of a conflict with the Rules of the 'Olympic Charter' the rules contained in the latter (Olympic Charter) shall prevail.
(h) The IOA will affiliate and approve, with the exception of widely played Indian Games, only such NSF/Associations, the games of which is on the approved list of the IOC for the Olympic Games, on the approved list of the Commonwealth Games Federation for the Commonwealth Games, and on the approved list of the Olympic Council of Asia the affiliated State Olympic Associations of the IOA will also follow this procedure.
(i) It shall be binding on all the NSFs, Associations, State Olympic associations and other units affiliated to the IOA to forward their annual report and audited statement of account every year. The affiliated units to also conduct their election as and when due or in special circumstances as and when directed by the IOA. However in the elections held by all or any of the unit(s) to reconstitute its/their Executive Council or to elect new office-bearers, the date and time of the election shall be intimated to the IOA and the President IOA shall nominate an election observer to attend the election meeting and who shall submit his/her report to the President IOA for appropriate action. The non-compliance of these requirements may result in disaffiliation of the defaulting units by the IOA General Assembly on the recommendations of the Executive Council.
(j) All the NSFs, Associations and State Olympic Associations will forward to the IOA a copy of their current and valid Constitution along with amendments whenever made. Important and significant information and statistics shall also be likewise supplied by them to the IOA from time to time.

342. Any appeal by a member of an NSF, Association or State Olympic Association complaining against the procedure adopted by the concerned NSF, Association or State Olympic Association for holding 'Elections', or any other issue connected with this subject must be made in writing, to the IOA within thirty days of the occurrence of the incident. No complaint will be considered valid or entertained by the IOA if it is made after the expiry of the thirty-day period. The complaint must be specific and contain documentary evidence to prove the issue that is disputed.

Chapter 3. Major National Federations

343. Government deals only with the National Sports Federations (NSFs) and grants recognition to them to become eligible to receive financial as well as other forms of assistance. Total number of fifty-six NSFs are recognized by the government for different sports disciplines. Normally, elections are held by the NSFs at the intervals prescribed under the by-laws of the concerned NSFs. In order to ensure that NSFs function in a democratic manner, Government has prescribed model election guidelines to be followed by the NSFs for their elections which has been made an integral part of the National Sports Development Code of India, 2011 (NSDCI). NSDCI, *inter alia*, contains instructions on democratic and healthy management practices, age and tenure limits of office-bearers, holding of elections as per model election guidelines devised by the government.

§1. The Football Federation

I. Introduction

344. Football was introduced during the days of the British Rule. Many football clubs were created and predate many of the organizations and clubs, such as FIFA, which are predominant in the game today. Initially games were played between army teams; however, clubs were soon set up around the country. Mohun Bagan Athletic Club was set up in what is now West Bengal and is considered the oldest football club in Asia. The club became famous in 1911 when it became the first Indian team to lift the Indian Football Association (IFA) Shield, a tournament previously won only by British teams based in India. It defeated the Eastern Yorkshire Regiment 2-1 in the final of the tournament in a victory that is still regarded by many as the greatest by an Indian team before independence.

345. India lacked a structured national football organization before the foundation of the AIFF, with only a few provincial associations administering the sport regionally. IFA, the association governing football in the State of West Bengal, was recognized as the sport's de facto governing body. The IFA at this time was affiliated to the FA, the Football Association of England, and hence, all foreign tours were organized by the former. In 1935, the IFA organized a conference of the representatives of the football associations of Assam, Bihar, UP, Delhi, Mysore and Bombay at Darbhanga with an aim to finding a national body for the running of the sport. However, no unanimously acceptable decision was arrived at. Though the IFA delegates (late) S.N. Banerjee and (late) Pankaj Gupta, as well as the Maharaja of Santosh (now in Bangladesh), walked out in protest, the remaining delegates formed a body, naming it All India Football Association. The Raja Bahadur of Darbhanga was appointed Secretary.

346. In 1937, a meeting was held at Delhi and there was an attempt at discussion with the protesting group. A resolution was finally reached, the All India Football Association was liquidated, and the AIFF came into being, with one representative from each affiliated association and two each from the IFA and the Army Sports Control Board. Brigadier V.H.B. Mejendine was elected the first president, Major A.C. Wilson the first Honorary Secretary and Pankaj Gupta the first Treasurer.

II. Structure

347. The AIFF is the apex body for management and administration of football at national level. This body is affiliated to the regional Asian Football Confederation, as well as to the worldwide body FIFA. There are also State level Football Federations and some of them are very old.

The football is one of India's most popular sports, and ranks second only behind cricket in popularity, although some reporting considers football to be more popular. Football is played in almost all over India and said to be the top sport in the States of Goa, Kerala and West Bengal. Kolkata (formerly Calcutta), in the State of West Bengal, is considered to be the home of Indian football. The city contains the two most famous Indian teams East Bengal Club and Mohun Bagan.

III. Functions

348. The AIFF is the amateur organization. It administers the running of the national team and also controls the National Football League, India's premier domestic club competition, in addition to various other competitions. The AIFF was founded in 1937, and gained FIFA affiliation in 1948, after India's independence in 1947. India was one of the founder members of the Asian Football Confederation when it was set up in 1954.

349. State level games are administered by State football associations, some of which predate the AIFF. The IFA, which is responsible for the game in the State of West Bengal, used to be in de facto charge of the game in India before they pushed for the creation of a national body in association with other State associations. Some of these predate the AIFF and were instrumental in its founding. Club teams compete at national, State and district levels in India. There are also interstate and interdistrict competitions.

IV. Leagues

350. The highest level club teams in India compete in the National Football League. Women's football has its own separate interstate and State competitions. The national football team was also quite successful until the 1970s, qualifying for Olympic tournaments and the FIFA World Cup. The team qualified for the 1950 World Cup finals in Brazil, but could not appear as they still played in their bare feet at that time. The Indian team also won the 1951 and 1962 Asian Games gold medals in football. In 1956, the team finished fourth at the Melbourne Olympics.

Women's football has not had the relative head start over the rest of the world that the men's game has had, and also has not had the chance to spread through the country like its male counterpart. The game was administered by the Women's Football Federation of India until the early 1990s when they were absorbed into the AIFF. The women's game, like the men's game, also has its early pioneers in the State of West Bengal. The large Kolkata teams, East Bengal and Mohun Bagan, started women's club sides in the 2000–2001 season, and they participated with other teams in the Calcutta Women's Football League. However, players from Manipur have also made advances in the game. Players from these two States make up a large part of the team.

V. Sports Clubs

351. Football is one of the popular sports, and ranks second only behind cricket in popularity. Football is played almost all over India and said to be the top sport in the States of Goa, Kerala and West Bengal. West Bengal is considered to be the home of Indian football. The Kolkata city in West Bengal is the base of some famous football clubs namely East Bengal Club, Mohammedan Sporting and Mohun Bagan Club.

§2. Federation of Athletes

I. Introduction

352. Athletics activity in its present form started in India sometime in the last decade of nineteenth century. Nothing much is known of its early stages, till first known participation of Norman G. Pitchard in second Olympic Games in 1900 at Paris, where he won a Silver Medal in 200 m. History does not speak much of this sport between 1900 and 1920. However, Athletic Competition was held as Inter-Provincial Athletic Championship every two years. With the formation of IOA in 1926, its affiliation with IOC in 1927 and taking over the reigns of IOA by late Maharaja Bhupinder Singh as President and Professor G.D. Sondhi as Secretary in 1928, Athletic Championship became a part of Indian Olympic Games held every two years.

353. India in the meantime participated (unofficially) in the 1920 Olympic Games at Antwerp (Belgium) with four athletes and 1924 Olympic Games at Paris with eight athletes under the leadership of H.C. Buck of YMCA Madras. The official participation of Indian athletes started in the 1928 Olympic Games at Amsterdam with a seven-member team. Since then, India participated under the IOA Banner in 1932 Olympic Games at Los Angeles and 1936 Olympic Games at Berlin with three and five athletes, respectively. Mr M.C. Dhawan, who participated in 1932 Olympic Games at Los Angeles later became the Secretary of Amateur Athletic Federation in 1950.

II. Bodies and Objectives

354. Amateur Athletic Federation of India (AAFI) was formed in 1946 at the initiative of Maharaja Yadvinder Singh, the then President of IOA with Professor G.D. Sondhi as its first President. The AAFI got affiliated to IAAF (International Amateur Athletic Federation) in 1946). But it followed the IOA for holding the National Athletic Championship once in two years. It was in 1949 that AAFI took the decision of holding the National Athletic Championship every year. The AAFI for the first time selected eight athletes (six men and two women), who participated in 1948 Olympic Games at London. Indian women competed in the Olympic Games for the first time in 1948.

Mr M.C. Dhawan was elected Secretary of AAFI in 1950 and was the Technical Secretary in the first Asian Games held at New Delhi in 1951. It was for the first time that AAFI held a Coaching Camp for six weeks duration at Sabathu in the Simla Hills in 1950 to prepare the team for the New Delhi Asian Games. Raja Bhalindra Singh became the President of AAFI in 1952 and continued to guide athletics till 1968. Mr M.C. Dhawan who was elected Secretary in 1950 and ten years partnership with Raja Bhalindra Singh. AAFI was the real pioneers of Coaching in India. Mr P.K. Mathur of Railways succeeded Mr M.C. Dhawan as Secretary AAFI in 1962. Raja Sahib continued as the president.

355. The introduction of age Group Competitions, the addition of Open National Championship and Zonal and Inter-Zonal Championships was the contribution of this team. Raja Bhalindra Singh left the presidentship of AAFI in 1968 to devote more time to IOA and Olympic Movement as he had also become the IOC Member. A new team of Mr P.K. Mathur as President and Mr M.L. Jadam as Secretary came into power in 1969 and held the position for one term till 1972. During this period, maximum numbers of Indian Athletes were sent out for international competition. First Indian woman, Kamaljeet Sandhu won a Gold Medal in Asian Games. S. Umrao Singh and Mr M.L. Jadam were elected President and Secretary of the newly formed Asian Amateur Athletic Association at Bangkok in 1970 respectively. The year 1972 saw a change in the team to lead AAFI and S. Umrao Singh, and Mr L.R. Khanna were elected the new President and the Secretary of the AAFI respectively. Mr Umrao Singh was elected IAAF Council Member in 1972 at Munich for four years. He has the distinction of being the only Indian to be elected, as IAAF Council Member; this team made a great personal effort to organize more coaching camps to ensure better participation in International Meets and improved performance in the Asian Games and Olympic Games. The Indian athletes gave the best ever performance in the 1976 Olympic Games. Indian athletes (Statistical Book) were published and so was the AAFI Rule Book. The 1974 Asian Games also saw a very good performance by Indian athletes and won fifteen medals including four Golds. These were the only Golds won by the Indian Contingent in the Asian Games at Tehran (1974) T.C. Yohanan became the first Indian to Jump over 8.00 m barrier in this Asian Games.

356. The period 1976–1980 saw a new team of S. Buta Singh (President) and Col. Kirpal Singh (Secretary) which further strengthened the AAFI. The proof of it was good performance of Indian Athletes in the 1978 Asian Games winning eight Gold Medals in a total of nineteen medals. A number of foreign teams visited India including a team of Russian athletes, who provided excellent competition to Indian Athletes before the Bangkok Asian Games. In 1980–1984, yet another change took place in the team with S. Buta Singh continuing as President, Mr G.S. Sivia became the new Secretary. This team made a great contribution in the organization, technical conduct of athletic events including officiating in Asian Games held at New Delhi. The National and International Clinics for Officials produced an excellent team which flawlessly conducted athletic competition in the Asian Game. A great emphasis on coaching of athletes was laid. Teams were sent to Germany (East and West) for training cum competitions. For the first time a high altitude training camp was held in 1982 at Dagshai (Simla Hills) in preparation for the Asian Games.

In 1984–1988, Maharaja Jaideep Singh of Baria became the new President and Mr V.K. Verma the new Secretary. They worked with great enthusiasm and tried to give a new direction to popularize athletics. Emphasis was to have more and more athletes in the coaching camps. To increase the number of competitions, Master's Meet was introduced. In addition, a beginning was made for holding International IAAF Meet and involve big names (Foreign Athletes) in it to popularize and strengthen the athletic programme. Maharaja Baria suddenly died in late 1987, and his place was taken by Mr Suresh Kalmadi. The Juniors Competition was separated from the Seniors and the first Junior Championship was held in 1986–1987 at Hissar.

357. Mr Suresh Kalmadi and Mr Lalit K. Bhanot formed the new team of President and Secretary respectively. Junior Development Programme, in collaboration with ITC and SAI, as well as IAAF Permit Meets were initiated along with a new strong competition calendar, falling in line with the International Competition Calendar. Domestic Circuit Meets and all year round coaching plans were initiated.

§3. Swimming Federation

I. Introduction

358. In olden days, swimming was one of the warfare activities for the warriors and a lifesaver. It has off late grown into the world famous recreation game. Swimming is widely popular in India both as a general activity and as sporting event. It appeals to people of all ages. It is one of the original games of the Olympics; however, competitive swimming in India is one such Olympic event which has not seen any notable triumph at international competitions. The Federation International Association (FINA) is the governing body of international swimming.

II. Objectives

359. The Swimming Federation of India (SFI) is the apex body for swimming sport in India. The SFI is affiliated to FINA, the world governing body. The SFI came into existence after the amalgamation of its predecessors, the National Swimming Association and the Indian Swimming Federation (ISF). The two rival associations were at loggerheads over affiliation issues. While the Kolkata-based National Swimming Association got affiliation from FINA in 1932–1933, the ISF was supported by the IOA. The issue was resolved in 1948 and the Swimming Federation of India came into being.

§4. The Basketball Federation

I. Introduction

360. This game is of recent origin. Dr James Naismith of USA invented this game at Springfield college in 1891. The purpose was to provide for a game that could be played indoors during winter months. The final set of rules were formulated by Dr James Naismith in 1892 and later on standardized in 1915. Graduates of Springfield's college, YMCA men and soldiers of America carried and popularized this game in other parts of the world. In 1932, the International Basketball Federation was formed.

II. Objectives

361. In India YMCA College of Physical Education, Madras played this game about ninety years back. It was only in 1950 that Basketball Federation of India (BFI) was formed. This game is popular in all parts of India. BFI controls this game in the country. The State Basketball Associations are affiliated to this central body. Since 1936, Basketball championships are being held as part of Olympic Games. In India, affiliated State Basketball Associations conduct national basketball championship for men and women. Besides, National Junior Interstate Championship for boys and girls and National Boys Championship are also conducted.

§5. Volleyball Federation

I. Introduction

362. The game of Volleyball was invented in 1895 at Holyoke YMCA Gymnasium in USA by a physical Director named William Morgan. However, the first complete set of rules was formulated in 1917. The International Volleyball Association was formed in 1947 with headquarters in Paris, France. The first World Volleyball Championship was held in 1949 at Prague, Czechoslovakia.

II. Objectives

363. In India, Volleyball was introduced by the YMCA. In 1950, the Volleyball Federation of India was established to coordinate the activities of various State associations and to promote the game at national level. The first Asian Volleyball Championship was held at Tokyo in 1955 and India beat Japan in the finals.

III. National Leagues and Associations

364. The Volleyball Federation of India coordinates the activities of various State associations and to promote the game at national level. The first National Volleyball Championship was held in Madras in 1952. The National School Games Volleyball Championship is held every year at different venues as a part of National School Games.

§6. Board of Control for Cricket in India

I. Introduction

365. Cricket, like hockey, was brought to the Indian subcontinent by the British. There are references to cricket having being played in India in the early parts of the eighteenth century. By the beginning of the nineteenth century, the game was being played in the cities of Bombay, Calcutta and Madras. The presidency matches began in 1892–1893 between Parsis and Europeans, and the tournament became the Bombay Triangular, with the Hindus fielding a team in 1907–1908. In 1912–1913, the tournament became quadrangular with the entry of Muslims in the field. With the efforts of several Princes, H.E. Grant-Gloven and A.S. de Mellow, the national championship, the Ranji Trophy began in 1935.

366. BCCI is the national apex body of cricket with headquarters at Mumbai, and it controls and regulates the activities related to cricket in the country. It enjoys a monopoly status as regards regulation of cricket under the terms of its Memorandum of Association and Articles of Association. It enjoys tax exemption and other benefits such as the right to use any stadium across the country at a nominal annual rent. As a member of the International Council, BCCI represents the country in international fora. It has the authority to select players, umpires and officials to represent the country in international events and exercises control on them. Without the recognition of BCCI, no competitive cricket involving Indian players can be hosted within or outside the country.

The game of cricket was introduced in India by the soldiers of East India Company in 1792. After many developments, a Provisional Board of Control was formed with headquarters at Delhi in 1927. In 1928, a representative Board of Control for Cricket was established with Mr R.E. Grant Goran as the first President and Mr A.S. de Mello as the Honorary Secretary. BCCI got affiliated to ICC in 1929. The first international tour of Indian team was to England in 1932. Simultaneously the first national cricket championship Ranji Trophy was introduced in the name of Ranjit Singh, the Maharaja of Patiala and Captain of Indian team.

367. The Supreme Court pointed out the background of BCCI as follows:
It is then necessary to understand the nature of the respondent organization, namely, CAB. It cannot be disputed that the BCCI is a non-profit making organization which controls officially organized game of cricket in India. Similarly, Cricket Association of Bengal (CAB) is also non-profit making organization which controls officially organized game of cricket in the State of West Bengal. The CAB is one of the Founder Members of BCCI. Office-bearers and Members of the Working Committees of both BCCI and CAB are all citizens of India. The primary object of both the organizations, among others, is to promote the game of cricket, to foster 'the spirit of sportsmanship' and the ideals of cricket, and to impart education through the media of cricket, and for achieving the said objects, to organize and stage tournaments and matches either with the members of ICC or other organizations. According to CAB, BCCI is perhaps the only sports organization in India which earns foreign exchange and is neither controlled by any Governmental agency nor receives any financial assistance or grants, of whatsoever nature.

368. It was further observed that 'It cannot be disputed that to arrange any international cricket tournament or series, it is necessary and a condition precedent, to pay to the participating member countries or teams, a minimum guaranteed amount in foreign exchange and to bear expenses incurred for travelling, boarding, lodging and other daily expenses for the participating cricketers and the concerned accompanying visiting officials. A huge amount of expenses has also to be incurred for organizing the matches. In addition, both BCCI and CAB annually incur large amount of expenses for giving subsidies and grants to its members to maintain, develop and upgrade the infrastructure, to coach and train players and umpires and to pay to them when the series and matches are played.' (Secretary, Ministry of Information and Broadcasting, *Govt. of India and Others v. Cricket Association of Bengal and Others* (AIR 1995 SC 1236: (1995) 2 SCC 161; (1995) 1 SCR 1036).

II. Structure

369. The BCCI's membership generally includes the State Cricket Associations. However, some States have more than one association like Maharashtra State has Maharashtra Cricket Association (MCA), Mumbai Cricket Association and Vidharva Cricket Association. The Gujarat State has Gujarat Cricket Association, Baroda Cricket Association and Saurashtra Cricket Association. Besides, Railways and Services are also members of BCCI. In *Zee Telefilms Ltd. and Another v. Union of India* (AIR 2005 SC 2677), the Supreme Court deliberated as to structure and importance of BCCI as follows:

It is accented by the Union of India that the Board is an autonomous organization and the Government of India does not hold any cricket match series as it is the function of the Board, but that is all the more reason as to why it has its own responsibilities towards officials, players, umpires, coaches administrators and above all the cricket loving public.

However, we may place on record that there are a number of documents filed by the Union of India which clearly show that either for sending Indian Team abroad or inviting a foreign team on the soil of India, the Board has invariably been taking permission from the MYAS. In the counter affidavit filed before the Bombay High Court, the Board raised a contention that it seeks permission of the Union of India for obtaining visas, foreign exchange and matters connected therewith; but the said contention cannot be accented in view of the fact that had the same been the position, the Ministry of Human Resource Development (which has nothing to do in these matters), would, not have been approached therefore and that too in the form prescribed in the guidelines.

The Board's activities representing the country are not confined to international forums only. The Board within the country organizes and conducts the Ranji Trophy, the Irani Trophy, the Duleep Singh Trophy, the Deodhar Trophy and the NKP Slave Challenger Trophy. Although, there are domestic events, indisputably only those who are members of the Board and/or recognized by it can take part therein and none else. This also goes to show that the Board regulates domestic competitive cricket to the fullest measure and exercises control over its members which represents the five zones in India. All the States Federations besides a few other clubs which are its members, two of which will bear representation to State, are governmental organizations.

Indisputably, the Board is a regulator of cricket played at the country levels both off and on the fields including selection of players and umpires. ICC possesses and exercises all the powers to regulate international competitive cricket. It exercises disciplinary power also as in case of violation of the rules, a country member or the player may be derecognized. The ICC exercises a monopoly over the sports at the international level whereas Board does so at the country level. It is the Board only, to the exclusion of all others that can recognize bodies that are entitled to participate in the nominated tournaments. Players and umpires also must be registered with it. In the event of violation of its rules and regulations, which may include participation in an unauthorized tournament without its permission, a player or umpire would forfeit his right to participate in all official cricket matches which for all intent and purport shall be the end of career of a professional cricketer or umpire. In our constitutional scheme, rule of law would, by all means, prevail over rule of cricket. A body regulating the game of cricket would be compelled by the court to abide by rule of law.

370. BCCI undertakes activities of entering into contracts for telecasting and broadcasting rights and allows advertisements in the stadium. While considering the status of the Board vis-à-vis Article 12 of the Constitution of India, the Central Government's reluctance to interfere with its day-to-day affairs or allowing it to work as an autonomous body, non-assistance in terms of money or the administrative control there over may not be of much relevance as it was not only given de facto recognition but also it is aided, facilitated or supported in all other respects by it. It would not be correct to contend that a monopoly status upon a body must be conferred either by way of statute or by the State by issuing an appropriate order on that behalf. The question as regard exercise of monopoly power by the Board must be determined having regard to the ground realities, i.e., it not only represents the country but also controls and regulates the entire field of competitive cricket.

Despite the fact that the relationship between the Board and the players is not that of an employer and employee, but the players are within its complete control. Sports activities of the countries being not a commercial activity, as has been held in Cricket Association of Bengal, the same must be considered from a larger spectrum of the Indian citizens as a whole. It is not disputed that as of now except the Board there is no other authority in the field. The rules framed by the Board do not spell out as to how without virtual recognition of the Union of India as also the patronage of States whether de facto or de jure it could become a national federation and how it could become a member of the ICC. It does not furthermore disclose as to how it could having regard to its professed function as a private club, could grant to itself enormous powers as are replete in its rules and regulations. Rules and regulations framed by the Board speak out for themselves as to how it represents Indian cricket team and regulates almost all the activities pertaining thereto. It also legislates law of sports in India in the field of competitive cricket. There is no area which is beyond the control and regulation of the Board. Every young person who thinks of playing cricket either for a State or a zone or India must as of necessity be a member of the Board and if he intends to play with another organization, it must obtain its permission so as to enable him or continue to participate in the official matches. The professionals devote their life for playing cricket. The Board's activities may impinge on the fundamental rights of citizens.

There is no organization in the world other than the ICC at the international level and the Board at the national level that control the game of first-class cricket with enormous powers and wield great influence over the entire field of cricket. Cricket when it comes to competitive matches no longer remains a mere entertainment; it commands such a wide public interest. It is now recognized that game of cricket as an activity gives a sense of identity and pride to a nation.

371. In the landmark judgment of *Board of Control for Cricket in India v. Cricket Association of Bihar & Ors.* (2015 STPL (web) 131 SC (DB); 2015 AIR (SCW) 2258, dated 22 January 2015), the Supreme Court examined the status of BCCI as State under Article 12 as follows:
Article 12 of the Constitution of India gives an inclusive definition to the expression 'State', and says that for purposes of Part III of the Constitution the expression 'State' includes the Parliament of India, the Government and the Legislature of each of the States and Local or other authorities within the territory of India or under the control of the Government of India. A long line of decisions of the Supreme Court have examined and interpreted the expression appearing in Article 12 with a view to determining whether or not a given entity is 'State' within the meaning of Article 12. It is unnecessary to refer to all such decisions pronounced over the past few

decades not only because the law is by now fairly well settled by a long line of decisions but also because the question whether or not BCCI is 'State' within the meaning of Article 12 may not make any material difference to the case at hand in view of the admitted position that respondent-BCCI does discharge several important public functions which make it amenable to the writ jurisdiction of the High Court under Article 226 of the Constitution of India. We may all the same refer to a few landmarks on the judicial landscape only as a reminder to what is settled and binding upon us.

372. In *Sukhdev and Ors. Etc. v. Bhagatram Sardar Singh Raghuvanshi and Anr. Etc.* ((1975) 1 SCC 421), one of the questions for considerations was whether an employee of statutory corporation like Oil and Natural Gas Commission established under the Oil and Natural Gas Commission Act, 1959, Indian Finance Corporation, established under the Indian Finance Corporation Act, 1948 and the Life Insurance Corporation (LIC) under the Life Insurance Corporation Act, 1956, was entitled to claim protection of Articles 14 and 16 against the Corporation. A Constitution bench of the Supreme Court answered the question in the affirmative by a majority of 4:1. Mathew J., in his concurring judgment referred to *Marsh v. Alabama* ((3) 326 U.S. 501: 19 L.21 ed. 265), to hold that even where a corporation is privately performing a public function, it is bound by the constitutional standard applicable to all State actions. *Marsh v. Alabama* arose out of a prosecution launched against a Jehovah's witness for her refusal to leave the side walk where she was distributing religious pamphlets. She was fined 5 USD but aggrieved by her prosecution she approached the Supreme Court to argue that the corporation that owned the town had denied the right of religious liberty available to Marsh. The US Supreme Court upheld the contention and declared that administration of public bodies like a town through private entities were tantamount to carrying out functions of a public body. Private right of the corporation could, therefore, be exercised only within constitutional limitations. Black J. speaking for the court observed:

The more an owner, for his advantage, opens up his property for use by the public in general, the more do his rights become circumscribed by the statutory and constitutional rights of those who use it. Thus, the owners of privately held bridges, ferries, turnpikes and railroads may not operate them as freely as a farmer does his farm. Since these facilities are built and operated primarily to benefit the public and since their operation is essentially a public function, it is subject to State regulation.

Justice Frankfurter in his concurring opinion added that the function discharged by the corporation as a municipal corporation was a public function hence subject to State Regulation. Borrowing support from the above decision and several others the Supreme Court in Sukhdev's case held:

Another factor, which might be considered, is whether the operation is an important public function. The combination of State aid and the furnishing of an important public service may result in a conclusion that the operation should be classified as a State agency. If a given function is of such public importance and so closely related to governmental functions as to be classified as a governmental agency, then even the presence or absence of State financial aid might be irrelevant in making a finding of State action. If the function does not fall within such a description, then mere addition of State money would not influence the conclusion. In America, corporations or associations, private in character, but dealing with public rights, have already been held subject to constitutional standards. Political parties, for example, even though they are not statutory organisations, and are in form private clubs, are within this category. So also are labour unions on which statutes confer the right of collective bargaining ... .

373. In *Ramana Dayaram Shetty v. International Airport Authority of India and Ors.* ((1979) 3 SCC 489), the Supreme Court held that while a corporation may be created by a statute or incorporated under a law such as the Companies Act, 2013, or the Societies Registration Act, 1860, the question is as to when the corporation can be described as an instrumentality or agency of the government and what are the tests to determine whether a corporation is or is not such an instrumentality or agency. While holding that there is no cut and dried formula that can provide an answer, American decisions in *Evans v. Newton* (382 US 296 15 L.Ed.-2nd 373, Ch 614 = 1963 1 All. E.R. 590) and *New York v. United States* (326 US 572) were referred to declare that if the functions of the corporation are of public importance and closely related to governmental functions, it would be a relevant factor in classifying the corporation as an instrumentality or agency of the State. The Supreme Court said:

> 16. There is also another factor which may be regarded as having a bearing on this issue and it is whether the operation of the corporation is an important public function. It has been held in the United States in a number of cases that the concept of private action must yield to a concept of State action where public functions are being performed. (Vide Arthur S. Miller: 'The Constitutional Law of the "Security State"'). It was pointed out by Douglas, J., in *Evans v. Newton* that 'when private individuals or groups are endowed by the State with powers or functions governmental in nature, they become agencies or instrumentalities of the State'. Of course, with the growth of the welfare State, it is very difficult to define what functions are governmental and what are not, because, as pointed out by Villmer, L.J., in *Pfizer v. Ministry of Health* there has been since mid-Victorian times, 'a revolution in political thought and a totally different conception prevails today as to what is and what is not within the functions of Government'. Douglas, J., also observed to the same effect in *New York v. United States*: 'A State's project is as much a legitimate governmental activity whether it is traditional, or akin to private enterprise, or conducted for profit.' *Cf. Helvering v. Gerhardt.* A State may deem it as essential to its economy that it owns and operates a railroad, a mill or an irrigation system as it does to own and operate bridges, streetlights or a sewage disposal plant. What might have been viewed in an earlier day, as an improvident or even dangerous extension of State activities may today be deemed indispensable. It may be noted that besides the so-called traditional functions, the modern State operates a multitude of public enterprises and discharges a host of other public functions. If the functions of the corporation are of public importance and closely related to governmental functions, it would be a relevant factor in classifying the corporation as an instrumentality or agency of Government. This is precisely what

was pointed out by Mathew, J., in *Sukhdev v. Bhagatram* where the learned Judge said that, 'institutions engaged in matters of high public interest or performing public functions are by virtue of the nature of the functions performed government agencies. Activities which are too fundamental to the society are by definition too important not to be considered government functions'.

374. In *Ajay Hasia and Ors. v. Khalid Mujib Sehravardi and Ors.* ((1981) 1 SCC 722), it was noted that the constitutional philosophy of a democratic socialistic republic requiring the government to undertake a multitude of socio-economic operations, and the practical advantages of functioning through the legal device of a corporation for various commercial and economic activities. But any such contrivance of carrying on such activities cannot, declared this Court, exonerate the government of its basic obligation to respect the fundamental rights of the citizens for otherwise it would be the easiest thing for any government to assign to a plurality of corporations, almost every state business and thereby cheat the people of this country of the fundamental rights guaranteed to them under the Constitution. The court went on to enunciate certain tests applicable for determining whether an entity is an 'instrumentality or the agency of the State', an expression that does not figure in Article 12 of the Constitution but which would constitute an authority under Article 12 of the Constitution.

375. In *Board of Control for Cricket in India & Anr. v. Netaji Cricket Club and Ors.* ((2005) 4 SCC 741), the Apex Court had an occasion to consider the role and the nature of functions being discharged by the BCCI and held that the Board's control over the sport of cricket was deep and pervasive and that it exercised enormous public functions, which made it obligatory for the Board to follow the doctrine of 'fairness and good faith'. The Board is a society registered under the Tamil Nadu Societies Registration Act. It enjoys a monopoly status as regards regulation of the sport of cricket is concerned in terms of its Memorandum of Association and Articles of Association. It controls the sport of cricket and lays down the law therefore. It *inter alia* enjoys benefits by way of tax exemption and right to use stadia at nominal annual rent. It earns a huge revenue not only by selling tickets to viewers but also by selling right to exhibit films live on TV and broadcasting the same. Ordinarily, its full members are the State associations except Association of Indian Universities, Railway Sports Control Board and SSCB. As a member of ICC, it represents the country in the international events. It exercises enormous public functions. It has the authority to select players, umpires and officials to represent the country in the international fora. It exercises total control over the players, umpires and other officers. The Rules of the Board clearly demonstrate that without its recognition no competitive cricket can be hosted either within or outside the country. Its control over the sport of competitive cricket is deeply pervasive and complete.

The question whether the BCCI is 'State' within the meaning of Article 12 fell directly for consideration of the Supreme Court in *Zee Telefilms Ltd. and Anr. v. Union of India and Ors.* ((2005) 4 SCC 649). The Supreme Court ruled that BCCI was not 'State' within the meaning of Article 12. The Board was neither created by any statute, nor was any part of the share capital held by the government. There was practically no financial assistance given to the Board by the government, and even

when the Board did enjoy a monopoly status in the field of cricket such status was not State conferred or State protected. So also there is no deep and pervasive State control. The control, if any, is only regulatory in nature as applicable to other similar bodies. The control is not specifically exercised under any special statute applicable to the Board. All functions of the Board are neither public functions nor are they closely related to governmental functions. The Board is not created by transfer of a government-owned corporation and was an autonomous body. It was held that the Board was not financially, functionally or administratively dominated by or under the control of the government so as to bring it within the expression 'State' appearing in Article 12 of the Constitution. The court also examined whether the Board was discharging public duties in the nature of State functions. Repelling the contention that the functions being discharged by the Board were public duties in the nature of State functions which would make the Board a State within the meaning of Article 12 the Supreme Court observed:
'It was then argued that the Board discharges public duties which are in the nature of State functions. Elaborating on this argument it was pointed out that the Board selects a team to represent India in international matches. The Board makes rules that govern the activities of the cricket players, umpires and other persons involved in the activities of cricket'. These, according to the petitioner, are all in the nature of State functions and an entity which discharges such functions can only be an instrumentality of State, therefore, the Board falls within the definition of State for the purpose of Article 12. Assuming that the abovementioned functions of the Board do amount to public duties or State functions, the question for our consideration is: would this be sufficient to hold the Board to be a State for the purpose of Article 12? While considering this aspect of the argument of the petitioner, it should be borne in mind that the State/Union has not chosen the Board to perform these duties nor has it legally authorized the Board to carry out these functions under any law or agreement. It has chosen to leave the activities of cricket to be controlled by private bodies out of such bodies' own volition (self-arrogated). In such circumstances when the actions of the Board are not actions as an authorized representative of the State, can it be said that the Board is discharging State functions? The answer should be no. In the absence of any authorization, if a private body chooses to discharge any such function which is not prohibited by law then it would be incorrect to hold that such action of the body would make it an instrumentality of the State. The Union of India has tried to make out a case that the Board discharges these functions because of the de facto recognition granted by it to the Board under the guidelines framed by it, but the Board has denied the same. In this regard we must hold that the Union of India has failed to prove that there is any recognition by the Union of India under the guidelines framed by it, and that the Board is discharging these functions on its own as an autonomous body.

376. The Supreme Court recognized the fact that the Board was discharging some duties like the selection of Indian Cricket Team, controlling the activities of the players which activities were akin to public duties or State functions so that if there is any breach of a constitutional or statutory obligation or the rights of other citizens, the aggrieved party is entitled to seek redress under the ordinary law or by way of a writ petition under Article 226 of the Constitution which is much wider than Article 32. The Supreme Court further observed:

> 31. Be that as it may, it cannot be denied that the Board does discharge some duties like the selection of an Indian cricket team, controlling the activities of the players and others involved in the game of cricket. These activities can be said to be akin to public duties or State functions and if there is any violation of any constitutional or statutory obligation or rights of other citizens, the aggrieved party may not have a relief by way of a petition under Article 32. But that does not mean that the violator of such right would go scot-free merely because it or he is not a State. Under the Indian jurisprudence there is always a just remedy for the violation of a right of a citizen. Though the remedy under Article 32 is not available, an aggrieved party can always seek a remedy under the ordinary course of law or by way of a writ petition under Article 226 of the Constitution, which is much wider than Article 32. (emphasis supplied) After above exposition, the Supreme Court held that:
>
> The majority view thus favours the view that BCCI is amenable to the writ jurisdiction of the High Court under Article 226 even when it is not 'State' within the meaning of Article 12. The rationale underlying that view if we may say with utmost respect lies in the 'nature of duties and functions' which the BCCI performs. It is common ground that the respondent-Board has a complete sway over the game of cricket in this country. It regulates and controls the game to the exclusion of all others. It formulates rules, regulations norms and standards covering all aspect of the game. It enjoys the power of choosing the members of the national team and the umpires. It exercises the power of disqualifying players which may at times put an end to the sporting career of a person. It spends crores of rupees on building and maintaining infrastructure like stadia, running of cricket academies and Supporting State Associations. It frames pension schemes and incurs expenditure on coaches, trainers, etc. It sells broadcast and telecast rights and collects admission fee to venues where the matches are played. All these activities are undertaken with the tacit concurrence of the State Government and the Government of India who are not only fully aware but supportive of the activities of the Board. The State has not chosen to bring any law or taken any other step that would either deprive or dilute the Board's monopoly in the field of cricket. On the contrary, the Government of India have allowed the Board to select the national team which is then recognized by all concerned and applauded by the entire nation including at times by the highest of the dignitaries when they win tournaments and bring laurels home. Those distinguishing themselves in the international arena are conferred highest civilian awards like the Bharat Ratna, Padma Vibhushan, Padma Bhushan and Padma Shri apart from sporting awards instituted by the Government. Any organization or entity that has such pervasive control over the game and its affairs and such powers as can make dreams end up in smoke or come true cannot be said to be undertaking any private activity. The functions of the Board are clearly public functions, which, till such time the State intervenes to takeover the same, remain in the nature of public functions, no matter discharged by a society registered under the Registration of Societies

> Act. Suffice it to say that if the Government not only allows an autonomous/private body to discharge functions which it could in law takeover or regulate but even lends its assistance to such a non-government body to undertake such functions which by their very nature are public functions, it cannot be said that the functions are not public functions or that the entity discharging the same is not answerable on the standards generally applicable to judicial review of State action. Our answer to question No. 1, therefore, is in the negative, qua, the first part and affirmative qua the second. BCCI may not be State under Article 12 of the Constitution but is certainly amenable to writ jurisdiction under Article 226 of the Constitution of India.

III. Functions

377. The functions and objects of BCCI are as follows:

(1) It controls the game of cricket in India and a dispute resolution forum in disputes referred by any State, regional or other association.
(2) Arranges, controls and regulates the visits of teams in and out of the country.
(3) Promotes the game and organizes matches in the aid of public charities and relief funds.
(4) Frames the rules and regulations for cricket in India and makes alteration, amendments and additions in such laws.
(5) Lays out grounds and provides pavilion, canteen and other facilities.
(6) Selection of the team to represent the country in test matches in India and abroad.
(7) Appoint *inter alia*, the representative of India in the ICC and other conferences, seminars connected with the game of cricket.

378. The nature of the functions of BCCI came for examination before the Supreme Court in the case of *Zee Tele-Films Ltd. v. Union of India* (AIR 2005 SC 2677). The court held as follows:

> The facts established in the case do not cumulatively show that the Board is financially, functionally or administratively dominated by or is under the control of the Government. The little control that the Government may be said to have on the Board is not pervasive in nature, and this control is only regulatory and nothing more (paragraph 24).

It is true that the Union of India has been exercising certain control over the activities of the Board in regard to organizing cricket matches and travel of the Indian team abroad as also granting of permission to allow the foreign teams to come to India. But this control over the activities of the Board cannot be construed as an administrative control.

The State/Union has neither chosen the Board to perform duties like the selection of an Indian cricket team, controlling the activities of the players nor has it legally authorized the Board to carry out these functions under any law or agreement. It has chosen to leave the activities of cricket to be controlled by the private bodies out of such bodies' own volition.

IV. Allocation of Seats in the Stadium and Provision of Tickets

379. In the matter of *Sudhir M. Mody and Others v. Bombay Cricket Association*, before the Bombay High Court (1994(2) Bom CR 601) Honourable Judge M.S. Rane, delivered the judgment. Facts of the case were as follows:

> The application herein which has been assigned to this Court is being disposed of as directed by the Supreme Court in its order dated March 5, 1993 passed in SLP No. 2472 of 1993.

Both the parties herein, who claim to have avowed object in promotion of sports in particular cricket, have been locked up in the court litigation. Record reveals the suit herein is fifth in the series in this Court – four filed by the plaintiffs and one by the defendants. These do not include some other suits filed and pending between the parties herein in the City Civil Court at Bombay so also appeals filed against the interim orders passed in the interim applications.

A. The Issues

380. The principal dispute between the parties revolves over: (i) allotment and allocation of seats during the Cricket test matches played at Wankhede Stadium, (ii) the rates of the tickets, (iii) allocation of place, (iv) issuance of such tickets, (v) rights and related claim in and over the Club House and other premises attached to the Club House and stadium. As would be pointed out herein below, the litigious history started in 1987 and since then, whenever the matches of the International Cricket teams are arranged on the stadium, for one reason or the other, parties have mostly the plaintiffs herein, as would be evident from the record of suits filed by them, knocked the doors of the Court. Applications for interim relieves are moved. Ad interim as also interim reliefs, depending upon the expediency, urgency and exigency, are granted. The aggrieved parties went further in appeals.

381. The suit herein has also been filed on the eve of such a first-class cricket test match, which was to be played between India and England on the same stadium, i.e., Wankhede Stadium from 19 February 1993. The suit is filed on 25 January 1993.

382. It is noticed or rather pointed out during the course of addresses to the court that proceedings and averments are repetitive and reliefs overlapping but revolve over the controversial issues between the parties listed earlier.

Before considering the reliefs in the suit herein, as also interim reliefs in the application, it would be useful to have brief appraisal of the background of the nature of dispute.

The plaintiffs are the members and office-bearers of the Managing Committee of the Club House known as Bombay Cricket Association (BCA) Garware Club House, which is an unregistered association. The defendant is a society registered under the Societies Registration Act as also under the Bombay Public Trust Act.

383. Somewhere in 1968, the defendants acquired on lease plot of land from the Maharashtra Government for setting up a stadium and semi-permanent structure for a Club House. It is noticed that after acquiring lease the defendants undertook the construction work of Stadium and Club House. The plaintiffs association also, it appears, came to be formed by then or about the same time. Late Shri Wankhede, in whose name the Stadium is named after, was a pivotal and central figure and record shows, that he was a Chairman of the plaintiffs Association as also defendants. The plaintiffs paid a sum of INR 12,000,000 to the defendants at the crucial stage, which helped the defendants in constructing the Stadium and Club House. One pavilion in the stadium is named as Garware Pavilion, which has very advantageous strategic location from the point of view of the game and the plaintiffs, it may be stated at the outset, are claiming and insisting with vehemence, that they be provided the seats for all the matches in the said Garware Pavilion (hereinafter referred to as 'Garware Pavilion' for brevity's sake). Exh-A to the plaint is the plan of the Stadium wherefrom the location and situation of the said Garware Pavilion becomes clear.

Somewhere in 1974, the arrangement and understanding was arrived at between the parties herein, eventually recorded in the resolutions and the minutes of the meetings of the parties documented in the correspondence exchanged between them, the reference of which finds place in the proceedings. The main term of the arrangement in brief according to the plaintiffs, were:

- The plaintiffs were to be allotted 6,000 seats by the defendants at a particular rate, which was concessional in view of their contribution as mentioned earlier.
- Seats were to be allocated permanently in the Garware Club only.
- Printing and issuance of such 6,000 tickets were to be done by the plaintiffs themselves.

The arrangement as above, it seems, worked without any major hurdle till 1977, as, it is stated, both the parties worked in hand. However, in 1977, the parties severed their ties and became separate from each other. Even after separation, till 1987, the arrangement in respect of distribution, allocation of tickets, etc. it appears, did not create any problem requiring any party to approach Court.

384. In 1987, on the eve of matches sponsored by Reliance, plaintiffs filed first suit in this Court being Suit No. 2604 of 1987, principal reliefs being: (i) distribution of their entitlement of 6,000 seats in Garware Pavilion, and (ii) at concessional rate. Ad interim reliefs were refused to the plaintiffs who filed appeal being No. 1069 of 1987, in which Honourable Shri D.M. Rege (Rtd.) Valluer was appointed by the order dated 18 August 1987. The Appellate Court disposed of the Appeal and 6,000 seats were allotted at the rate determined by the Valuer.

385. Plaintiffs filed second suit being No. 3148 of 1989 in this Court seeking principally the same relief as claimed in the previous suit of allocation of their quota of 6,000 seats and distribution on the basis of agreement in 1980, wherein, by and large, the arrangement with regard to the quota of seats and allotment, etc. was kept as before. With the grant of interim reliefs, the matter rested there although appeal by the defendants came to be dismissed on 8 February 1992.

386. The defendants filed suit being No. 1568 of 1990 against the plaintiffs, seeking various declarations, such as plaintiffs (the defendants in the suit herein) are the absolute owner of the stadium, club house, etc. and defendants have no right as owners or any title in the same, etc. The plaintiffs herein also filed a suit being No. 3268 of 1990, as Cross Suit, claiming almost identical reliefs in respect of portion of Club House, etc. The interim applications made by the parties in respective suit were disposed of by my brother Judge Dhanuka with common order dated 29 July 1991, prima facie upholding the case of the defendants in this suit in respect of the ownership of Stadium and Club House, and directing the plaintiffs herein to make various payments as specified in the said order. It is also noted in the said judgment that since the plaintiffs herein are unregistered association is not a legal entity capable of holding immoveable assets/properties. The plaintiffs have preferred two appeals being Nos 833 of 1991 and 835 of 1991 against the said order, which are still pending.

387. The suit herein is filed as stated, on the eve of test matches between England and India, which was to be played in February 1993. The main reason for the plaintiffs to rush to the Court, as is revealed from these proceedings, is the defendant's letter dated 19 November 1992 being Exh-L to the plaint. Vide said letter, defendants, while assuring the allocation of quota of 6,000 seats to the plaintiffs circumscribed quantified the allotment as under. (Extracted from the said letter itself):

Garware Pavilion	*Seats*
A Block	Upper 215
B Block	Upper 657
C Block	Upper 692
D Block	Upper 642
E Block	Lower 314
I Block	Lower 488
J Block	Lower 661
K Block	Lower 533

Garware Pavilion	*Seats*
L) M) Block	Lower 1,000
Guest Stand	898
Total Seats	6,000

The exact implication of the above communication is that: (i) as regards allocation of seats, 898 seats were offered in Guest Stand instead of Garware Pavilion. According to the plaintiffs, as stated earlier, they are entitled to all 6,000 seats allocated in Garware Club only and not elsewhere. (ii) that printing and issuance of such tickets would be done by the plaintiffs only and not by the defendants. (iii) that defendants are not entitled to insist for the checking of identity cards of the members of the plaintiffs.

388. The relief in the suit herein have been claimed on the basis as above and application herein has been made for ad interim and interim relief in consonance with main relief of the suit. The application of the plaintiffs for an ad interim relief so far allocation of seats in Garware Pavilion only was rejected on 8 February 1993, from which plaintiffs filed appeal being Appeal Lodging No. 74 of 1993, which was dismissed on 10 February 1993. The plaintiffs approached the Supreme Court and as stated, the matter, i.e., above Notice of Motion is before this Court for disposal. Although the test match scheduled in February 1993 is over, the relief still survives as the plaintiffs have included the matches which would be played in future.

At the outset, during the course of arguments, the learned counsel for the plaintiffs indicated that as far as printing of tickets and checking of identity cards are concerned, the plaintiffs are not pressing the same in this application and leave the same for consideration at the trial of the suit. It may also be stated that on behalf of defendants it was stated and made clear that the common procedure in that respect is made applicable and followed in respect of members of all other clubs, and no exception is made for the plaintiffs. Well this is all as far as these two sets of reliefs are concerned.

389. Now the only issue that requires consideration is the insistence by the plaintiffs to have their quota of 6,000 seats and that too allocated in Garware Pavilion only, for all the matches to be played in future. Great deal of submissions has been made, pleadings and various earlier Court orders referred to, and extensive correspondence relied upon, by both the parties.

As far as quota of 6,000 seats, the entitlement of the plaintiffs, on behalf of defendants it was reiterated and stated that never in the past there was any reduction therein nor the defendants want to do so in the future. That also sorts out the quantum of quota, needing no further probe.

390. The question remains how far plaintiffs are justified in demand, claim and insistence to have all the seats of their quota to have allocated in the Garware Pavilion only. As stated, the plaintiffs have sought to base and justify their said claim by referring to agreements between the parties, correspondence, resolutions passed in the meetings, the practice followed, etc. whereas, the defendants have countered the said demand of the plaintiffs, asserting that never in the past their all quota seats (6,000) were allotted in the Garware Pavilion only. They refer to and rely upon their letters from time to time allotting to the plaintiffs tickets in question. The defendants further contend that they are the main and authorized organization to hold and conduct internation cricket test matches as also other main matches in Bombay under the Central Organization namely, BCCI, which organizes the internation matches. The defendants have to hold, conduct and organize such test matches under the authority and instructions of the BCCI. They are required to allot 500 seats to BCCI in the main pavilion, i.e., Garware Pavilion. Further they have to allot seats in the various dignitaries, such as government, past cricketers, umpires, Ranji Trophy players, guests, the representatives of the other affiliated clubs, etc. In the circumstances, defendants plead, that they have to take into consideration the other claims as above. However, defendants clarified that they would offer maximum seats to the defendants in the Garware Pavilion and balance in the Guest Stand as done in the past.

391. It may be stated that the earlier Resolutions, referred to by the plaintiffs, passed by the parties in 1977 mention the allotment of seats to the plaintiffs in the Garware Pavilion. However, actual allotment made since the beginning of the arrangement claimed by the plaintiffs, does not support the claim of the plaintiffs. Inasmuch as, letter dated 2 December 1979, being Exh-C to the plaint from the defendants to the plaintiffs, allotting the seats, 245 seats are allotted from BCA Guest Stand to make total of 6,000 seats. Some allotment pattern is followed in 1987 as is evidenced in defendants' letter dated 21 September 1987 being Exh-D to the plaint. It is still pertinent to note that the agreement of the year 1980, which plaintiffs rely upon (being Exh-E to the plaint) which is comprehensive and in respect of which plaintiffs have filed Suit (No. 3148 of 1989) as valid and subsisting, some does not mention the exact place of allocation. This is how Clause 'C' of the said agreement provides:

> B.C.A. to charge BCA Garware Club House for test match tickets at the same rate as charged to the Gymkhana and Clubs affiliated to BCA. Total number of seats allotted to BCA Garware Club House will be 6,000.

392. The fact that plaintiffs were allotted seats also in BCA Guest Stand to make up their quota of 6,000 seats, and the plaintiffs accepted the same, without demur is manifested from their Suit No. 2604 of 1987 referred to earlier, in which in their interim application being Notice of Motion No. 2237 of 1987, vide prayer (a)(i) they have sought the relief to the effect:

> To issue and allot 319 seats in addition to 345 seats in BCA Guest Stand …

It is also of relevance to note that in the past the plaintiffs were unable to lift and avail of their said full quota of 6,000 seats, which is borne out from their own document, i.e., their Circular dated 4 November 1988, which shows that they could buy only 2,859 seats against their full quota.

393. It therefore clearly emerges from the conspectus of above, that the case and the contention of the plaintiffs that they are entitled to their full quota of seats or that they were allotted their full quota in the Garware Pavilion only is not correct. Apart therefrom, the explanation offered by the defendants, who are obliged to conduct and organize the test matches including of international teams, under the BCCI, have also to give due consideration to other compelling demands for allocation of seats to the dignitaries, renowned past players, artists and distinguished dignitaries, which adds to such demands. It is however clear from the evidence discussed above, that the seats have been allotted to the plaintiffs to make up their sanctioned quota from BCA Guest Stand and it is but fair that the defendants adhere to the same practice.

394. To sum up, therefore, I am of the view and in particular in view of the fact that the defendants have not refused and denied the seat quota of 6,000 to the plaintiffs and considering the fact that the seats are made available to the plaintiffs from BCA Guest Stand and further considering the fact that the defendants as organizers of the matches have also to meet demands for the seats as stated earlier, even on balance of convenience, I do not find the case in favour of the plaintiffs for grant of interim relief as claimed in this regard. Likewise in the matter of printing and issuance of tickets, checking of identity cards, etc. various factors would need due consideration, including the insurance of safety and security measures, which is major and current issue of the day, in course of organization of the matches. It is to be noted that in such aspects, plaintiffs have not separately identified, but common procedure is made applicable to the members of the other affiliated clubs, like plaintiffs. It is heartening that, as stated earlier, the plaintiffs have not made it a contentious issue, at least at such interim stage. As far as fixing of rates of the tickets is concerned, the earlier orders and directions of the court are still in force and circumstances neither warrant, nor case made out on that behalf for variation or substitution. It is noticed and so pointed out by and on behalf of the defendants that the principle in determination of the rates commonly made applicable to all members and it is indeed so, since in the past, when reference to the value was made, dispute was sorted out. Further, my brother Judge Dhanuka in his common order dated 29 July 1991, mentioned earlier, has ordered as under:

> The plaintiffs (i.e. the defendants herein) shall make 6,000 seats available to the defendants (i.e. to the plaintiffs) for Test Matches at the same rate as charged to the Gymkhana and Clubs affiliated to the Bombay Cricket Association (i.e. defendant herein).

Although the said order is in appeal, as far as this part of the order, it is stated its operation continues and is binding upon the defendants. It is neither unnecessary therefore to rock up the same issue in this application, nor any case made justifying Court intervention.

Hence the following order:

(1) The defendants shall issue and allot 6,000 seats to the plaintiffs allocating the same in the Garware Pavilion and BCA Guest Stand for the test matches. The

defendants shall offer such tickets to the plaintiffs with reasonable margin before the scheduled dates of the matches and the plaintiffs shall also collect the tickets, on compliance of requisite formalities well in advance of the commencement date of the matches.

(2) The defendants to charge the rate for the tickets on the same basis as charged to their affiliated other clubs and Gymkhanas.

(3) As far as printing of the tickets and checking of identity cards, no reliefs are granted in view of observation appearing in the body of the judgment.

V. Change in By-Laws of BCCI

A. BCCI v. Cricket Association of Bihar and Others

395. An interesting case which came up in the Supreme Court relating to by-laws was *BCCI v. Cricket Association of Bihar and Others* (2015 STPL (web) 131 SC (DB); 2015 AIR (SCW) 2258) wherein existing by-laws were amended and certain activities were excluded.

In a meeting of the Board of Cricket Control in India (BCCI) held on 13 September 2007, the working committee of the Board appears to have taken a decision to launch what came to be known as IPL to be run by a committee constituted by the general body of the BCCI to be called IPL Governing Council. In December 2007, the IPL Governing Council invited tenders for grant of IPL franchises on an open competitive bidding basis, in which only corporate bodies were allowed to participate. India Cements Ltd. was one of those who participated in the auction for the Chennai franchise and emerged successful in the same. The team it assembled was named as Chennai Super Kings. Jaipur IPL Cricket Private Limited emerged successful for the Jaipur Franchise and assembled a team called Rajasthan Royals. Franchise agreements were, pursuant to the auction, signed by BCCI with the franchisees concerned.

396. On 27 September 2008, Mr N. Srinivasan was elected as the Secretary of the BCCI in a General Body Meeting. In the same meeting, Regulation 6.2.4 of the IPL Regulations was amended to exclude from its operation events like IPL and Champions' League Twenty20. Amendment to Rule 6.2.4 was assailed before the High Court of Bombay on three principal grounds. The first ground was that the amendment was mala fide inasmuch as the whole object underlying the same was to protect the grant of Chennai Franchise to Mr Srinivasan's India Cements Ltd. which was as on the date of the grant in clear breach of Rule 6.2.4 as it existed before its amendment. As treasurer of BCCI, Mr Srinivasan was an administrator who could neither acquire nor hold any commercial interest in any BCCI event including IPL, Champions League and Twenty20 tournaments, as all these tournaments are fundamentally BCCI events. The question of conflict of interest arose, in breach of Rule 6.2.4, but the same was neutralized by amending the rule itself and taking the three events mentioned above out of the purview of Rule 6.2.4.

397. The second limb of the challenge to the amendment was that the same was brought hurriedly without any supporting recommendation from any Committee, without an agenda item for deliberations of the BCCI and without a proper notice to the members who were supposed to discuss the same. The amendment was pushed through under the residuary and omnibus 'any other item' appearing in the agenda even when it was an extremely important matter of far-reaching implications which when changed brought a fundamental change applicable to all the events organized by BCCI. In substance, the second limb of the challenge was also suggestive of the amendment having been brought about to serve the personal interest of those administering the affairs of BCCI rather than any ethically or morally correct proposition to ensure purity of the game or to nurture the confidence of those who are fond of it.

398. The third ground on which the amendment came under challenge was that the same is opposed to public policy and good conscience. The argument, it appears, was that inasmuch as the amendment permitted in perpetuity a conflict between administrator's duty and his commercial interest, it fell foul of the concept of fairness, transparency and probity in the discharge of public functions by the BCCI and its administrators. It has been discussed that BCCI is amenable to writ jurisdiction under Article 226 of the Constitution of India as it discharges 'Public Functions'. The natural corollary flowing from that finding is that all actions which BCCI takes, while discharging such public functions are open to scrutiny by the courts in exercise of their powers under Article 226 of the Constitution. It also implies that such actions shall when under scrutiny be judged by the standards and on principles that govern similar actions when taken by the State or its instrumentalities. The approach, which a Court exercising powers of judicial review of administrative action adopts, will remain the same irrespective of whether the action under review is taken by the State or its instrumentality or by any non-statutory, non-government organization like the BCCI as in the case at hand. It follows that Rule 6.2.4 will be subject to the same tests and standards as would apply to any similar provision emanating from a statute or the general executive power of the State.

Rule 6.2.4 before amendment was in the following words:

No Administrators shall have, directly or indirectly, any commercial interest in the matches or events conducted by the Board.

The impugned amendment added the following words at the end of the above Rule:

> excluding events like IPL or Champions League Twenty20.

B. Validity of Amendment in By-Laws

399. The Supreme Court observed that the validity of amendment to Rule 6.2.4 shall be tested on a three-fold basis namely: (i) whether the amendment is made by the authority competent to do so; (ii) whether such authority has followed the procedure prescribed for the same; and (iii) whether the amendment falls foul of any statute or principle of law, violation whereof cannot be countenanced.

Seen in the light of the Articles of Association, the Apex Court found no infirmity in the amendment to Rule 6.2.4 insofar as the legislative competence (if we may use that expression) of the authority that brought about the amendment is concerned. The court also stated that:
It is nobody's case that the amendment was beyond the competence of the authority that made it. So also, there is in our opinion no merit in the argument that the amendment should fall because the same did not figure as an item in the agenda for the meeting in which it was passed. It is true that the circumstances, in which the amendment came about, may create a suspicion as to the bona fides of the exercise but a mere suspicion may not be enough to strike it down. So long as the forum where the matter was taken-up, discussed and a resolution passed was competent to deal with the subject, procedural deficiencies, which do not affect the competence of the authority, do not matter much. We have, therefore, no hesitation in rejecting the contention that the amendment is bad because the same came up all too suddenly for discussion, without any real research or other work to support it and without adequate notice to the members to think about and usefully contribute to the deliberations.

400. The third aspect is that the amendment has not been questioned on the ground that the same violates the Tamil Nadu Registration of Societies Act under which BCCI stands registered as a society. It is also not challenged on the ground that any other statute regulating such societies is breached. What is contended is that inasmuch as the amendment permits commercial interest to be held by administrators in the events organized by BCCI it violates a fundamental tenet of law that no one can be a judge in his own cause, recognized universally as an essential facet of the principles of natural justice which must permeate every action that BCCI takes in the discharge of its public functions. That contention is not without merit and needs to be carefully explored from different angles.

401. The Honourable Court referred to the decision in *A. K. Kraipak & Ors. v. Union of India & Ors.* ((1969) 2 SCC 262) where a Constitution bench was examining whether Principles of Natural Justice have any application to purely administrative actions as distinguished from those described as quasi-judicial in nature. The question there arose in the context of a selection process in which Naqishbund who was a member of the selection committee was himself a candidate along with others for induction into the Indian Forest Service. The challenge was founded on the plea that there was a conflict between the duty, which Naqishbund was required to perform as a member of the selection committee and his interest as a candidate for selection. In defence of his role and the selection made by the committee, it was argued that the selection committee discharged administrative functions to which the principles of natural justice had no application. Repelling the contention this Court held that horizons of natural justice were constantly expanding, and that the principles apply only in areas not covered by any law validly made. The court observed:

> 20. The aim of the rules of natural justice is to secure justice or to put it negatively, to prevent miscarriage of justice. These rules can operate only in areas

not covered by any law validly made. In other words they do not supplant the law of the land but supplement it. The concept of natural justice has undergone a change in recent years. In the past it was thought that it included just two rules namely: (1) no one shall be a judge in his own case (Nemo debet esse judex propria causa) and (2) no decision shall be given against a party without affording him a reasonable hearing (audi alteram partem). Very soon thereafter a third rule was envisaged and that is that quasi-judicial enquiries must be held in good faith, without bias and not arbitrarily or unreasonably. But in the course of years many more subsidiary rules came to be added to the rules of natural justice. Till very recently it was the opinion of the courts that unless the authority concerned was required by the law under which it functioned to act judicially there was no room for the application of the rules of natural justice. The validity of that limitation is now questioned. If the purpose of the rules of natural justice is to prevent miscarriage of justice one fails to see why those rules should be made inapplicable to administrative enquiries.

Enquiries which were considered administrative at one time are now being considered as quasi-judicial in character. Arriving at a just decision is the aim of both quasi-judicial enquiries as well as administrative enquiries. An unjust decision in an administrative enquiry may have more far-reaching effect than a decision in a quasi-judicial enquiry. The rules of natural justice are not embodied rules. What particular rule of natural justice should apply to a given case must depend to a great extent on the facts and circumstances of that case, the framework of the law under which the enquiry is held and the constitution of the Tribunal or body of persons appointed for that purpose. Whenever a complaint is made before a court that some principle of natural justice had been contravened the court has to decide whether the observance of that rule was necessary for a just decision on the facts of that case.

C. Applicability of Principles of Natural Justice

402. On behalf of the appellant, it was contended that the amendment authorizes, contrary to what is demanded by the principles of natural justice, the creation and continuance of a conflict of interest situation. That is what is not permissible on a true and proper application of the principles of natural justice. The contention is that but for the amendment, Rule 6.2.4 would debar any conflict of interest, by forbidding administrators of BCCI from having any commercial interest in the events organized by the BCCI. That is according to the appellant an ideal situation which gets distorted and corrupted by the amendment permitting such commercial interests disregarding the fact that creation or continuance of such interests will bring about a serious conflict between the duties of administrators on the one hand and their personal/commercial interest on the other.

The respondents, on the contrary, argued that conflict of interest is a reality of life and exists in any number of situations some of them at times unavoidable. But, what is important is that the rules should provide for resolving the conflict. Relying upon rules applicable to conflict of interests in different sporting bodies, it was contended that unless, the conflict of interests is so palpable, that there is no room for any resolution, the rule cannot and should not be struck down simply because it may give rise to a conflict of interest at any time in future.

403. A conflict of interest situation may arise even when the rules or the norms do not specifically authorize acts or transactions that may lead to such a conflict. The scheme of the rules, may itself suggest that a conflict of interest is not welcome. And yet, such a conflict may at times arise, in which event, the rules can provide for a mechanism, to resolve the conflict as is the position in some of the rules in regard to some other sports. The question, however, is whether a rule can by a positive and enabling provision permit acts and transactions which would by their very nature bring about a conflict of interest. The court observed its answer in the negative and also observed that it is one thing to say that conflict may arise even when rules do not specifically permit such a conflict situation and a totally different thing to permit acts which will per se bring about such a conflict. The case at hand falls in the latter category. Rule 6.2.4 after amendment, permits creation of commercial interests in the events organized by BCCI by its administrators. This enabling provision disregards the potential conflict of interest which will arise between an administrator's duty as a functionary of the BCCI on the one hand and his interest as the holder of any such commercial interest on the other. The respondents may argue as indeed they have done, that commercial interest held by India Cements Ltd. in the IPL and other events do not constitute a conflict per se so as to fall foul of the principle that such conflicts are impermissible on the touchstone of fairness, reasonableness and probity in the discharge of public functions by the BCCI. But that contention is specious and deserves notice only to be rejected. Three real-life situations that have arisen in the past, qua India Cements owned by Mr Srinivasan's family and captained by him, simply demonstrate how such conflicts have arisen between the duty which Mr Srinivasan owes to BCCI and through the BCCI to the cricketing world at large and his commercial if not personal interest in the events which BCCI organizes. The first instance arose when BCCI awarded compensation of a sum of INR 10.40 crores to Chennai Super Kings, on account of the cancellation of the Champions League Tournament 2008. It is not in dispute that Mr Srinivasan was one of those who contributed to the taking of the decision to award that amount towards compensation to his own team. True it is that a similar amount was awarded to Rajasthan Royals the other finalist also, but that does not, mean that to the extent Mr Srinivasan, participated and deliberated in the proceedings leading to the award of a hefty amount of compensation, he was not privy to a self-serving decision that benefited India Cements Ltd. a company promoted by Mr Srinivasan. The fact that some others also participated in the decision-making process as members of IPL Governing Council does not cure the legal flaw arising out of the benefactor also being the beneficiary of the decision.

D. Likelihood of Bias

404. The test of bias is not whether bias was actually at work when the decision was taken. It is the reasonable likelihood of bias that determines whether the action can be faulted. A reasonable likelihood of bias is evident when the decision to award compensation was taken by the governing council of IPL with Mr Srinivasan, present and participating as a member. A similar award of a sum of INR 13.10 crores came in 2009 which too fell foul of his duty on the one hand and interest on the other. This amount was returned by ICL subsequently, but such return does not improve the matters. The decision to award an amount higher than the one awarded earlier appears to have led to public criticism raising the pitch for Mr Srinivasan's removal from the BCCI on the principles of conflict of interest. Return of the amount because of a public outcry may no doubt mean that Mr Srinivasan tried to come clean on the subject even when his company may have suffered a loss, but it may as well mean that the return of the amount came only under public pressure and in recognition of the fact that the amount was not actually due and payable and yet was paid to the detriment of BCCI who is a trustee of general public interest in the sport of cricket and everything that goes with it.

In view of the above discussion, it can be said that amendment to Rule 6.2.4 was the true villain in the situation. It was the amendment which attempted to validate what on the date of the award of the franchise was invalid as Rule 6.2.4 did not as on that date permit an administrator to have any commercial interest in any event organized by BCCI. While it may not have been feasible at that stage to interfere with the award of the franchise to ICL especially when hundreds of crores had been invested by the franchisee, the amendment, which perpetuates such a conflict was ordered to be struck down.

E. Amendment Opposed to Public Policy

405. The Supreme Court held that the validity of the Rule 6.2.4 as amended could be examined also from the standpoint of it being opposed to 'public policy'. But for doing so it first needs to examine what is meant by 'Public Policy' as it is understood in legal parlance. The expression has been used in section 23 of the Indian Contract Act, 1872 and in section 34 of the Arbitration and Conciliation Act, 1996 and a host of other statutes but has not been given any precise definition primarily because the expression represents a dynamic concept and is, therefore, incapable of any straitjacket definition, meaning or explanation. That has not, however, deterred jurists and courts from explaining the expression from very early times. Mathew J. speaking for the court in *Murlidhar Agarwal and Anr. v. State of Uttar Pradesh and Ors.* ((1974) 2 SCC 472) referred to Winfield's definition of Public Policy in *English Common Law* 42 *Harvard Law Review* 76 to declare that:

> 31. Public policy does not remain static in any given community. It may vary from generation to generation and even in the same generation. Public policy would be almost useless if it were to remain in fixed moulds for all time.

The court then grappled with the problem of ascertaining public policy if the same is variable and depends on the welfare of the community and observed:

> 32. If it is variable, if it depends on the welfare of the community at any given time, how are the courts to ascertain it? The Judges are more to be trusted as interpreters of the law than as expounders of public policy. However, there is no alternative under our system but to vest this power with Judges. The difficulty of discovering what public policy is at any given moment certainly does not absolve the Judges from the duty of doing so. In conducting an enquiry, as already stated Judges are not hidebound by precedent. The Judges must look beyond the narrow field of past precedents, though this still leaves open the question, in which direction they must cast their gaze. The Judges are to base their decisions on the opinions of men of the world, as distinguished from opinions based on legal learning. In other words, the Judges will have to look beyond the jurisprudence and that in so doing, they must consult not their own personal standards or predilections but those of the dominant opinion at a given moment, or what has been termed customary morality. The Judges must consider the social consequences of the rule propounded, especially in the light of the factual evidence available as to its probable results. Of course, it is not to be expected that men of the world are to be subpoenaed as expert witnesses in the trial of every action raising a question of public policy. It is not open to the Judges to make a sort of referendum or hear evidence or conduct an inquiry as to the prevailing moral concept. Such an extended extra-judicial enquiry is wholly outside the tradition of courts where the tendency is to 'trust the judge to be a typical representative of his day and generation'. Our law relies, on the implied insight of the judge on such matters. It is the Judges themselves, assisted by the bar, who here represent the highest common factor of public sentiment and intelligence. No doubt, there is no assurance that Judges will interpret the mores of their day more wisely and truly than other men. But this is beside the point. The point is rather that this power must be lodged somewhere and under our Constitution and laws, it has been lodged in the Judges and if they have to fulfil their function as Judges, it could hardly be lodged elsewhere.

406. In Central Inland Water Transport Corporation, the Supreme Court was also considering the import of the expression 'Public Policy' in the context of the service conditions of an employee empowering the employer to terminate his service at his sweet will upon service of three months' notice or payment of salary in lieu thereof. Explaining the dynamic nature of the concept of public policy, the court observed:

> Public policy, however, is not the policy of a particular government. It connotes some matter which concerns the public good and the public interest. The concept of what is for the public good or in the public interest or what would be injurious or harmful to the public good or the public interest has varied from time to time. As new concepts take the place of old, transactions which were once considered against public policy are now being upheld by the courts and similarly where there has been a well-recognized head of public policy, the

courts have not shirked from extending it to new transactions and changed circumstances and have at times not even flinched from inventing a new head of public policy.

407. Thus, the principles governing public policy must be and are capable, on proper occasion, of expansion or modification. Practices which were considered perfectly normal at one time have now become obnoxious and oppressive to public conscience. If there is no head of public policy which covers a case, then the court must in consonance with public conscience and in keeping with public good and public interest declare such practice to be opposed to public policy. Above all, in deciding any case which may not be covered by authority, the courts have before them the beacon light of the Preamble to the Constitution. Lacking precedent, the court can always be guided by that light and the principles underlying the fundamental rights and the directive principles enshrined in our Constitution.

408. The decision in *Oil & Natural Gas Corporation Ltd. v. Saw Pipes Ltd.* ((2003) 5 SCC 705), can be referred where Supreme Court considered the expression 'Public Policy of India' as a ground for setting aside an arbitral award. Speaking for the court M.B. Shah, J. held that the expression 'Public Policy of India' appearing in the Act aforementioned must be given a liberal meaning for otherwise resolution of disputes by resorting to arbitration proceedings will get frustrated because patently illegal awards would remain immune to courts interference. This Court declared that what was against public good and public interest cannot be held to be consistent with Public Policy. The following passage summed up the approach to be adopted in the matter, the Supreme Court pointed out:

> Therefore, in our view, the phrase 'public policy of India' used in section 34 in context is required to be given a wider meaning. It can be stated that the concept of public policy connotes some matter which concerns public good and the public interest. What is for public good or in public interest or what would be injurious or harmful to the public good or public interest has varied from time to time. However, the award which is, on the face of it, patently in violation of statutory provisions cannot be said to be in public interest. Such award/judgment/decision is likely to adversely affect the administration of justice. Hence, in our view in addition to narrower meaning given to the term 'public policy' in *Renusagar* case it is required to be held that the award could be set aside if it is patently illegal. The result would be that an award could be set aside if it is contrary to:
>
> a. fundamental policy of Indian law; or
> b. the interest of India; or
> c. justice or morality, or
> d. in addition, if it is patently illegal.
>
> Illegality must go to the root of the matter and if the illegality is of trivial nature it cannot be held that award is against the public policy. Award could

> also be set aside if it is so unfair and unreasonable that it shocks the conscience of the court. Such award is opposed to public policy and is required to be adjudged void.

409. In *Oil and Natural Gas Corporation Ltd. v. Western GECO International Ltd.* ((2014) 9 SCC 263), the court was examining the meaning of 'Fundamental Policy of Indian Law' an expression used in Saw Pipes' case (*supra*). Extending the frontiers of what will constitute 'Public Policy of India' Supreme Court observed:

> 35. What then would constitute the 'fundamental policy of Indian law' is the question. The decision in ONGC does not elaborate that aspect. Even so, the expression must, in our opinion, include all such fundamental principles as provide a basis for administration of justice and enforcement of law in this country. Without meaning to exhaustively enumerate the purport of the expression 'fundamental policy of Indian law', we may refer to three distinct and fundamental juristic principles that must necessarily be understood as a part and parcel of the fundamental policy of Indian law. The first and foremost is the principle that in every determination whether by a court or other authority that affects the rights of a citizen or leads to any civil consequences, the court or authority concerned is bound to adopt what is in legal parlance called a 'judicial approach' in the matter. The duty to adopt a judicial approach arises from the very nature of the power exercised by the court or the authority does not have to be separately or additionally enjoined upon the fora concerned. What must be remembered is that the importance of a judicial approach in judicial and quasi-judicial determination lies in the fact that so long as the court, tribunal or the authority exercising powers that affect the rights or obligations of the parties before them shows fidelity to judicial approach, they cannot act in an arbitrary, capricious or whimsical manner. Judicial approach ensures that the authority acts bona fide and deals with the subject in a fair, reasonable and objective manner and that its decision is not actuated by any extraneous consideration. Judicial approach in that sense acts as a check against flaws and faults that can render the decision of a court, tribunal or authority vulnerable to challenge.

Equally important and indeed fundamental to the policy of Indian law is the principle that a court and so also a quasi-judicial authority must, while determining the rights and obligations of parties before it, do so in accordance with the principles of natural justice. Besides the *audi alteram partem* rule, one of the facets of the principles of natural justice is that the court/authority deciding the matter must apply its mind to the attendant facts and circumstances while taking a view one way or the other. Non-application of mind is a defect that is fatal to any adjudication. Application of mind is best demonstrated by disclosure of the mind and disclosure of mind is best done by recording reasons in support of the decision which the court or authority is taking. The requirement that an adjudicatory authority must apply its mind is, in that view, so deeply embedded in the jurisprudence that it can be described as a fundamental policy of Indian law.

No less important is the principle now recognized as a salutary juristic fundamental in administrative law that a decision which is perverse or so irrational that no reasonable person would have arrived at the same will not be sustained in a court of law. Perversity or irrationality of decisions is tested on the touchstone of Wednesbury principle of reasonableness. Decisions that fall short of the standards of reasonableness are open to challenge in a court of law often in writ jurisdiction of the superior courts but no less in statutory processes wherever the same are available.

410. The Supreme Court concluded that Public Policy is not a static concept. It varies with times and from generation to generation. But what is in public good and public interest cannot be opposed to public policy and vice versa. Fundamental Policy of Law would also constitute a facet of public policy. This would imply that all those principles of law that ensure justice, fair play and bring transparency and objectivity and promote probity in the discharge of public functions would also constitute public policy. Conversely, any deviation, abrogation, frustration or negation of the salutary principles of justice, fairness, good conscience, equity and objectivity will be opposed to public policy. It follows that any rule, contract or arrangement that actually defeats or tends to defeat the high ideals of fairness and objectivity in the discharge of public functions no matter by a private non-governmental body will be opposed to public policy. Applied to the case at hand Rule 6.2.4 to the extent, it permits, protects and even perpetuates situations where the administrators can have commercial interests in breach or conflict with the duty they owe to the BCCI or to the people at large must be held to be against public policy, hence, illegal. That is particularly so when BCCI has in the Anti-corruption Code adopted by it recognized public confidence in the authenticity and integrity of the sporting contest as a fundamental imperative. It has accepted and, in our opinion rightly so, that all cricket matches must be contested on a level playing field with the outcome to be determined solely by the respective merits of the competing teams. The Anti-corruption Code of the BCCI does not mince words in accepting the stark reality that if the confidence of the public in the purity of the game is undermined then the very essence of the game of cricket shall be shaken. The BCCI has in no uncertain terms declared its resolve to protect the fundamental imperatives constituting the essence of the game of cricket and its determination to take every step in its power to prevent corrupt betting practices undermining the integrity of the sport including any effort to influence the outcome of any match. Unfortunately, however, the amendment to Rule 6.2.4 clearly negates the declarations and resolves of the BCCI by permitting situations in which conflict of interest would grossly erode the confidence of the people in the authenticity, purity and integrity of the game. An amendment which strikes at the very essence of the game as stated in the Anti-corruption Code cannot obviously coexist with the fundamental imperatives. Conflict of interest situation is a complete antithesis to everything recognized by BCCI as constituting fundamental imperatives of the game hence unsustainable and impermissible in law.

411. It was contended that IPL was conceived as a commercial enterprise, structured in a manner that it eliminated all possibility of conflict of interest. That is because all decisions, financial or otherwise relating to the IPL, are already known to all the participants leaving no discretion with any official of the BCCI. The commercial interest of an administrator in the IPL can never be in conflict with the administrator's duty in the BCCI. That apart, every franchise is treated equally since the contractual obligation with the BCCI is identical for each franchise leaving no possibility of differential treatment by BCCI. It was also argued that IPL is distinct from other matches/events conducted by the BCCI so that there is no question of any conflict of interest between the role of a person as an administrator of BCCI and an owner of an IPL franchise. The following distinguishing features were in this regard relied upon:

- IPL is not a tournament to test the players' ability to play representative cricket since the record of each player in the IPL is not considered for national selections. IPL is only a platform provided to cricketers – both Indian and international, to make a living from the sport outside of playing representative cricket, which is not as remunerative.
- The IPL teams revolve around a business structure and each team is formed pursuant to winning a franchise for a particular stadium in a commercial tender floated by BCCI, whereas in representative cricket it is the BCCI, a not-for-profit society which manages the teams selected by it.
- The franchise in the IPL has a contractual arrangement by which the franchise fee is paid to the BCCI and in return the franchisee gets a share of the broadcast and sponsorship revenue. In representative cricket, the income from sponsors and broadcast fee goes exclusively to the BCCI.
- IPL was started as a commercial venture by BCCI to bring more money into the game from the private sector for being ploughed back into the sport in the form of infrastructure development of the game, players' benefit and ground facilities in all parts of the country. Income from broadcast rights of the national team is incidental to the membership of the BCCI to ICC that permits the BCCI to field the India team against other teams of other member nations.
- In IPL, the selection committees of BCCI for various age groups have no role to play. Players from all over the world through their respective national boards enrol for the auction. Players cannot pick or choose a franchisee to play once enlisted for the auction. The player intake by a franchisee is dependent on open market principles. In the IPL, the players are allowed to be traded between franchisees within the rules of permitted salary caps as detailed in the players regulations.
- Entertainment of the public hitherto not interested in the sport, i.e., bringing in newer fans to the game has been a goal of the IPL whereas representative cricket is the more serious version and a pathway to the national selection.

On the above contention, the Supreme Court held that, no doubt, it is right to contend that in certain areas the BCCI or anyone of its administrators/office-bearers does not have any discretion except to go by what is prescribed as a uniform pattern for all the franchisees. But, to say that there is no possibility of any conflict of interest arising in IPL format between an administrator's duty and the commercial interest if any held by him is not correct. The conflict of interest is not only possible but ominously looming large if an administrator also owns a competing team. So also, the contention that, IPL being a commercial venture of BCCI and a platform for Indian and international cricketers to make a living from the sport, takes neither here nor there. Neither has anyone found fault with IPL as a format, nor is there any challenge to the wisdom of BCCI in introducing this format for the benefit of cricketers or for its own benefit. The question is whether the BCCI can afford to see the game lose its credibility in the eyes of those who watch it, by allowing an impression to gather ground that what goes on in the name of the game is no more than a farce because of sporting frauds like betting, match-fixing and the like. Can the BCCI live with the idea of the game being seen only as a means to cheat the unsuspecting spectators watching the proceedings whether in the stadium or on the television with the passion one rarely sees in any other sporting enterprise.

412. BCCI's commercial plans for its own benefit and the benefit of the players are bound to blow up in smoke, if the people who watch and support the game were to lose interest or be indifferent because, they get to know that some business interests have hijacked the game for their own ends or that the game is no longer the game they know or love because of frauds on and off the field. There is no manner of doubt whatsoever that the game enjoys its popularity and raises passions only because of what it stands for and because the people who watch the sport believe that it is being played in the true spirit of the game without letting any corrupting influence come anywhere near the principles and fundamental imperatives considered sacrosanct and inviolable. All told whatever be the format of the game and whatever be the commercial angles to it, the game is what it is, only if it is played in its pristine form free from any sporting fraud. In addition, it is because of that fundamental imperative that these proceedings assume such importance. The fundamental imperatives, to which BCCI is avowedly committed in the Anti-corruption Code, cannot be diluted leave alone neglected or negated.

413. In *K. Murugon v. Fencing Association of India, Jabalpur and Ors.* ((1991) 2 SCC 412), the Supreme Court held that sports in India has assumed a great importance for the community while international sports have assumed greater importance over the past few decades. Despite this, however, several sports bodies in this country have got involved in group fights leading to litigation in the process losing sight of the objectives which such societies and bodies are meant to serve and achieve. This Court therefore emphasized the need for setting right the working of the societies rather than adjudicating upon the individual's right to office by reference to the provisions of law relating to meetings, injunctions, etc. The following passage from the Murugon's decision (*supra*) is a timely reminder of the need of the hour:

> 12. This does not appear to us to be a matter where individual rights in terms of the rules and regulations of the Society should engage our attention. Sports in modern times has been considered to be a matter of great importance to the community. International sports have assumed greater importance and has been in the focus for over a few decades. In some of the recent Olympic games the performance of small States has indeed been excellent and laudable while the

performance of a great country like India with world's second highest population has been miserable. It is unfortunate that the highest body in charge of monitoring all aspects of such sports has got involved in group-fight leading to litigation and the objectives of the Society have been lost sight of. The representation of India in the IOA has been in jeopardy. The grooming of amateurs has been thrown to the winds and the responsibility placed on the Society has not been responded. This, therefore, does not appear to us to be a situation where rights to office will have to be worked out by referring to the provisions of the law relating to meetings, injunction and rights appurtenant to elective offices. What seems to be of paramount importance is that healthy conditions must be restored as early as possible into the working of the Society and a fresh election has to be held as that seems to be the only way to get out of the malady.

F. BCCI and Institutional Integrity

414. The Supreme Court also referred to its decision in *N. Kannadasan v. Ajoy Khose and Ors.* ((2009) 7 SCC 1), where Court examined the question relating to qualities required for appointment of a candidate as President of the State Consumer Commission. The petitioner was in that case found unfit to be appointed as a permanent Judge of the High Court. The question was whether his being unsuitable for appointment as a permanent judge could be a reason for denying to him an appointment as President of the State Consumer Disputes Redressal Commission. The following was observed:

> The superior courts must take into consideration as to what is good for the judiciary as an institution and not for the Judge himself. An act of balancing between public interest and private interest must be made. Thus, institution as also public interest must be uppermost in the mind of the court. When such factors are to be taken into consideration, the court may not insist upon a proof. It would not delve deep into the allegations. The court must bear in mind the limitations in arriving at a finding in regard to lack of integrity against the person concerned.

415. The decision in *Kannadasan* case (*supra*) was relied upon by a three-judge bench of the Supreme Court in *Centre for PIL and Anr. v. Union of India and Anr.* ((2011) 4 SCC 1) where the court dealt with the importance of institutional integrity and declared that an institution is more important than an individual. The following was observed:

> 45. … Thus, we are concerned with the institution and its integrity including institutional competence and functioning and not the desirability of the candidate alone who is going to be the Central Vigilance Commissioner, though personal integrity is an important quality. It is the independence and impartiality of the institution like the CVC which has to be maintained and preserved in the larger interest of the rule of law (*see* Vineet Narai (1988) 1 SCC 226).

416. BCCI is a very important institution discharging important public functions. Demands of institutional integrity are, therefore, heavy and need to be met suitably in larger public interest. Individuals are birds of passage while institutions are forever. The expectations of the millions of cricket lovers in particular and public at large in general, have lowered considerably the threshold of tolerance for any mischief, wrongdoing or corrupt practices which ought to be weeded out of the system. Conflict of interest is one area which appears to have led to the current confusion and serious misgivings in the public mind as to the manner in which BCCI is managing its affairs, held the Apex Court.

It was lastly argued by the counsel of BCCI that if administrators were held to be disentitled to have any commercial interest in BCCI events including IPL, the same may adversely affect not only the IPL format but certain outstanding sportspersons who by reason of their proficiency in cricket and its affairs are often engaged as coaches, mentors, commentators or on similar other positions may also be rendered disqualified to get such engagements. This would mean that the teams will lose the advantage of having these outstanding sportspersons on their side while the sportspersons will lose the opportunity to earn a livelihood only because they hold or have at an earlier point of time held an administrative office in BCCI. Such an interpretation or disqualification would not be in the interest of the game or those who have distinguished themselves in the same.

417. The expression 'administrator' appearing in Rule 6.2.4 has been defined to mean and include present and past presidents, Honorary Secretaries, Honorary Treasures, Honorary Joint Secretaries of the BCCI. Presidents and Secretaries present or past of members affiliated to BCCI are also treated as administrator along with representative of a member or an associate member or affiliate member of the Board. That apart, any person connected with any of the committees appointed by the Board are also treated as administrator; none of whom could have any commercial interest in any BCCI event but for the impugned amendment to Rule 6.2.4. What is important, however, is that the challenge in the present proceedings arises in the context of Mr Srinivasan, President of BCCI having commercial interest in the IPL by reason of the company promoted by him owning Chennai Super Kings. It is common ground that the owner of a team buys the franchise in an open auction. India Cements Ltd. owner of CSK has also bought the Chennai franchise in an open auction held by BCCI. This sale and purchase of the franchises is a purely commercial/business venture for India Cements Ltd. involving investment of hundreds of crores. The franchise can grow as a 'brand' and in terms of franchise agreement executed between franchisee and the BCCI be sold for a price subject to the conditions stipulated in the agreement. There is, therefore, no manner of doubt that the investment made by India Cements Ltd. is a business investment no matter in a sporting activity. To the extent, the business investment has come from India Cements Ltd. promoted by Mr Srinivasan and his family, India Cements and everyone connected with it as shareholders acquire a business/commercial interest in the IPL events organized by BCCI. The association of India Cements Ltd. and Mr Srinivasan with IPL is being faulted on account of this commercial interest which India Cements Ltd. has acquired for itself. It may well be argued that there is a difference between commercial interest referred to in Rule 6.2.4 and 'professional engagement' of a player on account of his proficiency in the game. It may be logically contended that the engagement of a player even though made on a remuneration remains a professional engagement because of his professional skill in the game of cricket and not because he has made any investment like India Cements Ltd. has done in acquiring a franchise or in any other form. Whether or not a player who is an 'administrator' by reason of an existing or earlier assignment held by him can acquire or hold a commercial interest in any BCCI event, will depend upon the nature of the interest that such person has acquired and whether the same is purely professional or has any commercial element to it. Therefore, amendment to Rule 6.2.4 permitting administrators of BCCI to acquire or hold commercial interests in BCCI like IPL, champions league and Twenty20 held to be bad.

VI. Indian Premier League

418. The IPL is a domestic league for Twenty20 cricket competitions in India, initiated by BCCI. The inaugural season started on 18 April 2008. The franchises have players from different countries. The IPL has a grand brand value. IPL has been a grand success and largest money earner for BCCI. The franchisee acquires a player in the annual auction, buying domestic players, signing uncapped players through trading and buying replacements.

§7. Indian Hockey Federation

419. Hockey, in which India has an impressive record with eight Olympic gold medals, is officially the national sport. Other popular games are football, cricket, basketball, volleyball and badminton. Cricket has become a very popular game in India. After the IX Asian Games in New Delhi in 1982 and Common Wealth Games in 2010, the city now has modern sports facilities. Such facilities are also being developed in other parts of the country. Besides sports and games included in the international sporting agenda, there are many which have developed indigenously. Among these are wrestling, kabaddi, kho kho and several traditional systems of martial arts.

420. Hockey is considered as world's oldest ball and stick game. The International Hockey Federation known as Federation Internationale de Hockey was formed on 7 January 1924 with headquarters at Vienna (Austria) which was later on shifted to Paris. It was in 1908 that hockey was introduced in the Olympic Games at London. British soldiers brought hockey to India. The IHF was formed on 7 November 1925 at Gwalior to control this game. The federation, for the first time, organized Inter-Provincial Hockey Tournaments at Calcutta to select team for the Olympic Games at Amsterdam. The All India Women's Hockey Federation was formed in 1947. Since 1944, National Hockey Championship is organized by the federation every year. This game was considered as the national game of the country.

§8. Role of Federations

421. The government will not recognize more than one NSF for each sport discipline enlisted in the First Schedule of National Sports Development Bill, 2013. The recognized NSF shall represent India in the International Federation and regulate sport in India (sections 7 and 8). The NSFs receiving grant of INR 10 lakh or more have been declared as 'public authority' under section 2(h) of the RTI Act.

Financial assistance from the government is available only to such recognized NSFs for sending their teams abroad for training and participation in international tournaments, holding international tournaments in India, conducting National Championships and for procuring equipment. Federations are also assisted by the SAI for organizing coaching camps for preparing national teams and for engaging the services of foreign coaches. The salaries of joint/assistant Secretaries of the federation are also reimbursed. The Ministry has laid down procedures for making a request for assistance.

§9. Role of NGOs

422. The Ministry provides financial assistance to voluntary agencies and NGOs, etc. under the four schemes; namely the Scheme for Development and Empowerment of Adolescents, Scheme for Promotion of Youth Activities and Training, the Scheme for Promotion of Adventure and Scheme for Promotion of National Integration.

I. Application from NGOs

423. The Ministry invites applications from NGOs after advertising in newspapers. The applicant NGOs are required to submit proposals in triplicate to the prescribed recommending authorities under the scheme. The recommending authority will forward NGO applications in duplicate to the Secretary Youth Affairs in their respective State government and UT Administration after verification and countersigning as required under the scheme. The last date for receipt of application by State/UT Government is fixed for current financial year. The State government and UT Administration constitutes a Screening Committee under the chairpersonship of the Secretary, Youth Affairs in the State and UT for screening, scrutiny, pre-appraisal, technical feasibility, trained manpower for the proposed activity and past performance and credibility of the NGO including their financial soundness and non-involvement in the antisocial or anti-national activities, etc. The Screening Committee will consist of a Vice Chancellor or Head of any reputed educational institution, Zonal Director, NYKS, one non-official representing an NGO or civil society who is not a beneficiary applicant and the Director of Youth Affairs. The Screening Committee will shortlist a limited number of proposals commensurate with the tentative Statewise allocation.

II. Screening and Short Listing

424. Any proposal received directly in the ministry during the year is referred back to the State government for their consideration by the Screening Committee. The State government forwards proposals shortlisted by the Screening Committee to Government of India scheme by scheme. It also indicates the priority in which the proposals may be considered by the Government of India. A last date for receipt of applications is prescribed by Government of India. Proposals of NYKS, National Services Scheme, Central Organizations and Central Universities including Association of Indian Universities, SAI, Bharat Scouts and Guide will be entertained directly by the Ministry, provided the proposal is self-appraised by their respective Head Offices. Proposals from Himalayan Mountaineering Institute, Jawahar Institute of Mountaineering and Winter Sports and Indian Mountaineering Foundation will also be considered directly by the ministry.

All India NGOs (referred as consultative NGO) will also be allowed to submit proposals directly to the ministry. For this purpose, an expert group will be constituted by the ministry who, on the basis of specific performance benchmark to be laid down in advance, will notify such NGOs for a fixed time period and such NGOs will require renewal thereafter for availing the benefit of applying directly. The proposals recommended by the State government received directly from the notified institutions will be valid for the relevant financial year only and will not be carried forward to the next financial year.

Part III. Sports and Employment

Introduction

425. There are a large number of issues related to employment of those who are associated with sport. The problem related to unfair terms and conditions of employment contract, breach of such contract. Further, age fraud, and taking care of sportspersons after their retirement are also big issues. The suspension and termination of the sportsperson may be resorted to as per the employment contract and sportsperson may allege that such suspension or termination has been resorted to with mala fide intention. However, it is not only sportspersons who have issues and problems, but also many others who are directly or indirectly associated with sporting activities. There are also problems related to one-sided employment contracts. The sport associations and clubs being in dominant position sometime get signature of the sportsperson on dotted lines or otherwise have one-sided terms favouring them. In case of any dispute the sportsperson has to suffer. Further, generally the rules and regulations of sports federations/associations or clubs oust the jurisdiction of the courts, so aggrieved sportsman cannot go to the court as well for ventilation of grievances.

There is also problem of sex discrimination as well as exploitation of female sportspersons. Sport not only requires sportsman but also require a broad range of other staff from full-time management executives athletes to dedicated 'volunteer' supporters who are also having their own employment issues. The sports professions group includes all persons who engage in a sporting activity for remuneration and those who supervise this activity. There are following type of persons associated with sports:

(i) 'professional sportspersons', participating in a limited number of sports and, in general, depending on the sporting events which constitute their livelihood;
(ii) 'sports officials', i.e., all those who, as referees, judges or timekeepers, directly supervise the conduct of sporting competitions Beyond the scoreboard: global and regional opportunities;
(iii) 'sports activity leaders', who use sport as a means of getting specific groups of the population (elderly people, the disabled, young people, etc.) involved in team activities;

(iv) 'sports instructors', who teach one or more specific sporting activities to groups of the population who learn from scratch or wish to develop their abilities; and 'sports coaches', responsible for preparing and guiding systematic performance in a given sport;
(v) sport-related professions.

There is also a full range of professions that, although they belong to other large occupational groups, require a high level of specific skills in the field of sport.

426. As for sport-related activities, those who could be identified as involved in a 'sport-related profession', must show certain characteristics of institutionalization like professional trade unions, specific training, recognized designations, etc. These professions are classified as follows:

(i) professional managers of sports or sports-related organizations;
(ii) sports doctors;
(iii) physical education and sports teachers in the school environment; sports journalists and other specialists in communication through or on sport;
(iv) physiotherapists specialized in sport;
(v) agents or promoters of events or professional sportspersons;
(vi) sellers of sports goods;
(vii) caretakers of sports facilities and other reception staff;
(viii) sports facilities maintenance workers.

However fact remains that the above categories of professionals described are not the only ones present in the sports and sport-related sectors. A large number of people who work there come under other occupational categories that are not specific to their enterprise. All these categories may face problems with respect to employment.

Chapter 1. Sources of Employment Law

427. The main sources of employment law in sports are the rules and regulations of sport bodies, clubs and institutions. Further, the contractual terms agreed among the sportsman and clubs and other sport bodies and general law of employment also constitute source of employment law. The judgments of the courts on general law of employment also form an important source of employment law.

§1. Ordinary Law

428. The principal sources of law and regulations relating to employment relationships in India are the Constitution of India, labour statutes, judicial precedence and collective and individual agreements. There are as many as 165 labour laws, including nearly 50 central (federal) laws. Most of the employment laws are applicable to employees in the worker category. A worker is defined under the Industrial Disputes Act 1947 as a person who is employed to do any manual, unskilled, skilled, technical, operational, clerical or supervisory work for hire or reward, excluding a person: who is employed mainly in a managerial or administrative capacity; or who, being employed in a supervisory capacity, draws a salary exceeding a particular amount per month or exercises functions mainly of a supervisory or managerial nature. Apart from certain employment statutes that may be applicable to the non-worker category of employees, the employment relationship with a non-worker is governed by the employment contract.

429. In a major development, the government has subsumed forty-four central labour laws into four Board labour codes, which are – code on wages; industrial relations; occupational safety, health and working conditions (OSH) and social security. The same has already received the president's nod. While the Code on wages was passed in Parliament in 2019, the other three codes were approved by both the houses in 2020. The Labour Ministry is now all set to implement the new rules under these four labour codes. The rules under the four codes have been finalized which are required to implement the four labour code and ready to be notified. The States are doing their work to firm up rules under the four codes. Pertaining to the new labour rules, companies will be required to make major changes in the employees' salary structure. These include an increase in gratuity and the exclusion of benefits such as bonus, PF and HRA from the wages.

§2. Collective Bargaining Agreements

430. The Constitution of India in the chapter on fundamental rights and directive principles of State policy provided for collective bargaining. Article 19 gives every citizen to form an association, which can be understood as the permission of organizing the trade union and right to collective bargain. The directive principles also can be interpreted as to improve the condition of the labour. In the Article 43-A, the State shall ensure the participation of workers in the management which can be seen as a direct cause for the right to collective bargaining.

The relationship of an employer and an employee comes into existence when, pursuant to an agreement of the parties, one person, the employee as sportsman, agrees to work under the direction and control of another namely the employer for compensation. The contract may be an express or implied. The sportsman may have right to form a labour union and requires employers to deal with a duly elected union as the bargaining agent for the employees. It may prohibit employers from interfering with employees and from discriminating against an employee as a result of the employee's union activity. Collective bargaining agreements (CBAs) govern the rights and obligations of employers and sportsman in many employment relationships. Collective bargaining involves representatives of the employees bargaining with a single employer or a group of employers for an agreement. This agreement covers wages, hours of work and working conditions for the employees. The employees may make a union and elect members to represent, and negotiate for, them with the employer. In the process of bargaining, the parties create new solutions and arrive at new terms and conditions and act as a source of employment law.

431. Employment contracts in sport may come out of collective bargaining process by entering into agreements or individual employment contracts may be entered into directly between a club and player. Sometimes agent conducts negotiation of contract terms on behalf of the sportsman. Contract terms may also be derived from CBAs entered into between a sport's governing body and players' trade unions and applied in future contracts which may give rise to standard contract forms. Major examples include footballers' and cricketers' contracts negotiated by the Professional Footballers' Association and the Professional Cricketers' Association respectively. Such standard contracts are supplemented by confidential personal terms covering issues such as salaries, performance bonuses, sponsorship deals and image rights. Express terms in a player's standard contract deal with issues such as fitness, exclusivity and discipline.

Chapter 2. Status of Players

432. Sportsmen carry out a sporting activity as a career for remuneration or as amateur on a continuous basis. The applicability of law differs whether individual sportsperson has taken to sports as amateur or as professional. Further, setting a line of demarcation between amateur and professional sports activities is sometimes difficult, but in general amateur sportsperson participates in sports as a vocation. In case of amateur sports, the activities are organized and managed by individual groups which establish rules for eligibility and compensation.

§1. Professionals

433. In the majority of sports which feature professional players, the professionals participate at a higher standard of play than amateur competitors, as they can train full time without the stress of having another job. The sports bodies namely IOA and SAI promote amateur sports and not professional sport. The Memorandum of Association of IOA as mentioned hereunder provides that it is to develop and promote Olympic movement and amateur sport; to educate the public as to the value of amateurism in sports. IOA to guard and enforce amateur rules in connection with NSFs or Associations and to maintain the highest ideals of amateurism and to promote interest therein. Thus there is very limited scope for professional sport.

434. In case of professional sports the leagues generally have a standard player contract entered between players and owners and serves as model employment contract. Courts are generally reluctant to interfere in sport matters provided that rules are reasonably applied.

§2. Amateurs

435. In amateur sports participants engage largely or entirely without remuneration. The professional sporting participants are paid for the time they spend competing and training and are also used for sponsorship and promotion of products. The IOA Eligibility Code prescribes requirement for a sportsman and terms it as competitor. According to the rules of IOA, to be eligible for participation in the Olympic Games and other international competitions and tournaments a competitor must:

(i) Observe and abide by the rules of the IOC and, in addition, the rule of International Federation, as approved by IOC, even if the federation's rules are more strict than those of the IOC, as well as Asian Games, Commonwealth Games and any other international competitions, recognized by the IOC, Commonwealth Games Federation and Olympic Council of Asia.

(ii) Not have received any financial reward or material benefit in connection with his or her sports participation, except as permitted in by-laws to this rule.

436. The by-laws with respect to a competitor provide as follows:

(i) A competitor may: be a physical education or sports teacher who gives elementary instruction.
(ii) During the period of preparation and actual competition shall be limited by the rules of each International Federation:
   - Accept assistance administered through his or her National Olympic Committee or NSF or Association for:
   - The cost of food and lodging.
   - The cost of transport.
   - Pocket money to cover incidental expenses.
   - The expenses for insurance cover in respect of accidents, illness, personal property and disability.
   - The purchase of personal sports equipment and clothing.
   - The cost of medical treatment, physiotherapy and authorized coaches.
   - Accept compensation authorized by his or her National Olympic Committee of NSF or Association, in case of necessity, to cover financial loss resulting from work or basic occupation on account of preparation for, or participation in the Olympic Games and other international sports competitions. In no circumstances shall payment under this provision exceed the sum which the competitor would have earned in his work in the same periods. The compensation may be paid with the approval of the NSFs or Associations at their discretion.
(iii) Accept prizes won in competition within the limits of the rules established by the respective international federations.
(iv) Accept academic and technical scholarships.

437. A competitor must not:

(i) Be, or have been, a professional athlete in any sport.
(ii) Have allowed his person, name and picture or sports performance to be used for advertisement, except when his or her International Federation, National Olympic Committee or NSF or Association enters into a contract for sponsorship of equipment. All payments must be made to the International Federation, National Olympic Committee or NSF or Association concerned, and not the athlete.
(iii) Carry advertising material on his person or clothing in the Olympic Games, World or Continental Championships and Games, under the patronage of the IOC, Commonwealth Games Federation and Olympic Council of Asia, other than trademarks on technical equipment or clothing as agreed by the IOC, Commonwealth Games Federation or Olympic Council of Asia with international federations.
(iv) Have acted as a professional coach or trainer in any sport.

438. The majority of worldwide sporting participants are amateurs. By the early twenty-first century the Olympic Games and all the major team sports accepted professional competitors. However, there are still some sports which maintain a distinction between amateur and professional status with separate competitive leagues. The most prominent of these are golf and boxing.

§3. Others

439. Problems can arise for amateur sportsmen when sponsors offer to help with an amateur's playing expenses in the hope of striking lucrative endorsement deals with them in case they become professionals at a later date. This practice, dubbed, 'shamateurism', a portmanteau of sham and amateur, was present as early as in the nineteenth century. As financial and political stakes became higher, shamateurism became all the more widespread, reaching its peak in the 1970s and 1980s, when the IOC started moving towards acceptance of professional athletes.

Chapter 3. Employment Relationship

440. The status of the sportsperson vis-à-vis employment is extremely varied and every sport as well as relationship of sportsperson with its employer has peculiar characteristics. Sometimes a sportsperson plays for his employer and sometimes represents his or her nation individually or as part of a team. The employment may be full time and sportsperson is considered and treated for all practical purposes as employee. In case he is with some club or federation, it is generally based on term contract basis or membership basis as the case may be.

§1. Employment Agreement

441. Indian law does not in general prescribe any format for entering into any contract. There can be a valid and legally binding oral contract by words of mouth. Therefore, it depends on with whom one is entering into contract. The associations and federations can have their own standard contract specially designed and drafted for their purpose. However individual contract terms widely differ as these depend on reputation and recognition of the sportsperson meaning thereby that respective bargaining power of the parties determines the terms and conditions of the contract.

These contracts are generally in writing whereas Indian law recognizes an oral contract as well. However, certain contract like a contract for refereeing the matters to arbitration is by law required to be in writing. The contract is required to be on a non-judicial stamp paper, and the value of stamp paper is prescribed by the State government of the place where contract is enforced or to be produced in the court for implementation.

I. Dismissal

442. The taking of drug, acts of violence by sportsman give rise to disciplinary issues justifying dismissal on the grounds of breach of contract. The clubs have an extremely wide discretion in these matters ranging from leniency towards the imposition of penalties that could be considered harsh. The recreational drug-taking viewed more seriously than acts of violence on or off the field of play. During playing seasons, the use of drugs, or alcohol, is considered to be potentially in conflict with players' duties to keep themselves fit. A dismissal is only wrongful where it is a breach of contract on the part of the employer. There is an important interrelationship between express and terms judicially implied into all employment contracts. Employees are subject to express and implied terms to obey instructions of the employer and the latter is subject to a judicially implied term to maintain trust and confidence. Where treatment of an employee constitutes a breach of this term and the employee responds by resigning, then the resignation constitutes a wrongful constructive dismissal entitling the employee to claim damages.

443. In cases where the employee resigns in response to the employer's breach it matters not that the employee had previously indicated that he might be prepared to leave the employment if suitable terms were offered to him. It may be noted that managers are most often dismissed not for misconduct but for the failures of the team on the pitch. Such dismissals are wrongful but claims of damages are normally pre-empted by agreements on the amount of compensation the manager will receive.

A right to claim for unfair dismissal may be a legal right and not dependent on an employer dismissing in breach of contract. Rather, a dismissal will be unfair where the employer has acted unreasonably, that is, has acted in a way that no reasonable employer would act. A dismissal may be substantively unfair because the employer did not have an adequate reason for dismissing the employee. It may be procedurally unfair because the employer has failed to act reasonably in failing to follow an appropriate procedure before reaching a decision to dismiss. A failure to follow a proper procedure will not always render a dismissal procedurally unfair as there will be circumstances where an employer will have acted reasonably, despite procedural defects, because following procedure could be viewed by a reasonable employer as futile or useless.

II. To Be Heard

444. An individual has the right of audience before an employment tribunal, and therefore employees are often represented by officials of trade unions or appropriate professional associations. Although costs can be awarded against the losing party it is normal for the parties to bear their own costs.

A player will be able to claim unfair dismissal even where the dismissal is in accordance with the player's contract or the dismissal is in the form of the non-renewal of a player's contract that has expired. The player may contend that he should have been informed at an earlier date of the decision to dispense with his services. The failure to do this adversely affected his chance of finding a new club for the following season.

§2. Players' Obligations

445. The obligations of the player are governed by the contract which player has with the sport federation or association, rules of such bodies and other general rules which may be applicable to professionals. As sportspersons are always in competition with other sportsmen, so they have to adhere to and play their game as per the rules of the game. Perhaps in no other sphere of human activity, decisions and results are as quick as in sporting activity as umpires, referees and judges are available to give on the spot decision.

I. Sporting Contracts and Restraint of Trade

446. The doctrine of restraint of trade plays an important part in the context of sports employment contracts. One aspect of this is where a club imposes a contractual period of 'garden leave' on a manager before he is able to leave the club in order to take up an appointment with a new club. If the period of 'garden leave' is too long then it will constitute an unreasonable restraint of trade and will be unenforceable. The departure of a manager to another club not infrequently results in other members of the coaching and playing staff joining him shortly thereafter.

§3. Player's Rights

I. Fundamental Rights

447. The Constitution of India contains fundamental rights which are general in nature and available to sportsman and players as well. Under the Constitution of India, sports participants are protected from acts of unlawful direct and indirect discrimination on the grounds of age, disability, gender reassignment, marriage and civil partnership, pregnancy and maternity, race, religion or belief, sex and sexual orientation. The prohibition of unlawful harassment is particularly relevant to sports participants given the levels of racist and homophobic abuse to which players have been historically subjected by fans, coaches and fellow players on and off the field of play.

448. If a player is subjected to racist or homophobic abuse or other forms of harassment by other employees of the club, and his club has failed to take reasonable steps to protect the player from such acts, then the club will be directly or vicariously liable. However, the law cannot provide an effective mechanism for protecting players who are the victims of discriminatory abuse during a match by a member of the opposing team. Effective deterrents in this regard could be in the form of such racist or homophobic abuse automatically constituting a sending-off offence, and for clubs to incur points deductions if their players are shown to be regular offenders.

A. Right Against Discrimination

449. The Constitution of India prohibits terminating an employee or refusing to hire an applicant because of caste, race, colour, sex, religion. It prohibits treating one sportsman less favourably than another because of race, sex, etc. Certain tests which an employer might give to a job applicant might be found to be culturally biased and therefore have a disparate impact against a minority. This is not to say that all tests will be declared illegal by a Court. However, a test must have a reasonable relation to the job for which it is to be used. The Pregnancy Discrimination laws require that an employer treat pregnancy in the same manner that other disabilities are treated. Women that are temporarily disabled by pregnancy or childbirth must be provided with the same benefits as other disabled workers. This includes sick leave, insurance and similar benefits.

B. Invocation of Article 311 of the Constitution

450. In the case of *Md. Azharuddin v. Dr A Muthaiiah and Others* (AIR 2002 AP 409) wherein the matter related to a life ban imposed by BCCI on the cricketer, the High Court of Andhra Pradesh at Hyderabad dealt with the nature of contract which a cricketer has with the sporting association and held that 'On behalf of the petitioner-plaintiff it is contended that there is a service contract between the plaintiff and the first defendant and therefore, the plaintiff is entitled to move the Civil Court seeking redressal of his grievances for violation of his rights under Article 311 of the Constitution of India. I am of the view that this submission is untenable inasmuch as Article 311 of the Constitution of India provides a mechanism for redressal of grievances of persons who are members of a Civil Service of Union of India or of civil servant of a State or holds a civil post under the Union or a State. As the petitioner is not holding any of these posts but only has entered into a private contract with the first defendant on certain terms and conditions to play cricket matches for the Indian Team for which certain amount of remuneration per match is paid, the petitioner is not entitled to invoke the provisions of Article 311 of the Constitution of India.'

II. Other Rights

A. Right Against Sexual Harassment

451. The sexual harassment is another issue which may involve supervisory personnel seeking sexual favours from employees/sportsman/sportswomen under them in return for job benefits such as continued employment, promotions, raises, or a favourable performance evaluation. Another form of sexual harassment is the hostile working environment. This is a situation where a supervisor's conduct has sexual connotations and causes anxiety and poison the work environment. This type of conduct may include unwelcome flirtations, propositions, or any other abuse of a sexual nature. If this type of conduct causes a sportsperson to quit his or her job, the employer may be liable for any damage caused to the employee.

452. Coaches and other authorities in control of sport, may use their power over athletes for sexual favours. In 2011, an official of Tamil Nadu Boxing Association was arrested on charges of sexual harassment.[24] In another case, in 2009, a female

24. Times of India, Boxing Association Official Arrested on Sexual Harassment Charges, 2011, available at: http://Boxing association official arrested on sexual harassment charges.

athlete committed suicide because she was being sexually harassed by her coach.[25] Studies show that 2-8% of minor-age athletes are victims of sexual abuse in the field of sport.[26] An analysis of 159 cases of sexual abuse in sports reported in the print media revealed that the perpetrators of the abuse were coaches, teachers and instructors in 98% of the cases.[27]

453. The provisions for prevention of sexual harassment of women were introduced under the National Sports Development Code of India, 2011 and Hockey India adopted a Sexual Harassment policy which was in line with the Sports Code, however most other sporting federations failed to adopt such a policy. The Supreme Court in Vishakha and Ors v. State of Rajasthan (AIR 1997 SC 3011) issued guidelines that defined sexual harassment and stipulated conditions for its prevention and redressal.

454. The outrage over the December 16, 2012, rape case in Delhi led to enactment of the Sexual Harassment of Women at Workplace (Prevention, Prohibition and Redressal) Act, 2013. 'Workplace' as defined in section 2(o)(i) of the Act, includes any department, organization established, owned, controlled or wholly or substantially financed or funded provided directly or indirectly by the government. The fact that most sports federations are financed or funded by the government brings them within the ambit of workplace under the Act. Further, workplace also includes sports institutes, stadiums, sports complex or competition or games venue, whether residential or games venue, whether residential or not used for training, sports or other related activities. It is therefore shocking to note that most sport federations and other organizations have not implemented the provisions of this Act. These organizations are required to constitute Internal Complaints Committee to address complaints.

B. Right to Form Association

455. Freedom of Association is a fundamental right recognized under Article 19(C) of the Constitution under which players may form associations or unions. So sportsperson can form trade unions, and as per decision in *Bangalore Water Supply and Sewage Board v. A. Rajappa and Others* (AIR 1978 SC 548), sporting bodies like BCCI may fall under the term 'industry' with respect to contract of service entered into with sportsperson and degree of control would be a determining factor to call sportsperson a workman. The footballers are represented by Football Players Association of India, but an attempt of cricket players in 1989 was not encouraged by the authorities.

---

25. Adrija Bose, 7 times Indian Sportswomen Reported Sexual Harassment but Nothing Changed, Huffington Post, available at::http://www.huffingtonpost.in/2016/12/14/7-times-indian- sportswomen-reported-of-facing-sexual-harassment/.
26. A. Sandra L. Kirby et al., *The Dome of Silence* (1st ed., Fernwood 2000).
27. Celia H. Brackenridge et al., *The Characteristics of Sexual Abuse in Sport: A Multidimensional Scaling Analysis of Events Described in Media Reports*, 6 Intl. J. Sport Exercise Psychol. 385–406 (2008).

C. Right to Strike

456. Striking is a tool in collective bargaining and has been considered as part of the freedom of association. Because in the absence of right to strike, the basic purpose of formation of association will be defeated; therefore, it forms part and parcel of freedom to form associations.

§4. Clubs Obligations

457. The transfer of a sportsman from one club or federation to another sometimes creates problems, as these clubs may be competitors. The transfer of player may depend on individual contract, sportsperson has entered into with the club or federation as the case may be and rules of such club or federation. Normally, when an employee's current contract comes to an end that employee has complete freedom to seek employment with a new employer. In professional games, a player can only play for the club that holds his registration and the club is not obliged to release that registration when the player's current contract comes to an end. A player is only free to negotiate a move to a new club if he is permitted to do this by his current club. In this case he is literally a free agent who can move to a new club on whatever terms he can negotiate. The offer must be made after the end of the domestic season. The player is permitted to reject this offer and thereby become 'free' to negotiate a move to another club but this is subject to the clubs agreeing on a transfer fee. If a fee cannot be agreed between the two clubs the player's registration can be transferred to the new club provided that club agrees to pay a fee as determined by the concerned games Compensation Committee. In practice, a player's desire to move may be frustrated if the other club is not prepared to pay the required fee or accept that the amount of the fee should be determined by the Compensation Committee.

§5. Termination Contracts

458. The termination of a sportsman's contract may occur because of efflux of time, by mutual consent, or by unilateral action of the sportsperson or entity with which it has employment or sponsorship contract. The termination in case of an employment contract is affected by resignation. Termination can also be brought about by operation of law. Ordinarily a contract of employment may be terminated in the same manner as any other contract. If it is to run for a definite period of time, the employer cannot terminate the contract at an earlier date without justification. If the employment contract does not have a definite duration, it is terminable at will. This is called employment at will. Under the employment at will doctrine, the employer has historically been allowed to terminate the contract at any time for any reason or for no reason. However, exceptions have been carved out to this doctrine when the discharge violates an established public policy, such as discharging an employee in retaliation for insisting that the employer complies with a law. Courts may sometimes construe an employer's statements concerning continued employment as a part of the employment contract, and therefore require good cause for the discharge of an at-will employee.

Chapter 4. Agents Regulations

459. The basic function of a sports agent is to represent sportsperson in professional dealings with outside parties. An agent may interact with sponsors for negotiating and signing the contracts, receiving payments on behalf of sportsperson, etc. He also deals with the press and other persons for getting exposure for performances of the sportsman represented. The agent is appointed so that sportsman can focus on sport rather than on non-sporting activities which can be taken care by any other person like agent. Further, an agent is expected to have contacts, connections and expertise to open, sponsorship and other business opportunities for the sportsman. The prudence dictates that even after appointment of an agent, the sportsman should also maintain direct relations with sponsors, the press and others and do not leave all to the agent. Even if sportsman does not spend a lot of time with these people, a relationship with these people will help in receiving feedback on agent's actions.

§1. Regulations

460. No specific legislation, code or rules regarding regulation of activities of agents exists in India at present. The provisions or regulations regarding relationship of sportsman with agent can be incorporated in the agreement between the two. Player representatives have a free hand, which sometimes results in players and sports bodies not getting proper advice. This is evident from the cases of IPL cricketers who were disciplined for failure to comply with player rules in their communications with other franchises while being contracted to their existing teams. Thus, there is need to regulate the activities in order to protect the younger players from making decisions which might jeopardize their careers. The scope of agent regulation in India may include:

(a) licensing and registration of agents through certification programmes and examination;
(b) transparency and limitations on agent commissions and length of contracts;
(c) regulation of agent communication with athletes and parents under the age of majority;
(d) prohibition of inappropriate communication and other conduct between agents and selectors/administrators; and
(e) confidentiality and reporting obligations to player-clients and avoidance of conflict of interest.

As the amount of money involved in Indian sports grows and laws and regulations become more complex, the need for qualified, ethical and well-regulated player representatives increases. The sportsman being the owner of all commercial rights relating to name and image so no one can use it without permission and license his name or photos or other images that represent a sportsman. There can be a number of other commercial opportunities that will arise in the course of one's career. Sportsman might be invited to public events such as product launches, inaugurations, etc. or to participate in corporate activities such as team-building, speaking opportunities, etc.

I. Important Terms of Agent Agreement

A. Solus Clause

461. The agent would like to have total control on commercial aspects of the sportsman and would like that sportsman work only with him or her. If contract includes this, solus clause one will not be able to associate with another agent during the period of contract. One must enter into an exclusive relationship only when one is confident that the agent in question will be able to provide to the sportsman all the services one requires.

B. Minimum Guarantee

462. Minimum guarantee refers to the amount of money that sportsman is entitled to receive from the agent regardless of whether or how the agent creates commercial opportunities. The sportsman should understand clearly the structure of the minimum guarantee and entitlements under the clause.

C. Availability Clause and Territorial Extent

463. This clause contains number of days that a sportsman makes available to the agent for ad shoots, commercial appearances, etc. In turn, the agent attempts to sell these days to brands for various sponsor and endorsements opportunities. The territorial area of activities of the agent rights must be clear in the contract, whether the agent is representing the sportsman worldwide, in India or in any other territories.

D. Duration and Right of First Refusal

464. The agent may like to renew his or her association with sportsman even after the term of the contract is over. The clause dealing with right of first refusal aims to give the agent the right to match the best commercial offer that one receives from another person and continue the relationship on these revised terms. The Supreme Court of India has held that it is illegal to have a right of first refusal clause that extends beyond the period of the contract. This means that a sportsman is free to negotiate with anyone once the contract period is over without obligations to the previous agent.

§2. Agents Rights

465. The agent is entitled to a commission for representing sportsman which is generally a percentage of the amount generated by the agent's activities. A minimum guarantee is an assured minimum payment is made to sportsman by the agent every year. This payment may be guaranteed to sportsman regardless of whether agent secures commercial opportunities for the sportsman or not. The agent makes this minimum payment (and takes the associated risk) for the privilege to deal exclusively with the athlete. But few athletes at the very highest level may receive minimum guarantees.

§3. Agents Obligations

466. The agent's duty is to coordinate with coaches, trainers and others who monitor performances. The agent assists in planning career and getting access to the various services such as coaches, trainers and others who create opportunities and contribute to the growth of sportsman. Sportsman must clearly understand all the implications of and obligations under the contract. There should not be any conflict of interest between sportsman and agent. If it exists, the agent may sometimes compromise sportsman interest to further his own. To avoid ambiguity and disputes later on, there must be a written agency agreement dealing with all the issues and matters of importance.

467. While entering into contracts or other legal obligations, the agent may create the opportunity and carry on negotiations but the contract should always be closely examined and signed by the sportsman. Under Indian contract law, one cannot sign a contract until attaining the age of 18 years. In case of a minor, a contract may be signed on behalf of minor by parent or legal guardian. When one turns 18, all contracts that were signed between the guardian and others must be signed once again directly with the sportsman. At this time, one can also decide to change contracts as he or she cannot be forced to continue with existing terms agreed to by the guardian.

§4. Employment and Economic Dispute Resolution

468. At a time when sportsmen are becoming more professional and the stakes are becoming higher than ever, dispute resolution takes on an increasingly important and significant role. In many respects arbitration offers the solutions with regards to the rapidity, diversity and professionalism of the decisions rendered. The disputes when referred to courts take a long time to come up as Indian courts are already piled up with a number of pending cases. There is a need to have an authority for sports that offers flexible, quick and inexpensive method of resolution of disputes.

I. Ousting Court Jurisdiction

469. It may be noted that the rules of IOA through voluntary surrender take away the right of all NSFs, Associations, State Olympic Association affiliated to IOA, to go to the court for redressal of the grievances and settlements of disputes. The National Sports Development Bill, 2013 also provides that no Civil Court shall have jurisdiction to entertain any suit or proceeding in respect of any matter which the Appellate Sports Tribunal is empowered by or under this Act to determine and no injunction shall be granted by any court or other authority in respect of any action taken or to be taken in pursuance of any power conferred by or under the Act (section 32). The Rules of IOA also deal with the nature and type of remuneration, which a sportsperson as competitor in international games can accept.

II. Economic Dispute Resolution

470. There are various ways of dispute resolution of issues arising out of economic interests of the sportsman. The general law to deal with professional aspects of and with respect to employment and labour matters is also applicable to sports which provides modes of dispute settlement as well. The relationship of sportsman with their sponsor or sports federation is governed by the contract which a sportsman has with the sponsor or sports federation. Such contract may include arbitration clause for resolution of disputes if any arise. Similarly mediation which is another mode of settlement of disputes may also be resorted to.

A. *Arbitration*

471. The arbitration clause may be a part of the contract which sportsperson enters into with a sporting club, association or federation. The rules of IOA also provides for arbitration in case of disputes between the NSF, associations, State Olympic association affiliated to IOA. An individual player, group of individuals belonging to an association, federation or club taking recourse to Civil Court of law without utilizing the available resources of IOA General Assembly, can be expelled from National Sport Federation, Association or State Olympic Association. Clubs, association or federations are required to follow the statutes related to matters affecting the well-being of the sports professionals. As IOA is registered under Societies Registration Act XXI of 1860, therefore, its provisions are also applicable to IOA. Introducing arbitration clauses into the documents governing any high-profile appointments can help to prevent disputes being fought in public as arbitration being a private form of litigation. Whilst such a clause is unlikely to prevent going to the Employment Tribunal, it would stop a breach of contract claim being brought in the Court. In many sports disputes, a contractual claim will be most valuable to the employee.

B. Labour Law

472. The labour laws require payment of a minimum wage as well as the payment of overtime after particular hours of work per week. The Occupational Safety and Health laws ensure safe and healthy working conditions for employees. For most kinds of employment, workers' compensation statutes govern compensation for injuries. The injured employee is entitled to compensation for accidents occurring in the course of employment.

473. Ignoring an enforcement notice can lead to criminal liability and an organization being named publicly as an employer contravening NMW legislation. Having a robust grievance policy in place will help in dealing with complaints swiftly and appropriately and can lead to a resolution without the need for formal legal action.

C. Mediation

474. If a matter is particularly serious or sensitive, one might consider instructing an external investigator to delve deeper into the details of the complaint to demonstrate how seriously it is being taken. Workplace mediation is often overlooked by employers, but it can help to reach an amicable solution and avoid ending up in court.

Chapter 5. Social Security

475. The social security of a sportsperson is ensured by means of employment, insurance, pension and other schemes, etc. so that in case of disability, injury and old age at least basic needs can be taken care of.

§1. Legal Framework

476. In India, there is no specific law exclusively dealing with social security of sportsperson but a scheme with the name of 'Incentive for Promotion of Sports Activities' has been implemented by the Ministry which includes the social security aspects like pensions, other monetary benefits and grants in case of illness in its ambit. Besides, government, public and private companies provide employment opportunities to sportsman.

I. Pensions to Meritorious Sportsperson

A. Background

477. A scheme of Sports Funding for Pensions to Meritorious Sportspersons was started in July 1994 with the objective that government would reward their outstanding achievements in the Olympic, Commonwealth Games and World Cup or World Championships in Olympic and Asian Games disciplines with lifetime assistance in the form of an assured monthly pension. The pension payments are made through LIC of India, for which Ministry purchases annuities for individual pensioners by making onetime lump sum payment to LIC.

478. The Khelo India Scheme was formulated by merging Rajiv Gandhi Khel Abhiyan, Urban Sports Infrastructure Scheme and National Sports Talent Search Scheme. The Khelo India Scheme was launched in 2016. The scheme was revamped in October 2017 with twin objectives of mass participation and promotion of excellence in sports. The mission is to encourage sports all over the country, thus allowing the population to harness the power of sports through its cross-cutting influence, namely, holistic development of children and youth, community development, social integration, gender equality, healthy lifestyle, national pride and economic opportunities related to sports development.

479. In 1997, a new scheme named 'Sports Scholarship Scheme' came into force by merging the scheme of Sports Talent Search Scholarship and Promotion of Sports and Physical Education among women. The Scheme of NSDF was started in 1998 to administer and use the monies of the fund for promotion of sports in general and specific sports disciplines and individual sportspersons in particular for achieving excellence at the national and international levels. On the recommendations of the Planning Commission in the context of zero-based budgeting exercise, the Ministry decided to amalgamate these five schemes into one scheme. The new scheme is called as ‘Incentive for Promotion of Sports Activities’.

B. The Components of the Scheme

480. This scheme has the following components:

(a) Pension to Meritorious Sportspersons.
(b) Rural Sports Programme.
(c) Promotion of Sports and Games in School.
(d) Sports Scholarships.
(e) NSDF.

C. The Objectives of the Scheme

481. The following are the objectives of the scheme:

(a) To provide incentive as well as an added measure of financial security to sportspersons in recognition of their outstanding performance in identified international competitions.
(b) To provide incentive to promote sports and to generate sports consciousness and mass participation in sports in the rural areas.
(c) To provide incentives to promote sports and games among the school children.
(d) To recognize the achievements of young sportspersons and their outstanding performance at the national, State, college and university levels.
(e) To apply the monies of the NSDF for promotion of sports in general and specific sports disciplines and individual sportspersons in particular for achieving excellence at the national and international levels.

D. Contribution Rates

482. The main sources of funding are the following:

(a) By contribution to the fund from National Welfare Fund for sportspersons.
(b) By contribution and donations received from private and public corporate companies and institutions.
(c) Government grant.

E. Sports Fund for Pension

483. The pension for the sportspersons is operated through a fund, named as ‘Sports Fund for Pension to Meritorious Sportspersons’. For the management and administration of the fund, a general committee is constituted with Minister of State for Youth Affairs and Sports as its Chairman.

F. Eligibility for Pension

484. To get the pension benefits, eligible sportspersons have to apply in prescribed proformae duly recommended by the concerned NSFs. Those sportspersons, who are Indian citizens and have won medals in Olympic Games, World Cup, World Championships, Asian Games, Commonwealth Games and Para Olympic Games can apply and are given life pension from the age of 30.

G. Calculation of Pension Allowances

485. The pension is payable to a sportsperson on attaining the age of 30 and will continue during the lifetime, provided that the sportsperson at the time of applying for such pension would have retired from an active sports career. An undertaking to this effect is to be given by the sportsperson in the application form itself. The pension is given at a varying rate.

486. Sportspersons availing themselves of a pension under the scheme will not be deprived of financial benefits, scholarships, ex gratia, grants or any other monetary benefit admissible from any other source and, vice versa, any sportsperson availing of any such benefit will not be deprived of the admissible pension under this scheme. However, the above benefits will not include service pay and service pension from any establishment, whether government, public or private.

II. Social Security Through Employment and Other Opportunities

487. Social security can also be provided through providing employment to the sportsperson. There are various avenues of employment open for sportspersons through placements in government departments and public sector undertakings and companies. Many government departments and public sector undertakings like Indian Railways, Indian Airlines, Air India, SAIL, Bharat Heavy Electric Limited, Tata Iron and Steel Company, ONGC, Armed and Paramilitary Forces, Custom Excise and Indian Postal Services offer placements to sportspersons in their organizations.

488. The sportspersons generally join at the initial placement level and are promoted according to their performance and as per the rules of the company. Graduates and even matriculate (Senior Secondary Certificate (SSC) or equivalent) students who have performed in the inter-university or inter-school sports events that include athletics, tennis, badminton, football, hockey, wrestling – in all about twenty-five disciplines, are qualified for such employment. There are more than a thousand sportsmen who are working in the armed and paramilitary forces.

489. Border Security Force has very good teams of hockey and football; the Central Reserve Police Force employs young men who are good in swimming, hockey and athletics. The Indo-Tibetan Border Police (ITBP) exclusively arranges winter games. ITBP also has a section for competitive shooting. A promising national level player is inducted as a constable and is promoted later on, according to his performance.

III. Medical Facilities

490. Sports Medicine and Sports Sciences Centre at J.N. Stadium established under the Plan Scheme of SAI in 1984 aims to provide comprehensive sports medicine and sports science backup to sportspersons with the help of specialists in sports medicine, sports scientists, physiotherapists and other support staff. The centre provides comprehensive sports-based programmes to treat and prevent injury, aid recovery and enhance performance through different scientific tests. The sportspersons who are provided medical and scientific support are national campers, sportspersons from various SAI schemes, regular trainees, sportspersons under Come and Play Schemes and others. To provide the best possible medical support to national athletes, specialists from Departments of Orthopaedics, Ophthalmology, Surgery and Medicine visit the centre from the leading hospitals of Delhi like All India Institute of Medical Sciences, Gangaram Hospital, etc. SAI has also roped in Medical Institutions running Masters in Sports Physiotherapy Courses wherein interns are being posted for their clinical duties at SAI. Jamia Hamdard, Jamia Islamia, Indian Institute of Spinal Injury from Delhi and Amity University, Noida are feeder institutions posting interns to SAI who are assisting doctors attached to national camps. Besides providing in-house medical care to National players, SAI has also entered into an agreement with Jai Prakash Trauma Centre under AIIMS, Delhi and Safdarjung Sports Injury Centre, Delhi to take care of medical emergencies for which special staff have been designated to treat the players on priority. Medical cover is also provided to national campers, sportspersons from SAI schemes, regular trainees, Sportspersons under Come and Play Schemes and others round the year and as per need basis.

IV. Incentives and Other Benefits

491. Incentives provide recognition and financial security to distinguished sportspersons, during and after their sporting careers, and also motivate youth in the serious pursuit of sports activities. Adequate and proper assistance is extended for insurance cover and medical treatment in the event of such eventuality or requirement. Job reservation is also there for sportspersons as per the prescribed categories. Social recognition, the conferment of awards and honours at the national, State and district levels, incentives in the form of cash awards and avenues of employment are important elements of the National Sports Policy, 2001 and the draft Comprehensive Sports Policy 2007. Alongside sportspersons, suitable incentives are provided to coaches, judges and referees for developing skills and enriching their experience.

A. Sports and Tourism

492. The policy recognizes the interdependence and interrelationship between the sports and tourism sectors; the integrated development of these two is capable of generating very substantial revenues and ensuring a high volume of tourist traffic from within the country and from overseas, while simultaneously promoting a sports and fitness culture in the country. Adventure sports, in particular, have great potential for the promotion of tourism. Towards this end, the concerned ministries and departments of the Union and State governments, that is those handling sports, tourism and related subjects, will strive to draw up joint and unified plans and proposals for various parts of the country, with due reference to the possibilities in the north-eastern region, and to execute these programmes in a systematic and coordinated manner.

B. Resource Mobilization for Sports

493. Except in case of cricket, insufficiency of financial resources has been a constraint in promoting sports in the country. While the Union and State governments would need to arrange higher budgetary provisions, special efforts are equally called for to mobilize corporate funds for the development of sports. Accordingly, corporate houses would be approached and encouraged to adopt and support particular disciplines (as well as sportspersons) in the longer term for this purpose. Tripartite agreements between the government and the concerned sports federations and the corporate houses can be entered into for different sports disciplines. In the context and background of the Policy of Economic Liberalization, the private and corporate sectors would be more closely involved with the promotion of sports, in general, and to build and maintain sports infrastructure, in particular, with requisite emphasis on the latest technologies. A suitable package of incentives can be evolved for this purpose. Eminent sportspersons of established merit will be encouraged to set up and manage sports academies.

494. All contributions from within or outside the country to the NSDF which has been created with initial contributions from the Union Government have been extended with 100% exemption from Income Tax. The revenues generated by the sale of broadcasting television rights of sports events are to be shared between the concerned sports federation or association and the broadcasting or telecasting agency, public or private, on mutually agreed terms, through appropriate revenue-sharing arrangements.

C. Mass Media

495. The role of the mass media is central to the popularization of sports among the people at large. The electronic media, including the national broadcasters, the private channels and the print media would be suitably mobilized for strengthening a sports culture in the country. Since it has a commercial aspect as well and generates more revenue for the sportsperson as well as federations, clubs or associations than available from pure sporting activity, therefore, mass media is very important from every angle. The earning of the sportsman from this source provides and adds up to economic security.

D. Assistance to Promising Sportspersons

496. Under this scheme, assistance is provided to promising sportspersons. The selected sportspersons holding national records in the priority disciplines are provided a package of assistance on yearly basis for coaching, equipment, participation in national and international tournaments, etc., on a long-term basis. The coaches, sports scientists and other sportspersons would also be assisted for upgradation of their skills and assisting the promising sportspersons for achieving excellence in international level sports.

E. Grants to NSFs

497. The government provides financial assistance to recognized NSFs for conducting National Sports Championship at sub-junior, junior and senior levels. Financial assistance to priority and general category of sports disciplines is also provided for participation in international sports tournaments and championships abroad and also for organizing international tournaments in India.

F. Pension to Medal Winners

498. Under the scheme launched in 1994, a monthly pension is given to winners of medals in Olympic, World Cup and World Championships, Asian Games, Paralympic Games and Commonwealth Games. Pension is given, to those sportspersons who have Indian citizenship on attaining the age of 30, which continues till their lifetime. The monthly pension varies with the event and with the level of medal won like gold, silver or bronze medal.

G. National Welfare Fund for Sportspersons

499. The National Welfare Fund for sportspersons was created in 1982 primarily to assist sportspersons of yesteryear who are living in straitened circumstances and who had won glory for the country in sports. Financial support was initially given in the form of a monthly pension but from July 2009 was converted in lump sum ex gratia assistance for medical treatment. The sportspersons suffering from grievous and fatal injuries in the course of participation in sports events during training are also helped through this fund. The fund is managed and operated by a committee. The Minister of Sports and Youth Affairs is the Chairman of this Committee. There is a separate scheme of pension for meritorious sportsperson.

H. National Sports Development Fund

500. An NSDF had been set up in 1998 under the Charitable Endowments Act, 1890 to mobilize financial resources from government, corporate and private sectors as well as individuals for promotion of sports and games in the country. To make the contributions to the fund attractive, 100% exemptions from income tax is available on all such contributions. The contribution of the government is on matching basis to the contributions received from other resources. Initially the Government of India made a contribution of INR 20 million as the seed money.

§2. Specific Conditions Applied to Sports

501. There are some specific opportunities and benefits which are available to sportspersons only. Some of them may not be directly related to social security but help the sportspersons in time of need.

I. Awards

502. The Ministry has the following schemes of awards in the Youth and Sports Sectors.

A. National Sport Promotion Award: Rashtriya Khel Protsahan Award

503. This award introduced in 2009, aims at encouraging and motivating sportspersons and coaches. The scheme has four categories namely community sports development, promotion of sports academies of excellence, support to elite sportspersons and employment to sportspersons.

B. National Adventure Awards

504. Under this scheme, National Adventure Awards are given as the highest national recognition of outstanding achievements in the field of adventure activities on land, sea and air.

C. Arjuna Awards

505. The Arjuna Awards were instituted in 1961. The government has recently revised the scheme for Arjuna Award for outstanding performance in sports and games. As per the revised schematic guidelines, to be eligible for the award, a sportsperson should have had not only good performance consistently for the previous three years at the international level with excellence for the year for which the award is recommended, but also have shown qualities of leadership, sportsmanship and a sense of discipline. The awardee is given a statuette, a scroll of honour, ceremonial dress and a cash award.

D. Rajiv Gandhi Award

506. Rajiv Gandhi Khel Ratna Award was launched in 1991–1992 with the objective of honouring sportspersons to enhance their general status and to give them greater dignity and place of honour in society. Under this scheme, a cash award is given for the most spectacular and outstanding performance in the field of sports by an individual sportsperson or a team.

E. Special Awards to Medal Winners in International Sports Events and Their Coaches

507. To attract the young generation to take sports as a career and to encourage the outstanding sportspersons for even higher achievements, special awards to medal winners of international sports events and their coaches were introduced in 1986. The coaches who have trained the medal winners for at least 240 days immediately preceding the grant are eligible for cash award under the scheme which is 50% of the award money given to sportsperson. To be eligible for this award, a sportsperson should have had not only good performance consistently for the previous three years at the international level with excellence for the year for which award is recommended, but also has to show qualities of leadership, sportsmanship and a sense of discipline. The awardees are given a statuette, scroll of honour, ceremonial dress and a cash award.

508. Cash awards are given for winning medals in the Olympic, World Cup or World Championships, Asian and Commonwealth Games and Championships. These awards are also given for victory in chess and billiards or snooker. Special awards are also given to junior sportspersons for winning medals in the World, Asian and Commonwealth Championships. This scheme was reviewed in August 2009 and concerned federations can submit the application for cash awards within one month of the completion of sports event. The basic objective of the awards is to provide an incentive to the achievers and an inspiration to the upcoming sportspersons. It is also intended to help the sportspersons of outstanding calibre to be able to maintain themselves with dignity and continue to give their best in further pursuit of the sports of their choice.

F. Dronacharya Award

509. The Dronacharya Award, instituted in 1985, honours eminent coaches who have successfully trained sportspersons or teams and enabled them to achieve outstanding results in international completions. The awardee is given a statuette of Guru Dronacharya, a scroll of honour, ceremonial dress and a cash prize.

G. Maulana Abul Kalam Azad Trophy

510. The Maulana Abul Kamal Azad Trophy, instituted as a Running Trophy in 1956–1957, is awarded annually to the university, which has given the best all-round performance during the year of award. The winner receives a replica of the trophy and a cash award to be utilized for acquiring sports equipment. The second and third position winner universities also get award money.

H. Dhyan Chand Award for Lifetime Achievement in Sports and Games

511. The Dhyan Chand Award for Lifetime Achievement in Sports and Games has been instituted from 2002 to honour those sportspersons who have contributed to sports by their performance and continue to contribute to promotion of sports even after their retirement from active sporting career. The award carries a cash award, a plaque, a scroll of honour and a ceremonial dress.

II. Working as Sports Coach or Teacher

512. In schools, physical education is a subject with a curriculum which is taught by a sport teacher and there may also be a sports coach to be present in the field. Physical education instructors train students on how to remain fit and fine; they also encourage them to participate in various games and sporting events. There is no limit as to how long can one coach or teach provided that he is fit to do so. For those who start early, there lies ahead a long career since experience has a bearing and counts a lot in sports. Coaching can mean anything from coaching a beginner to an Olympic athlete.

III. Working as a Leisure Club Manager

513. Many hotels and clubs in India are providing sports facilities these days, covering a wide range of interests like archery, judo and gymnastics. Managers who take care of these leisure clubs provide a number of services to the clients. Their responsibilities are mostly of administrative nature. They manage accounts, do planning for the general public and arrange for specialized coaching in sports like aerobics and swimming. They have to ensure that the premises, pool and equipment such as badminton nets and cricket mats are properly maintained.

IV. Sports Journalism

514. Another facet of sports that has interested a lot of young men and retired professionals is sports journalism. One who has a knack for writing and can understand the rules of the game can join a newspaper or a magazine as a sports reporter or a columnist. A sports photographer is expected to capture the most thrilling action of the game, be it soccer, hockey or cricket, for which he should not only be alert but also be a bit intuitive. With sports programmes hitting popularity charts week after week, there is also a rush to produce sports-based items for the small screen. It has opened up doors to a lucrative second career for many retired sports personalities. If one has a good voice and is confident to speak without a pause, then probably a career as a commentator is best suited for him. Breathless commentaries, after all, contribute a lot in making the turn of the event all the more exciting and enjoyable.

V. Scheme for Sportsman Living in Indigent Conditions

515. Pandit Deendayal Upadhyay National Welfare Fund for Sportspersons (PDUNWFS) was set up in March, 1982 with a view to assisting outstanding sportspersons of the past, living in indigent circumstances, who had brought glory to the country in sports. The scheme was reviewed and revised in July 2009. Scheme of National Welfare Fund of Sportspersons has been revised in May 2016. Scope of the scheme has been expanded and more sportspersons are being considered for financial assistance. The scheme has been renamed as Pandit Deendayal Upadhyay National Welfare Fund for sportspersons on 22 September 2017. The scheme was again reviewed and revised on 29 January 2019 incorporating the time lines for processing the application received in a time bound manner in the Ministry. Quantum of assistance from the fund has also been substantially enhanced. The scheme was further reviewed and revised on 15 May 2020. The amount of annual income for being eligible for getting financial assistance from the fund has been raised to INR 8 lakh from all sources.

516. The sportspersons and family members of the sportspersons will be eligible for following amounts of financial assistance:

(i) Financial assistance to an outstanding sportsperson now living in indigent circumstances, subject to a maximum of INR 5 lakh. In addition to this, a provision of monthly pension of INR 5,000 (Rupees five thousand) may be considered for specific period taking into consideration merit of request of a sportsperson.
(ii) Financial assistance subject to a maximum of INR 5 lakh may be granted to families of deceased sportspersons.
(iii) Financial assistance not exceeding INR 10 lakh may be provided for Medical Treatment to sportspersons or family members.

(iv) Financial assistance not exceeding INR 10 lakh may be provided for injuries sustained during training for and participation in sports competitions listed in the scheme but will also include sub-junior and junior category competitions.

(v) Financial assistance not exceeding INR 2.5 lakh may be provided for training, procurement of equipment and participation in national and international sports events to sportspersons, whose parents are living in indigent circumstances.

Sportspersons belonging to those sport disciplines whose federations are either derecognized or whose recognition has been suspended by the government or the federations, who has so far not got the recognition of the government, will also be eligible for assistance for this purpose.

(vi) Financial assistance up to INR 2 lakh may be provided to coaches and support personnel who have been attached with national coaching camps for senior category players and national teams (senior category), and umpires, referees and match officials, who have been associated with recognized national championships (senior category) and international tournaments (senior category) in the sports disciplines included in Olympics, Asian Games and Commonwealth Games who are living in indigent circumstances or to family members of such deceased support personnel living in indigent circumstances.

(vii) Financial assistance up to INR 4 lakh may be provided for medical treatment to coaches and support personnel who are living in indigent circumstances or to family members of such deceased support personnel living in indigent circumstances.

Part IV. Doping in Sports

Introduction

517. The problem of doping has now assumed alarming proportions in the sports world. Every now and then, the instances of doping are reported. In pursuit of gold, glory and fame some sportspersons use performance-enhancing substances in an effort to gain competitive edge over the others so that they can win but are caught in the process. Sport is about fair play which requires proper attitude and behaviour with the belief that sports is an ethical pursuit. The achievement in sports should not be through drug abuse or any other form of exploitation. By resorting to doping for winning a game, the true competitive spirit and purpose of sport is lost.

§1. Doping Defined

518. In the broadest sense of the term, doping signifies use and consumption of a foreign substances or agent to enhance one's sporting performance. Doping is the deliberate or inadvertent use by sportspersons of a substance or method banned by Medical Commission of IOC and World Anti-Doping Agency (WADA). Doping is prohibited because its presence undermines the fundamental joy of sports, collective pursuit of human and sporting excellence and gives an unfair advantage to the user of the drug or method against their competitors. Besides, this, doping also adversely affects the health of the sportspersons and can have a number of side effects. New challenges are posed in the field of doping as new and more complicated substances are being used by the sportsman which are sometimes difficult to trace. So at the same time testing methods must be able to meet with the challenge.

§2. Origin of the Word 'Dope'

519. The history of doping is very old and it may be as old as competitive sports itself. Ancient Greek athletes used special diets to strengthen the body and stimulating portions. There are many views with respect to origin of the word 'dope'. The word 'doping' is probably derived from the Dutch word 'dope', an alcoholic beverage made of grape skins used by Zulu warriors. The word 'doping' has either originated from 'Boer language' or from English. In Boer language, word 'dope' means strong liquor used as a stimulant in religious festivals. The English verb 'to dope' which means 'to administer a stimulant' and noun 'dope' meaning 'stimulating substance' can also possibly be the originator of this term. However, the use of the word 'doping' in sports perhaps started around the end of the nineteenth century, and it stood for a particular blend of opium, other narcotics and tobacco given to race horses in North Africa.

§3. Types of Doping

I. Synthetic Hormones

520. The emergence of synthetic hormones, invented in the 1930s has altered the basic nature of doping. By the 1970s, anabolic steroids were widely used, especially in those sports where muscle strength was required. Anabolic steroids are substances that assist in muscle growth. The most common type is anabolic-androgenic steroids like nandrolone and stanozolol which are synthetic chemicals which simulate the hormone testosterone.

The beta-blockers, medicines used by heart patients to reduce blood pressure and heart rate were used in sports where calming the nerves could be useful, like archery or shooting. Beta-blockers are banned only in some sports.

521. The next stage in doping came with the 'designer steroids' like tetrahydrogestrinone. These chemically manufactured substances had effects similar to anabolic steroids, but were superior to them from the doper's point of view, as these escape the tests that were meant to detect steroid use.

522. Another development was the entry of erythropoietin (EPO), which induces the production of red blood cells in the body. Since the Red Blood Corpuscles determine how much oxygen is carried by the blood and is a carrier and distributor of oxygen to the entire body and the amount of oxygen reaching muscles in turn determines how well they perform, EPO clearly helps to enhance performance.

523. The use of EPO in that sense seeks to achieve exactly what 'blood doping' did earlier. This was the practice of an athlete enhancing the amount of blood in the body just before competition. This could be done either by the athlete using extra blood from a donor, or by extracting some of his own blood, waiting for the body to make up the deficit and then re-injecting the extracted blood.

II. Genetic Doping

524. Genetic doping is not different from earlier forms of doping in the effect it has on the body. What is different is the method of achieving the results. Thus, while earlier an athlete may have injected testosterone or EPO, what now seems possible is that a gene can be introduced into the body to make the body itself produce more of these substances than it normally would.

III. Masking Agents

525. These are drugs (like diuretics) that can be used by athletes to mask the presence of other drugs. Since most tests involve the urine of the athlete, what they try to do is prevent the excretion of the banned substance in the urine. This is why anti-dope authorities have included masking agents in the list of banned substances.

§4. Medication of Sportspersons on Falling Ill

526. In case a sportsperson falls ill and requires administration of a drug which is banned drug from a sport point of view, the World Anti-Doping Code (WADC) allows for 'therapeutic use exemptions' in such cases but subject to very stringent guidelines.

§5. Treatment of Doping

527. Following the institution of the WADA, there has been increasing standardization and formation of a code. This code is the first one that has to be adopted by all countries that want to participate in the Olympics, or in any other international sport event.

Apart from treatment, the problem can also be averted by providing and dealing with dissatisfaction before these turn into complaints, problems or conflicts. Problem may arise out of confusion, indifference, frustration, anger, etc. Therefore, it is necessary that proactive approach is to be adopted which may include consultation with the sportsperson against whom allegation is there, follow up and then rehabilitation of such a sportsperson.

528. There is dire need of enacting specific anti-doping legislation. Such a legislation must be framed with the help of experts from the field of medicine, sport, ethics and of course law. The National Sports Ethics Commission Bill, 2016 is an attempt in this direction. But it is still in the Bill form and has not become law.

§6. Reasons for Using Drugs

529. There is always enormous pressure on sportspersons to excel in competition so that they can remain in the team and in the race for medals and awards. Winning a game can reap a sportsperson a lot of money, fame and change his or her fortunes. Some drugs and other practices can boost their efforts and give them a shortcut even as they risk their health and athletic careers. Drugs are also misused to relax, cope with stress or boost the confidence of the users.

I. Building of Physique

530. An athlete may want to build mass and strength of muscles and/or bones, increase delivery of oxygen to exercising tissues, mask pain, stimulate the body, relax, reduce weight and hide the use of other drugs and for this purpose he uses the banned drugs. Once it is clear after testing that there has been use of banned drug, disciplinary action can be taken against him or her as the case may be.

II. Masking of Banned Drugs

531. Masking of banned drugs is the most crucial aspect of doping. There are certain drugs which mask the banned substances with agents that will not show in the testing process. Diuretics can be used to reduce the presence of drugs in urine samples. Other compounds, including epitestosterone, plasma expanders and secretion inhibitors, can be used to reduce the presence of banned substance in blood samples. There are various ways of taking care of and detecting this phenomenon, but these methods of detection must improve on continuous basis as new masking ways are discovered and used by the sportspersons.

532. The dope control mechanism was earlier suffering from a clear-cut policy and implementation. The problems being faced are as follows:

(a) No strict punishment to dope cheats.
(b) No action against federations, coaches, doctors in doping cases.
(c) Dope offenders have even managed to walk away with certain awards; very little anti-doping activity and no awareness campaigns.
(d) No proper professional care and medical advice for sportspersons, prompting them to take shortcuts to win.

After formation of NADA and NDTL, the anti-dope implementation mechanism has taken shape and situation has improved as India has complied with WADA Code and implemented NADA Rules to take care of any violation.

Chapter 1. Legal Framework

533. The alcohol, strychnine, caffeine and cocaine were often used by sportsmen involved in endurance sports in the nineteenth century. When Thomas Hicks won the Olympic marathon race in 1904, he used strychnine injections and shots of brandy. However, in modern sports, doping has taken a different complexion and it has culminated in use of substances that are known to have serious long-term side effects on the body of the sportsperson, but significantly enhance performance in the short term. The first moves to take action against doping were made in the 1920s. In 1928, the International Amateur Athletic Federation banned the use of stimulants. Other federations followed suit. However, these restrictions did not mean much, since there was no testing for the drugs.

534. This situation changed in 1966, when the UCI (cycling) and FIFA (football) introduced doping tests in their respective World Championships. In 1967, the IOC set up its medical commission and announced a list of prohibited substances. Drug tests were introduced at the Olympic Winter Games at Grenoble and at the Olympic Games in Mexico in 1968. Most international sports federations introduced drug testing by the 1970s. IOC was responsible for anti-doping in sports prior to the constitution of the WADA in 1999 in accordance with the convention. The first world conference on doping in sports was held in Lausanne, Switzerland in early 1999, which led to the establishment of WADA.

§1. Ordinary Legislation

535. India pledged its support to and has finally signed the Copenhagen Declaration of 2003 on doping in sports on 6 January 2004. It has paved the way for a more serious effort and establishment of a dope control regime. NADA and NDTL have been established. NDTL is WADA recognized and accredited dope control laboratory in India. The Copenhagen Declaration signed on 5 March 2003, by about eighty government representatives and a majority of the international sports federations, paved the way for the acceptance of the WADA Code. The declaration, as revised and adopted in Madrid in November 2007, sought to recognize the role of WADA in anti-doping measures around the world and supported its co-funding.

536. A large number of governments including all the major sporting powers of the world have signed the declaration. In addition to all the 202 National Olympic Committees (NOCs), all leading international federations including those in athletics, swimming, football, gymnastics, hockey, boxing, badminton, cycling, table tennis, basketball and volleyball, and national anti-doping organizations have also signed the declaration.

There is also an International Convention on Doping, namely, UNESCO Convention against Doping in Sport 2005 (Paris, 19 October 2005) which has been ratified by India.

I. The World Anti-Doping Code

537. The World Anti-Doping Agency (WADA) was established on 10 November 1999 in Lausanne to promote and coordinate the international fight against doping in sport. WADA was set up as a foundation under the initiative of the IOC with the support and participation of intergovernmental organizations, governments, public authorities and other public and private bodies fighting against doping in sport. The agency consists of equal representatives from the Olympic Movement and public authorities. Since 2004 when the World Anti-Doping Code (Code) came into force, a number of legal decisions have been rendered applying the rules of the World Anti-Doping Code (Code) by the CAS as well as other internal tribunals of international federations and national anti-doping organizations. WADA reviewed the global anti-doping code, which sets out common rules and sanctions for all sports and countries. At present, the amended WADA Code, 2021 has come into force.

II. The National Anti-Doping Bill 2021

538. The National Anti-Doping Bill, 2021 has been introduced in Lower House of the Parliament (Lok Sabha) on 17 December 2021. The Bill seeks to prohibit doping in sports and establish a NADA, which will replace the existing NADA. The Bill prohibits athletes, athlete support personnel and other persons from engaging in doping in sport. Support personnel include the coach, trainer, manager, team staff, medical personnel and other persons working with or treating or assisting an athlete. These persons must ensure that there is no violation of anti-doping rules which include: (i) presence of prohibited substances or its markers in an athlete's body, (ii) use, attempted use or possession of prohibited substances or methods, (iii) refusing to submit a sample, (iv) trafficking or attempted trafficking in prohibited substances or methods and (v) aiding or covering up such violations. If any athlete requires a prohibited substance or method due to a medical condition, they may apply to the NADA for a therapeutic use exemption.

539. Violation of rule by an individual athlete or athlete support personnel may result in: (i) disqualification of results including forfeiture of medals, points and prizes, (ii) ineligibility to participate in a competition or event for a prescribed period, (iii) financial sanctions and (iv) other consequences as may be prescribed. Consequences for team sports will be specified by regulations. Consequences for a violation will be determined by the National Anti-Doping Disciplinary Panel (ADDP) after a hearing.

540. Currently, anti-doping rules are implemented by the NADA, which was established as a society. The Bill provides for constituting this NADA as a body corporate headed by a DG appointed by the central government. Functions of the agency include: (i) planning, implementing and monitoring anti-doping activities, (ii) investigating anti-doping rule violations and (iii) promoting anti-doping research. The agency will have the power to collect personal data of athletes such as: (a) sex or gender, (ii) medical history and (iii) whereabouts information of athletes (for out-of-competition testing and collection of sample). The agency will also prescribe the procedure for collection, usage, processing and disclosure of such personal data.

The Bill to become a law has to be passed by both houses of Parliament and assented by the president. Thereafter, it is to be notified in official gazette.

III. The Narcotics Drugs and Psychotropic Substances Act, 1985

541. This Act prohibits possession of certain natural products and drugs as an offence and prescribe punishment dependant on the quantity of substance or drug. These substances are poppy, opium, cannabis manufactured drugs. The import and export of these substances and drugs are also prohibited and punishable. The quantity has been categorized as: (i) possession of small quantity; (ii) more than small but less than commercial; and (iii) commercial quantity. A special court has been set up to try cases arising out of this Act. This Act not only extends to the whole of India but is also applicable to all citizens of India even when they are outside India.

IV. National Sports Ethics Commission Bill, 2016 (Bill)

542. This Bill is an attempt to deter the doping by criminalizing it. It prescribes a jail term up to ten years. The Bill covers athlete, coach and member of sports federation and totally bans all those covered under the Bill. This Bill has not been passed so it has not become a law but is only a proposed legislation.

§2. Sports Regulation

I. National Anti-Doping Agency

543. The government has established and registered NADA and NDTL as societies so as to effectively deal with the problem of doping. NADA is an autonomous society. It is the main prosecuting agency and initiates proceedings against sportspersons who violate anti-doping norms. The Anti-Doping Rules of NADA, which are compliant with the Anti-Doping Code of WADA, have been finalized in consultation with IOA and NSFs and became effective from 1 January 2010. The various committees provided under Anti-Doping Rules have been established and became functional like ADDP, Anti-Doping Appeal Panel (ADAP) and Therapeutic Use Exemption Committee. NADA has taken a major step in sample collection process and dissemination of information.

A. Aims and Objectives of NADA

544. The following are the functions, aims and objectives of NADA:

(a) to promote, coordinate and monitor dope control programmes in sport;
(b) to act as prosecuting agency for initiating proceedings against alleged violations of anti-doping norms;
(c) to educate and train sportspersons, coaches and other supporting personnel about the harmful effects of dope;
(d) to develop the rationale for drug-free sports and national anti-doping policy;
(e) to get conducted in-competition and out-of-competition dope tests on sportspersons;
(f) to promote research and training and provide funding for the same;
(g) to harmonize the dope-related regulations in tune with the World Anti-Doping Code and the rules and regulations framed by the WADA from time to time.

B. NADA Code

545. The NADA Code has been amended to incorporate changes brought by WADA Code of 2021 and thus new NADA Code 2021 has been given effect. As per the Code, NSFs are required to adopt the NADA provisions in their rules. The government is fully committed to doping-free sport environment in the country. Financial assistance is extended to NADA and NDTL for anti-doping programmes.

C. Role of NADA

546. NADA has to play a major role by creating awareness among the sportspersons about anti-doping rules which is at present negligible. Another important aspect is availability of doctors and medical advisers whose supervision is required throughout so that inadvertently a player may not take a drug which is covered under the anti-doping norms. As Indian players are not very rich, so NADA has to provide all these facets and infrastructure without taking any charge from the sportspersons.

II. National Dope Testing Laboratory

547. The dope testing lab in India was first established in 1990 as Dope Control Centre under SAI. The lab got ISO/IEC 17025 accreditation in 2003 by National Accreditation Board for Testing and Calibration Laboratories (NABL) and WADA accreditation in September 2008. The accreditation status of NDTL is upgraded gradually as per the latest guidelines of both accreditation bodies (NABL and WADA). The present NDTL is an autonomous body established in 2008 under the MYAS, Government of India. It is accredited by NABL for ISO:IEC17025:2005 and WADA for testing of urine and blood samples from human sports. NDTL is one of the WADA-accredited laboratories in the world. NDTL has state of the art facilities for both routine and research activities. NDTL was registered in 2008 under Registration of Society Act, 1860. Apart from Human Dope Testing, NDTL has diversified in the area of Horse Dope Testing. This facility of horse dope testing came into existence in 2014 and provides testing services to all the horse race clubs in India and neighbouring countries.

In the beginning, the laboratory was located inside Jawaharlal Nehru Stadium and later on shifted to new independent premises in May 2009 with modern and well-equipped infrastructure. NDTL had grown up in terms of routine testing and research in the field of Human Dope Testing and diversified in the field of Horse Dope Testing. NDTL is also experienced in handling the task of dope testing in various mega sport events starting from the first Afro-Asian Games, 2003.

548. The MYAS has constituted the General Body and Governing Body of NDTL. The NDTL Society consists of seven experts from the disciplines of medical, legal and science. It has five officials, one sportsperson and four representatives from the IOA and NSF. The governing body is constituted of twelve members. A website of NDTL (<www.ndtlindia.com>) has been launched on 6 January 2010.

III. Functioning of NDTL

A. Development of Testing and Research

549. The main aim and function of NDTL is to develop systems and procedures for dope testing and advance research. In the process, it has to maintain close association with WADA and WADA-accredited laboratories. NDTL is to conduct research in the field of dope analysis, develop and improve upon drug testing methods. It conducts training programmes for the postgraduate students in biochemistry, forensic science and chemistry.

B. Quality Management System

550. NDTL is to maintain the Quality Management System as per ISO:IEC:17025:2005 and WADA International Standard of Laboratories (Version 05). These accreditations are maintained by conducting annual surveillance audit and reassessment audit.

C. Collaboration with WADA-Accredited Laboratories

551. The NDTL interacts with WADA-accredited labs in order to test samples for mega sporting events like Common Wealth Games. Bilateral cooperation agreement was signed with Drug Control Centers (DCCs) London in January 2010.

NDTL has also engaged in international testing. After getting accreditation, the tariff of testing of samples was fixed, and a large number of samples have been tested as part of national and international testing by NDTL.

D. Tests in NDTL

552. According to the 2020 WADA Testing Figures Report, India once again finds itself among the top two nations on Adverse Analytical Findings (AAF). There was a limited collection in 2020 because of Covid-19 but as compared to India's 55 AAFs, United States has 136. In 2020, NADA collected just 1186 samples (including blood), while the US 7756. Percentage-wise, India stands at 4.6% while the US just 1.8%. As there were less competitions and collection of samples started somewhere in October so in competition collections stood at 708 and out-of-competition number was 423. The number of samples collected in the previous years was 4026 (2019 Testing Report), way more than what NADA collected during the Covid-affected year. In-competition urine sample numbers stood at 2248 while out of competition at 1778.

553. NDTL has also gone under Proficiency Testing (PT) which helps monitor the performance of the lab and to take corrective measures. Participation in PT programme is mandatory for ISO:IEC:17025:2005 accreditation which is in turn necessary for getting WADA accreditation. PT programme also establishes traceability of results in all WADA-accredited labs. NDTL has successfully participated in PT programmes of World Association of Anti-Doping Scientists, College of American Pathologists and Proficiency Testing of WADA.

554. As the government has signed the Copenhagen Declaration and the Indian Olympic committee has signed the World Anti-Doping Code, therefore India is to abide by the principles of the World Anti-Doping Code, which states: in Article 6.1 dealing with use of approved laboratories: 'Doping control samples shall be analysed only in WADA-accredited laboratories or as otherwise approved by WADA. Further, WADA's Code of ethics for the laboratories prohibits a laboratory from testing athletes by way of precaution before international events.' WADA recognizes only results of analyses made by its accredited laboratories.

IV. Doping Control Operational Guidelines

555. The operational guidelines have been designed to interpret the policy requirements and to provide operational direction for each of the venue positions. The following is the Doping Control Guide Policy:

(a) Doping controls involving urine and/or blood testing shall be undertaken in all sports. The procedures which follow are those applicable to in-competition and out-of-competition testing in relation to the national games, national level competitions, national coaching camps and selection trials.

(b) A condition of the competitor's entry in the national games, national level competitions, national coaching camps and selection trials is that the competitor agrees to comply with Anti-Doping Code and accordingly agrees to provide a urine sample being taken in accordance with the sampling procedure.
(c) Breath testing for alcohol shall also be undertaken in same sports as determined by the relevant national federation. The national federation shall select the competitors to be subjected to such testing and shall conduct the testing in accordance with the national federation's Doping Control rules and regulations.
(d) The doping control for urine testing includes the first four competitors in the final classification and others chosen at random.
(e) The national federations in consultation with other authorities will determine the means of selecting those competitors to be checked at random in competition. A Doping Control Protocol for urine testing outlining the agreed number and distribution of tests has been signed by all national federations and IOA Anti-Doping Commission (IOA ADC).
(f) Notwithstanding the planned test, the IOA ADC shall have the right to request, without justifying the reason therefore, that any competitor undergo a doping test at any time during the national games or national level competition/ coaching camps/selection trials.
(g) A competitor may be subject to doping on more than one occasion during coaching camps.

556. The sporting bodies in India are under the umbrella of the National Olympic Committee which has adopted the Code relating to doping, therefore sporting bodies are required to send their samples to NDTL which is WADA-accredited lab. This has been fully formalized as India has ratified the UNESCO Convention adopted by UNESCO General Conference. The UNESCO Convention is a legally binding document for governments, and India has to fully comply with the Code. Establishment of NADA and NDTL is a step in the direction of meeting obligations under UNESCO Convention against doping in sport. The government has established NADA as the apex body to implement anti-doping measures. The NADA Rules shall be deemed to have been notified under National Sports Development Bill, 2013. All the NSFs and National Olympic Committee shall be bound by NADA Rules (section 13(1)). NDTL accredited by the WADA shall be the NDTL (section 19(1)).

557. Further, the National Sports Development Bill, 2013[28] in Chapter IV provides for promotion of drug-free sport and provisions against other unethical practices. The government in furtherance of this objective has established NADA and NDTL and shall provide financial and other support to help discharge its duties effectively (section 13(2)). It shall be the duty of all NSF, the National Olympic Committee, the SAI and other sports bodies and officials and support personnel

28. Still not a law as it has not been passed by the Parliament.

including coaches, trainers, team doctors, team managers, physiotherapists to prevent doping in sports (section 13(4)). The Central Government is required to display on its website the anti-doping measures taken by it and the details of the financial assistance given.

The Indian sportspersons participating in major international competitions are being dope-tested before departure and then only cleared. The need of the hour is that general awareness about doping norms be created among sportspersons as to what are permissible, and prohibited substances and drugs listed by WADA. More importantly, sportspersons must be made aware of banned substances present in common drugs which may be taken by them in ordinary course. NADA has to examine practical and legal implication keeping in view Indian situations. Recently an Indian shot-put champion was suspended for four years by NADA for flunking four dope tests in 2017 and all competitive results were scratched from the date of suspension i.e., 20 July 2017. The athlete will lose gold won in the 2017 Asian Championship and other medals (The Times of India, 10 April 2019).

V. Efforts Made to Prevent Doping

558. The NADA, the IOAs and NSFs are primarily the action taking authorities against sportspersons who are found guilty of a doping offence. The Government of India, through SAI has made serious efforts to keep away sportspersons from use of any kind of prohibited drugs as per WADA Code. Ways which have been resorted to control the doping are more random dope tests; offenders to be stripped of all awards; increased awareness among sportspersons about side effects of doping; take action against coaches and officials involved; getting international accreditation for the dope testing lab.

A. Controlling the Environment

559. During the coaching camps, sportspersons are educated and regularly counselled about the banned drugs. Apart from this, the sports medicine doctors at NIS, Patiala and other regional centres conduct lecture, wherever camps are held, to educate the players not to use any banned drugs. At the time of commencement of the camp, each player is being provided with documents and brochures about the banned substances. The list of banned drugs and placards for education of players are put in the rooms of the campers. Rooms and belongings of the players are also searched and checked at regular intervals to see that no banned drugs are kept or used besides testing the urine samples of sportspersons during the coaching camps at random. Mere possession of a banned drug can be taken as violation of Anti-Doping Rule (Article 2.6(1)). However, WADA Code has made exceptions with respect to certain drugs in certain sports which can be taken under medical prescription and supervision. But these drugs are to be taken after following Therapeutic Use Exemption Provisions and Procedures. As per WADA Code, athlete is required to file his whereabouts information and make himself available for out-of-competition testing at all times during the year.

B. Urine Samples

560. The majority of performance-enhancing drugs used by athletes can be detected by testing the samples of urine. An athlete is told by a drug control officer to submit a urine sample for testing. The sample is then sent to a laboratory for analysis and the results are reported back to the governing athletic agency. For detection of some banned substances, blood samples are required and such samples are sent for testing.

VI. Action as per Rules

561. The NADA, the IOA and NSFs take action against guilty players as per their rules and the rules of the respective international sports federations. Sportspersons testing positive for dope are removed from the camp, and SAI Schemes benefit is not available to them and if they are already availing the benefits then it is withdrawn. If found guilty of doping, action is initiated against players as well as their coaches. The Government of India has stopped giving any assistance to sportspersons found guilty of doping offence under its sports promotion and other schemes.

562. As per the General Disciplinary Regulations of IOA, the president has the power to call for explanations from its member units where a sportsperson has been found guilty of use of dope or IOC prohibited substances, but no action has been taken by the concerned member unit. The recommendations of IOA President are placed before the General Body for appropriate disciplinary action. Further, under NADA Rules, the Anti-Disciplinary Panel, ADAP and the Therapeutic Use Exemption Committee have become operational so as to conduct fair hearings in an impartial way.

VII. Doping Instances

563. As per reports, the first doping instance in Indian sports was recorded in weightlifting. In 1986, three Indian lifters tested positive at the Asian Games and were banned for two years by the international body. Today, drugs are threatening the whole edifice of the game throughout the world and India is also having its share. It is significant to note that weightlifting is the game which has produced India's only woman medallist at the Olympics in the country. In the past couple of years, nine Indian weightlifters have been allegedly in the net of and charged for doping in international competitions such as the Asian Games, Asian Championship, World Championship and Juniors Championship. This menace grew as there were no clear-cut procedures and strict action could not be taken. Now systems have been streamlined and the IOA and Weightlifting Federation of India are required and ready to act in time. These bodies cannot remain moot spectator to this and have to take strict and timely action so that this menace can be prevented.

564. Nandrolone was the drug which one athlete was alleged to have taken at the 2002 Asian Games. However, athlete was later cleared by the Sushil Salwan Committee which was the first-ever inquiry held in the country on doping in sports. But again cases of twenty-two athletes emerged in Hyderabad. It was a grim reminder that the dope prevention system in the country is not very strong and effective so as to properly fight doping and requires strengthening. It cannot be efficiently enforced and accomplished simply by collecting urine samples during competitions and waiting for the report. For prevention, a whole system of checks and balances has now been evolved by which an eye is kept on sportspersons for the rest of the year. There is also periodic and proper counselling from time to time.

VIII. Responsibility of Athletes

565. The Anti-Doping Rules place a strict responsibility on athletes to be aware of what substances enter their bodies. In India, most athletes are not educated to the same level as in foreign countries and lack adequate access to resources which would enable them to identify the ingredients of what they consume. When athletes attend and reside at training camps for several months in a year, the camps are responsible for their food and supplements and the athletes cannot be expected to monitor or refuse the food being provided to them in these camps or by their coaches. In a case, six Indian athletes who were gold medallists in the Commonwealth Games were tested positive for the presence of anabolic steroids in their urine samples taken both in and out of competition.

566. The NDTL in New Delhi was given a special sanction to test all the supplements consumed by the athletes. The NDTL confirmed that Ginseng pills consumed by the athletes contained prohibited substances. It was not disputed that their coach provided these pills to them. It was the responsibility of the SAI to provide for all supplements but since this was not done in spite of repeated requests, the coach purchased bottles of these supplements.

567. The ADDP held that the athletes bore ‘no significant fault or negligence’ and issued a reprimand and suspension of athlete for a period of one year from the date of the positive test. The NADA and the WADA filed an appeal against the first instance decision of the ADDP and the athletes also filed cross-appeals against the first instance decision of the ADDP praying for a complete reprieve. In appeal, the ADDP upheld its first instance decision. Thereafter, the International Athletic Federation (IAF), the WADA and the NADA filed a second appeal against the decision of the ADAP before the CASs, Lausanne. The CAS, under the Anti-Doping Rules of the IAF and the WADC read with the NADA Anti-Doping Rules, held that the athletes were at fault and issued the full sanction of two years’ ineligibility for four of the athletes.

So, it is the athletes who ended up losing out the most. The NADA Anti-Doping Rules do not take the circumstances surrounding Indian athletes into consideration. One of the athletes involved in the proceedings was a tribal girl who was unable to converse in English or Hindi. She could not be expected to log on to the Internet and conduct research on the ingredients and dangers of supplements that contain Ginseng which were given to her by her coach.

568. The NADA Anti-Doping Rules specifically state that it is the fault of the athlete if the supplements consumed are contaminated. An athlete is expected to conduct research before consuming any supplement. However, there is a lack of laboratories in India that carry out such specific tests on supplements and if an athlete finds such a laboratory, the cost of carrying out the tests are very high. The NADA has to take steps to educate athletes about the dangers of doping. Athletes should be provided with safeguards against their seniors and coaches. They should be made aware of doping substances and methods. NADA should not only engage in deterrent measures by punishing athletes but should also educate and empower them so that they can avoid doping.

IX. Position of Coaches, Doctors and Federations

569. The sportspersons caught doping should not be let off with a warning or light punishment; they must be held accountable for bringing disgrace to the country. Problem was further compounded because of the fact that if athletes got away with light punishments, their coaches, doctors and federations – who stand also to gain from the success of a sportsperson – were never held to account. This is quite contrary to international rule. A landmark declaration on anti-doping signed at Lausanne (Switzerland) in 1999 by the IOC recommended that 'more severe sanction should apply to coaches, officials and doctors guilty of violation of the Olympic movement's anti-doping code'.

570. The Salwan Committee commented on the dubious role of the coaches when coaches took a line that they had never heard of nandrolone, which was found in the athlete's urine samples. As coaches, at least they ought to be aware of the names and descriptions of the banned drugs so that they can ensure that the athlete stays away from these.

X. Grant of Awards and Doping

571. Another reason why Indian sports were losing its fight against drugs was because while conferring the awards, which carried lucrative cash reward, cognizance of drug-offenders was not taken into account. Such award winners were getting cash award of substantial amount from the Sports Ministry. To discourage doping no award is now given to those athletes, who had earlier been caught for doping and had served a suspension.

To a large extent, the race to win at any cost has been triggered besides name and fame, by the rich incentives in sports today. Certain State governments like Andhra Pradesh had announced unprecedented hikes in prize money for the national games and such huge prize money could be one of the reasons why performance-enhancing drugs are becoming popular. Such trend may abet doping.

572. According to Salwan Committee, the monetary problem for sportspersons starts because federations do not pay adequate or handsome amounts so that they can look after themselves and their family well. There is also an urgent need for education of sportspersons on drugs and anti-doping activity. The awareness programmes are now being conducted by the NADA. Though creating awareness among athletes through conducting workshops and other programmes is mentioned as one of the prime duties of the National Olympic Committees by the world's highest body on anti-doping – WADA.

§3. Sports Courts

I. Anti-Doping Panel

573. To conduct fair hearings in an impartial way in regard to cases of Anti-Doping Rule violation, two panels namely, ADDP and ADAP have been constituted w.e.f. 16 October 2017. The panel has been constituted as per Article 8 and Article 13 of Anti-Doping Rules 2015.

II. The ADDP

574. This panel is headed by retired district and session judge with members from legal, medical and sports background. During the period 2017–2018 the panel held fifty-seven sittings. Total of fifty cases were decided and the athletes were imposed applicable sanctions. The remaining cases are under process of hearing.

III. The ADAP

575. This panel is headed by a retired High Court Judge and Sr. Advocate of Supreme Court who acts as Chairman/Vice Chairman and members are eminent persons from medical and sports field.

IV. Action Taken by IOA with Respect to Doping

576. The IOA is not a helpless body. It is making all efforts and taking actions so as to fight against dope. More comprehensive dope tests are to be conducted in the coaching camp. The tests should be conducted even on those who are not selected during trials so that to keep an eye on everyone. The Sports Ministry is putting one of the conditions that sportspersons testing positive for drugs will not be considered for the Arjuna Awards. IOA can take while dealing with cases of doping, all those actions which it otherwise is entitled to take in normal course

A. Disciplinary Actions

577. The IOA member units are liable to the following disciplinary actions:

(a) Caution.
(b) Warning.
(c) Suspension for a specified period of time.
(d) Expulsion from IOA.

The following conditions are to be satisfied in this respect:

- No penalty can be imposed before the unit at fault has been heard at the interrogation specially conducted for this purpose.
- Should an affiliate unit fail to present itself through its accredited office-bearer at the interrogation, it shall be considered as having been interrogated.
- As a general rule, except in special circumstances duly appreciated, suspension shall be applied as a temporary measure.

Disciplinary sanction will not be taken unless supported by two-thirds of the General Assembly Members present and voting.

B. Appeal

578. All NSFs as well as State Olympic Associations affiliated to the IOA commit themselves to appeal only to the President of the IOA in the event of any differences which may arise with regards to the functioning of the NSFs or Associations or State Olympic Associations within its laid down statutes and regulations. NSFs or Association is not allowed to appeal to any other body or jurisdiction.

C. Unsportsmanlike Behaviour and Acts of Violence

579. During the Olympic, Commonwealth Games, Asian Games, SAF Games and national games, or any other international competitions, any unsportsmanlike behaviour on the part of a sportsman or sportswoman, official or coach, which includes insulting, making undesirable gestures, abusing the decision of the judges or referees and provoking the opponents or spectators, etc., in a word, committing any act not in keeping with the propriety of sports, can be punished.

D. Residual Powers

580. In the event of disagreement concerning the Disciplinary Rules, the interpretation of these regulations falls within the competence of IOA Executive Council, which is the final authority in this respect.

E. Disaffiliation, De-recognition or Suspension

581. The IOA General Assembly, on the recommendation of the President IOA, either directly or through the IOA Executive Council, based on its discretion, can consider disaffiliation or de-recognition or suspension of the NSFs or Associations or State Olympic Association *inter alia* on certain grounds, after ensuring that a show-cause notice has been served and an explanation has been obtained from the organization, considered and recommended for disaffiliation, de-recognition or suspension. The decision of the IOA General Assembly must be supported by two-thirds majority votes of the members present and voting.

F. Expulsion

582. In the event of anybody related to sport is indulging in activities, which are prejudicial to the promotion of sports, including doping or the efficient functioning of the concerned NSF, Association or State Olympic Association without utilizing the available resources of the IOA General Assembly can issue a directive to take necessary action in the matter.

583. The IOA General Assembly before expulsion is to issue, a show-cause notice and an explanation to be obtained and considered from the individual, or group of individuals, recommended for disciplinary action. The decision for expulsion by the IOA General Assembly is required to be supported by two-thirds majority of votes of the members present and voting.

§4. CASE LAW

584. India is a signatory to the Copenhagen Declaration on Anti-Doping and the UNESCO International Convention against Doping. The Government of India set up the NADA as a registered society on 24 November 2005. NADA accepted a revised version of the WADC on 7 March 2008 and framed the Anti-Doping Rules of NADA in conformity with the WADC. The Anti-Doping Rules place a strict responsibility on athletes to be aware of what substances enter their bodies. However, in India, most athletes are not educated to the same level as in foreign countries and lack adequate access to resources which would enable them to identify the ingredients of what they consume.

I. Case Relating to Ginseng Pills

585. In one case, six Indian athletes who were gold medallists in the Commonwealth Games, tested positive for the presence of anabolic steroids in their urine samples taken both in and out of competition. The NDTL in New Delhi was given a special sanction to test all the supplements consumed by the athletes. The NDTL confirmed that Ginseng pills consumed by the athletes contained prohibited substances. It was not disputed that their coach provided these pills to them. It was the responsibility of the SAI to provide for all supplements but since this was not done in spite of repeated requests, the coach purchased bottles of these supplements.

The ADDP held that the athletes bore 'no significant fault or negligence' and issued a reprimand and suspension for a period of one year from the date of the positive test. The NADA and the WADA filed an appeal against the decision of the ADDP and the athletes also filed cross-appeals against the first instance decision of the ADDP praying for a complete reprieve. In appeal, the ADDP upheld its decision.

Thereafter, the IAF, the WADA and the NADA filed a second appeal against the decision of the ADAP before the CAss, Lausanne. The CAS, under the Anti-Doping Rules of the IAF and the WADC read with the NADA Anti-Doping Rules, held that the athletes were at fault and issued the full sanction of two years' ineligibility for four of the athletes.

586. The problem is that the NADA Anti-Doping Rules do not take the circumstances surrounding Indian athletes into consideration. One of the athletes involved in the proceedings was a tribal girl who was unable to converse in English or in Hindi. She could not be expected to log on to the Internet and conduct research on the ingredients and dangers of supplements that contain Ginseng which were given to her by her coach.

II. *Ms Dutee Chand* Case

587. In a landmark case, the CAS ruled on the International Association Athletes Federations ('IAAF') regulations on Hyperandrogenism where the challenge was brought by Ms Dutee Chand a renowned Indian athlete. The SAI, under whom the athlete had been training, supported the athlete's challenge of the regulations before the CAS. It was an accepted position of fact that the androgens in the athlete's body were naturally occurring and not a result of doping. The CAS ruled that it could not accept the Hyperandrogenism Regulations as the IAAF failed to discharge the burden of proving the degree to which performance was affected by testosterone levels; and set of hormones associated with masculinity. When it was found that her androgen levels were beyond the threshold prescribed in the IAAF Hyperandrogenism Regulations, she was prevented from participating in athletics events as a woman athlete.

588. The athlete contended that the Hyperandrogenism Regulations violated the non-discrimination principle of the International Olympic Charter by discriminating against her on the basis of a natural trait, i.e., naturally occurring androgens. Further, that the test of androgen levels on the premise that it affected athletic performance had no basis in science. The athlete also questioned the proportionality of the regulations, stating that the woman athlete was made to suffer stigma, loss of self-esteem, undergo medical procedures with harmful side effects, etc. as a result of the regulations.

The CAS, in an interim award, suspended the Hyperandrogenism Regulations for a period of two years, which time the IAAF was supposed to use to garner scientific evidence for the basis of the regulations, failing which they would be declared void.

III. *World Anti-Doping Agency v. Amit and NADA*

589. Amar, an Indian swimmer, tested positive to methylhexaneamine, a banned substance under the WADA Code, during an in-competition test at the Indian national championships in August 2010. The athlete was notified of the anti-doping rule violation in September 2010 (where he was provisionally suspended) but the case was subsequently heard for the first time by the ADDP two years later in September 2012. After further delays in the ADDP issuing its award, imposing a two-year suspension on 5 November 2012, taking into account the time Amar had served under his provisional suspension. Thus, the entire sanction was served by the time ADDP reached its final determination. While this delay illustrates procedural concerns, the athlete's appeal to the Anti-Doping Appellate Panel (ADAP) was heard on 13 March 2014, more than thirteen months after the required deadline under the NADA Rules and a decision was handed down by ADAP on 3 June 2014 – almost four years after the alleged anti-doping violation. On appeal, the CAS held that, in doing so, the NADA had 'undisputedly violated the Appellant's right to a procedure in line with the timing requirements'.

The sole arbitrator acknowledged that:

> Article 8.3 of the NADA ADR (which, in essence, follows Article 8.1 of the WADA Code) provides inter alia for detailed procedural rights of athletes as to being provided fair and timely information of the asserted anti-doping rule violation, an expedited hearing for a provisional suspension, and a fair hearing on whether the asserted anti-doping rule violation has been committed.

590. It was further acknowledged that this provision had not been complied with in the initial proceedings against the athlete. However, given that the CAS has the power for de novo review, the sole arbitrator determined that the procedural delays that took place before ADDP and ADAP can be cured by a full CAS hearing. Since the delay did not 'unduly prejudice his right to obtain evidence, interview witnesses, or adequately defend the claims brought against him'. The sole arbitrator held that 'while the NADA showed an alarming inability to effectively, timely, and appropriately handle the Appellant's case, such delay did not fundamentally violate the Appellant's procedural rights'. [(CAS 2014/A/3869), award of 23 November 2015].

Part V. Sport and Commerce

Introduction

591. Sports attract a large number of people, and sports events are not only seen in the field but everywhere as these are broadcast through electronic media. Further, sportspersons are liked and adored by the people. Some sportsmen have a large fan following and this factor is utilized and commercially exploited for promotion of consumer goods and other products. Hence, there is a commercial aspect to the sport which generates a lot of revenue for sportspersons and sport federations, clubs and associations. Therefore, there are various facets of commercial activities in sports which raise a number of issues. It may be related to prize money to be won, advertisements to be made on radio and televisions and other means of mass communication. The broadcasting rights of a game or any sport event fetch handsome returns. Without television revenue, some sports organization cannot even survive.

592. It is not only TV, print and radio advertising revenue that is growing but dynamic advertising, teams and franchise, and merchandise are all growing steadily. As each league gets stronger and the teams become known and popular, there will be more sponsorships. Non-cricket sports are no doubt a small but fast-growing segment. However, it might take time to reach the popularity cricket enjoys in India. Another advantage of developing other sports is that it gives advertisers multiple avenues to engage with their consumers on a year-long basis, across different sports.

593. IPL has been a real game changer and money spinner for the sport in India. It helped in establishing a successful model for packaging and marketing new leagues. But since IPL was a cricket league it had an inherent advantage being already popular. But the success story for some others has not been as smooth. For instance, the first professional league in India Premier Hockey League (PHL) – launched in 2005 by the IHF, Leisure Sports (a sports management company) and ESPN Star Sports, failed to get support from sponsors and viewers, and as a consequence was terminated in 2008. Similar was the fate of a few others as well.

594. There is immense scope for expansion of sports in India, especially since it is a high growth economy with an ever-growing middle class with more disposable income and leisure time. This situation has resulted in a rapid rise in advertising; most local and international companies are aggressively targeting this lucrative but underdeveloped market through sports.

Chapter 1. Public Regulations

595. The public regulation in the field of sports and commerce may include media and television rights; sponsoring; merchandising and ownership of club.

§1. The Media and Television Rights

596. In 2017, the TV-owning homes in India increased from 153.5 million in 2016 to 183 million. The number of rural households owning TV is 17% more than urban households. One of the major reasons attributed to this growth in TV sets is the increasing number of nuclear families without elders than ever before. India has a huge and expanding TV market which has still not been exploited to its fullest extent. India has a very large population which ensures large viewership. The cable industry in India has witnessed very high growth rate in recent years. The sports broadcasting in India has transformed significantly and broadcasters are looking to diversify their portfolios with a variety of sports other than cricket to keep the viewership rising. With over 675 million people having access to a TV in India, it is the second-largest market for broadcast media after China and has the potential to drive subscription revenue in addition to advertising revenue.

597. The content on television is regulated in multiple ways which range from statutory regulation to self-regulation. However, in India, there are on an average two new channels launched every month and a new show is launched every third day. Also, there are about 800 channels in India across more than twenty languages. A single monolithic regulatory mechanism is impossible to supervise and regulate the content of this magnitude. Hence, the content is classified to facilitate better regulation.

598. Each of the categories is regulated by statutes and self-regulatory codes supervised by statutory and self-regulated bodies. The content on TV is broadly classified as follows:

(i) Non-news and Current affairs (entertainment).
(ii) News and Current affairs.
(iii) Advertisements.
(iv) Films on Television.

1. Non-news and Current Affairs TV Channels

599. The content or 'programmes' on these channels are regulated by the Cable Television Networks (Regulation) Act, 1995 which consists of a programme code and the advertising code which all content transmitted or retransmitted on television must adhere to. The programme and the advertising codes are collectively called 'codes' and are mentioned in the Cable Television Networks (Rules), 1994.

The programme code largely regulates the content that should be shown on TV which includes content that may violate various statutes. For example, the programme code prohibits airing any content that may not be suitable for public viewing which may otherwise be prohibited under the Cinematograph Act, 1952. This code also prevents the airing of content that may be in contravention of the prevalent public policy such as obscenity, communal disharmony, etc.

600. The advertising code, on the contrary, regulates the content that can be advertised and prohibits advertising of those content that is in violation of public morality and decency and any other content that can create social disharmony, etc.

The above codes are enforced by the following bodies.

a. The Inter-Ministerial Committee(IMC)

601. This is a committee constituted by the Ministry of Information & Broadcasting (MIB) and looks into violations of any of the above codes and reports it to the MIB accordingly for various actions. A case in point was about NDTV India which was taken off-air by the MIB for a day due to violations of code that was not followed while reporting the terrorist encounter in Kashmir.

b. Electronic Media Monitoring Centre (EMMC)

602. This is another body established by the MIB to monitor the content of various TV channels for any violations of the above codes or statutes such as the Cable Act, etc. The EMMC after finding any violations reports it to the Inter-ministerial Committee for further action.

c. State Level and District Level Monitoring Committees

603. There are monitoring centres established at the district and the State levels. The district level monitoring committees are authorized to decide on any local content violating the code. In case of national level content violations, the district level committees may forward the complaints to the IMC through the State level committees.

604. All of the above-mentioned bodies are bodies of the State that have been constituted under certain statutory provisions. However, to ensure the independence of the media, a self-regulating provision has also been acknowledged by the State. To that end, an Indian Broadcasting Foundation (IBF) has been formed to form guidelines for regulating all content on TV across all forms of transmission, namely cable, terrestrial, DTH, IPTV, etc. The IBF has adopted Self-Regulation Guidelines and Content Code and Certification Rules, 2011, which are applicable to all non-news broadcast programmes on TV. The IBF has also established a Broadcast Content Complaints Council (BCCC), which receives complaints on any particular content broadcast on television. The complaint has to be filed with the BCCC within fourteen days of the first broadcast. Apart from this, the BCCC can also initiate Suo-Moto proceedings against any particular content broadcast on television.

2. News and Current Affairs TV Channels

605. Unlike the Press Club of India, which is a statutory body for regulating newsprint content, there is no statutory regulatory body to regulate content for the news channels in India. This has been a point of much debate as the news broadcasters invoke the freedom of fair and free media in a democracy is essential whereas the people on the other side advocate for some form of regulation as no institution is above the law. For the moment, there being no statutory regulatory mechanism, the news and the current affairs TV channels are regulated by a self-regulatory body known as the News Broadcasters Association (NBA) which has formulated a standards code known as the NBA Code.

606. The NBA has also laid down news broadcasting standards regulation as an industry standard and constituted under it News Broadcasting Standards Authority (NBSA) for disputes adjudication and to enforce the NBA code.

3. Advertisement

607. With increasing TV viewership, the advertisement revenue has become the main source of income and a very lucrative option for all the channels. However, the content of these advertisements has to be monitored. There is no statutory provision or body to regulate the ad content. Hence, a self-governing body called the Advertising Standards Council of India (ASCI) has been formed to regulate the ad content. The ASCI has prescribed an ASCI code to which all the ad content has to adhere to.

4. Films on Television

608. The State broadcaster known as the Broadcasting Corporation of India popularly known as the Prasar Bharti established under the Prasar Bharti (PB) Act, 1990, aims to conduct public broadcasting services to inform, educate and entertain the public and to ensure a balanced development of broadcasting on TV. The PB Act also provides for the establishment of a Broadcasting Council to receive any complaints with respect to content aired on different channels.

609. There has been a continuing debate as to the role of the State in controlling the media. The advocates of free media argue that independent media is essential for a sustainable democracy. On the contrary, any institution with unbridled freedom may lead to the creation of a Frankenstein monster. So, there has to be a line drawn to distinguish between regulation and censorship. With the advent of fake news and the repercussions it has, the State may be justified in placing restrictions where required, for example, in cases of national security reasons. Thus a combination of statutory and self-regulating bodies is the best way to protect the freedom of the content across all media.

610. In 2007, the Sports Broadcasting Signals (Mandatory Sharing with Prasar Bharti) Act was passed. The objective was to provide access to large numbers of listeners and viewers, on a free-to-air basis, of sporting events of national importance through mandatory sharing of sports broadcasting signals with Prasar Bharti. Any content right owner or holder television or radio broadcasting service provider shall not carry a live television broadcast on any cable or Direct-to-Home network or radio commentary broadcast in India of sporting event of national importance, unless it simultaneously shares the live broadcasting signal, without its advertisements, with the Prasar Bharti to enable them to retransmit the same on its terrestrial networks and Direct-to-Home networks in such manner and on such terms and conditions as may be specified.

611. The TRAI has, vide The Telecommunication Services (Broadcasting and Cable) (Eighth) (Addressable System) Tariff Order, 2017 dated 3 March 2017 and the subsequent amendment dated 30 March 2017 (Tariff Regulation), formulated a comprehensive framework for the broadcasting sector covering tariffs for Addressable TV distribution of TV broadcasting services across digital broadcasting delivery platforms (such as DTH, Cable TV, HITS, IPTV).

612. The provisions of the new Tariff Regulation have come into force. The provision requiring broadcasters to declare maximum retail price (MRP) per month payable by a subscriber for each pay channel offered on à la carte basis has now come into effect.

613. In TV broadcasting services, there are three main stakeholders, namely, broadcasters, distributors of TV channels and viewers/subscribers. Broadcasters provide channels, distributors establish their network and subscribers pay price for viewing TV channels. The amendment to the Cable Television Networks (Regulation) Act, 1995 (Cable TV Act) in 2011 implemented of digital addressable Cable TV system in India. The digitalization process was envisaged to be completed in four phases and is now complete.

614. Since the main source of revenue for broadcasters are advertisements and subscription fees, the existing Tariff Orders have led to reduction in revenues of broadcasters earned from advertisements resulting in lack of investment in niche and not so popular channels which in turn has led to a lack of choice for subscribers.

615. To facilitate choice for subscribers and to exercise their options in line with intention of lawmakers to choose individual channels, the new framework stipulates that broadcasters must declare to customer/subscribers the MRP of their à la carte channels and bouquets of pay channels. To ensure that prices of à la carte channels are kept reasonable, the maximum discount permissible for formation of a bouquet has been linked with sum of à la carte prices of the pay channels forming that bouquet. Full flexibility has been given to broadcasters to declare the price of their pay channels on à la carte basis.

616. Similarly, the bouquet offered by a distributor to a subscriber will be without any alteration in the composition of a bouquet by the broadcaster and a maximum discount of 15% can be provided while offering a bouquet by the distributor at a retail level. As far as à la carte price of pay channel by distributor is concerned, in no case it shall exceed the MRP per month declared by the broadcaster. Distributor can, also charge network capacity fee per month (with a cap of INR 130 up to initial 130 channels) from its subscribers for availing its distribution network capacity.

617. The net effect of fixing caps on discounts for bouquet by broadcaster and distributor will be a total maximum discount of approximately 30% on the bouquet of channels. Therefore, flexibility of formation of bouquet has been given to both broadcasters and distributors to such an extent that the total permissible discount does not kill à la carte choice.

618. The overhaul of the tariff plan was the need of the hour considering the limitation that subscribers can have the tariff plan in such a manner that even if distributor of TV channels would like to indulge in predatory pricing it will only have limited flexibility in determining the price of channels. The new framework will change the dynamics of business between the three stakeholders and will resolve certain long pending issues and at the same time is expected to give rise to new controversies.

619. The two major broadcasters namely Star India and Sony Pictures Networks (SPN) are competing intensely to acquire international sports properties. SPN, in fact, made a big move in August 2016 when it acquired Ten Sports from ZEE to diversify its portfolio. Before that, it joined hands with ESPN, marking the return of the global sports brand in India. Sports broadcasting has taken a new turn with the advent of various sports leagues. Broadcasters are vying for fresh properties, through global biggies and home-grown leagues, to increase their portfolio of TV channels as well as digital platforms. The major broadcasters such as Star and Sony understand viewers' pulse and know just what they want to watch. Their huge investments in non-cricketing sports have been reaping benefits for them. Five years ago, nobody was talking about kabaddi let alone watching it on TV. Today, it has become one of the top sports in the country. Another sport that has experienced similar rise is wrestling. During its first season in 2015, PWL was watched by an average of 31 million viewers per day.

I. Order Against Series of Infringers

620. In the case of *Ten Sports v. Taj*, the Delhi High Court came to the aid of the owners of broadcasting rights to the football World Cup. Owners of other Indian intellectual (IP) rights with a limited shelf life should be satisfied with the result. While Ronaldinho's perfect swerving goal against England was being celebrated by the Brazilian players at the FIFA World Cup in Japan, another team of men was busy taking photographs and recording evidence of the match as it was shown at a five-star hotel in Mumbai. This followed a landmark order by the Delhi High Court appointing a commissioner to enter the premises of any cable operator in India and record any evidence of unauthorized telecasting of the World Cup.

621. This court order in fact was an echo of the concept of 'John Doe' orders, familiar in the US, Canada, Australia and New Zealand granted against a class of unknown infringers. The Australian Copyright Council has defined these orders as 'a representative order against an identifiable class of defendants, rather than named persons, which allows the goods to be seized'. Generally, these orders are granted in the context of specific events, where the intellectual property rights have a limited shelf life and would lose its commercial value in a short time and there can be a series of infringers.

II. Marketing of Airtime

622. *Buddha Films Private Limited v. Prasar Bharti* (AIR 2001 Delhi 488) is an example of contractual aspects and interpretation of words 'signal' and 'airtime', and selling of broadcasting rights. The facts and other main aspects have been reproduced hereunder with certain modifications and are as follows:
The respondent Prasar Bharti Broadcasting Corporation of India (hereinafter to be referred as 'Prasar Bharti' for short) has made Doordarshan (DD) Sports Channel as an encrypted or any channel. Earlier to this it was free to air channel. This encryption of DD Sports Channel by Prasar Bharti has become cause of grievance to the appellant, namely Buddha Films Pvt. Ltd. According to the appellant this goes contrary to the agreement dated 17 February 2000 entered into between appellant and Prasar Bharti as per which there was an assurance given to the appellant the DD Sports Channel would remain free to air channel. The BCCI entered into contract dated 25 September 1999 with Prasar Bharti. As per this contract Prasar Bharti was given exclusive and full terrestrial (free to air or encrypted) and satellite (free to air and encrypted) rights and licences to telecast all domestic and international cricket matches played in India conducted by BCCI during the term of contract which is up to 30 September 2004. In turn Prasar Bharti invited bids for marketing of air time in India and overseas of the cricketing events conducted by the BCCI in India for the period from 1 January 2000 to 30 September 2004. The appellant also gave its bid. Bid of the appellant was accepted by Prasar Bharti vide letter dated 4 February 2000. It culminated into formal agreement dated 17 February 2000.

623. By the agreement dated 17 February 2000 Prasar Bharti granted to the appellant the rights for exclusive marketing or airtime in the Territory of Union of India in respect of all cricketing events conducted by BCCI during the period from 1 January 2000 to 30 September 2004. The agreement stipulates that domestic matches and test matches would be telecast live only on DD Sports (a satellite channel with a limited two hours live telecast of all test matches on DD-1 the National Channel which is both terrestrial and satellite). The highlights of the test matches shall also be telecast twice by Prasar Bharti on DD-1. In consideration for the award of the right for exclusive marketing of airtime, the appellant is to pay to Prasar Bharti minimum guaranteed revenue. Clause 8.1 while mentioning this consideration also stipulates the manner in which this amount is to be paid. It is also specified in this clause that if there are extra additional matches, then net revenue in excess of instalments of Minimum Assured Revenue (MAR) is to be paid. Provision is also made for reducing the MAR in the event countries named in the said clause are not able to participate or the series is not played due to any reason. Thus, genesis of the agreement is that appellant has to book advertisement by marketing airtime and generate revenue therefrom. It has to pay MAR of INR 450 crores to the Prasar Bharti for this purpose.

624. The channel is encrypted or coded in order to ensure that only that viewers or cable operator who has decoder can decode the signals and are able to view the same. After the channel has become encrypted pay channel, apprehension of the appellant is that the viewership would be affected thereby and in turn it would have adverse effect on the sale of airtime to prospective advertisers which will reduce the revenue and income of the appellant. The appellant therefore sent representations to Prasar Bharti for reviewing its decision to make DD Sports Channel as an encrypted channel. However, when it did not yield any results and in the meantime the test matches with Zimbabwe were to start, the appellant approached the court by filing petition under section 9 of the Arbitration and Conciliation Act, 1996 (hereinafter to be referred as 'the Act' for short).

625. The respondent argued that the contention of the appellant to the effect that Clause 1.2 of Part I of the tender enquiry which stipulated that DD Sports Channel was free-to-air was only a statement of fact prevailing as on that date and it did not contain any representation that this situation will continue forever or that situation will not change. Therefore, Prasar Bharti was within its right to convert DD Sports Channel into an encrypted or pay channel.

626. After converting DD Sports Channel into pay channel, Prasar Bharti has entered into contract with M/s. Modi Enterprises giving it right of marketing the encrypted channel or signal. The senior counsel for appellant argued that the matter was not considered in proper perspective. It was necessary to distinguish between 'signal' and 'airtime'. BCCI was the owner of the signal which was sold by it to Prasar Bharti and it is through this signal that the transmission is received. If the signal is free-to-air then any person can have access to the said signal. These are called satellite channels and are accessible to the viewers and cable operators without the installation of any decoder. No separate subscription is required to be paid by the viewers. On the contrary, if the signal is to be paid for, the channel is beamed through satellite, but a viewer cannot view the signal without a decoder which decodes the encrypted signal. Only those who pay for receiving the singles are provided with the decoders so that they can decode the signals and view the same.

627. Therefore, Clause 1.2 of Part-I was an assurance to the appellant that the channel would remain free-to-air. The learned counsel referred to various clauses of the agreement between BCCI and Prasar Bharti as well as in the tender enquiry forming part of contract between the appellant and Prasar Bharti, in order to demonstrate that it was almost a representation and assurance held out by Prasar Bharti to the appellant that during the period of this agreement the DD Sports Channel would remain free-to-air. The controversy on merit is that whether Prasar Bharti is obliged to continue Sports Channel on a free to air basis or is entitled to convert this channel into an encrypted or pay channel during the currency of agreement dated 17 February 2000 between the parties.

In a petition under section 9 of the Act court is to decide about the interim measures that can be made in the meantime.

628. After considering all the material aspect, the court felt:

> that balance of convenience is not in favour of granting any such order as claimed by the appellant and the injury which is likely to be suffered by Prasar Bharti in the event such order is granted and Prasar Bharti ultimately succeeds in arbitration would be much more than if such an order is not granted. Our conclusion rests on the following:
>
> 1. Prasar Bharti has admittedly entered into a contract with Modi Enterprises. Directing Prasar Bharti to make the channel free-to-air during the arbitration proceedings will have one definite consequence, namely, breach of contract between Modi Enterprises and Prasar Bharti.
> 2. This will not only have the effect of losing the revenue as settle in the said contract; it will also attract claims by Modi Enterprises on Prasar Bharti of such a breach. This will lead to litigation between Modi Enterprises and Prasar Bharti as well.
>
> Reversing the process at this stage would have adverse repercussions on the sale of foreign right, and it may even invite claims by such foreign parties against Prasar Bharti, thereby leading to further litigation. Even the image and good will of Prasar Bharti may come to disrepute in international arena.

629. 'The digital technology has definitely improved the picture quality of Sports Channel. The decoder is required for receiving the digital signals. It by adopting digital technology Prasar Bharti has also made it pay channel because of improved quality, its right to do so is difficult to question. Prasar Bharti has already made Sports Channel as encrypted or pay channel which is in vogue for quite some time. Judicial notice of the fact, as argued by learned counsel for Prasar Bharti, that all other Sports Channels like ESPN, Star Sports, etc. are paid channels can be taken. When all other Sports Channels are pay channels, it is not prudent to direct Prasar Bharti to revert back to free-to-air channel, that too by way of interim measure and pending arbitration which would ultimately decide the respective rights of the parties under the contract.'

630. 'The court came to the conclusion after the above deliberations that directing the Prasar Bharti to revert back to free-to-air channel will lead to more complications, chaos, unforeseen hardships and other difficulties including claims from various authorities on Prasar Bharti plus multiplicity of litigation. On the contrary, if the channel is allowed to continue as encrypted channel and the appellant ultimately succeeds in the arbitration, the Arbitral Tribunal can suitably compensate the appellant. Considerations regarding balance of convenience and irreparable loss and injury persuade us not to pass any order for interim relief. In the facts of the case, we are confident that the Arbitral Tribunal will be able to ultimately do complete justice. Therefore, at this stage no interim directions are called for.'

III. The Selling of Exclusive Rights

631. In the Taj Television case, the plaintiff was based in Dubai and owned and operated an exclusive sports channel, Ten Sports. The plaintiff had acquired exclusive rights to telecast the World Cup in India and certain other South Asian countries, from Kirch Sports, an entity that had in turn acquired the worldwide rights from FIFA. Ten Sports was broadcast from Dubai in an encrypted form and could be received only by cable operators with a decoder.

One of the plaintiffs was HMA Udyog, the exclusive distributor for the Ten Sports channel in India. On behalf of Taj Television, HMA Udyog had entered into specific licences with cable operators, allowing them to transmit the Ten Sports channel in India. Since the Ten Sports signal was an encrypted one, HMA Udyog also gave decoders to the licensed cable operators so they could decrypt the Ten Sports signal and transmit it to their subscribers.

632. Among the 40,000-plus cable operators (comprising MSOs, headends and link operators) in India, only about 3,500 had entered into licence arrangements with HMA Udyog. And of the large MSOs, only about 70% had entered into valid license arrangements. Even with the authorized MSOs, the practice was to extend licences unilaterally to areas not covered by the licence. In order to cater to a large, sport-loving audience, a number of unlicensed cable operators and MSOs were stealing the Ten Sports signals by tapping the wires of neighbouring cable operators which were licensed, and transmitting the stolen signals to their subscribers. This process known as return path or reverse path stealing is the most common form of cable piracy in India. Not only did the extensive volume of unauthorized transmissions cause the plaintiffs a huge loss of revenue, it also made it difficult to justify licence fees to those operators who had already entered into licences with them. In order to remain a commercially viable channel, the plaintiffs had no other option but to seek legal recourse.

A. *Broadcast Reproduction Rights*

633. Section 37 of the Copyright Act, 1957, grants certain exclusive rights to a broadcaster, known as the Broadcast Reproduction Right (BRR). The BRR is a special right that encompasses certain exclusive rights including rebroadcast of a broadcast or causing the broadcast to be heard or seen by the public. The BRRs subsist for a duration of twenty-five years from the beginning of the calendar year next following the year in which the broadcast is made.

In *Taj* case, the plaintiffs initially filed a lawsuit against a specific cable operator in Mumbai on the basis of a videotape that had been recorded from the home of one of the subscribers to the cable operator. The plaintiffs filed suit under section 37 of the Copyright Act, 1957. The BRR is a right distinct from the copyrights held for the contents of the broadcast. Therefore, in the case of a film that is broadcast, the film rights may belong to the producer, while the BRR may belong to the broadcasting organization. The court in this case issued an injunction preventing the party from transmitting the Ten Sports signals without authorization and appointed a commissioner to visit the premises of the defendant and seize equipment used in the illegal telecast.

634. During visit, the Commissioner observed that the unauthorized transmission was taking place at several other premises. In fact, with each passing day, the plaintiffs were also identifying more and more unauthorized cable operators. The plaintiffs became concerned that by the time they had identified and collected evidence of the specific infringing parties, the World Cup would be over. Therefore, the plaintiffs filed a second suit against certain specified cable operators and against fourteen unidentified 'John Does' who in the Indian context were referred to as 'Ashok Kumars', a common Indian name.

B. Foreign Judgments on the Issue

635. In the *Taj* case, the plaintiffs relied on a number of similar John Doe orders in various other jurisdictions to support an order of this kind in India. For example, in *Billy Joel and Root Beer Rags Ltd. v. Various John Does and ABC Co.* (499 F Supp 791), a US court restrained unidentified bootleggers from selling counterfeit merchandise bearing the name or likeness of Billy Joel outside concert halls where he was performing. The court captured perfectly the need for a John Doe order when it stated:

> Were the injunction to be denied, the plaintiffs would be without any legal means to prevent what is clearly a blatant infringement of their valid property rights. While the proposed remedy is novel, that in itself should not weigh against its adoption by this court. A court of equity is free to fashion whatever remedies will adequately protect the rights of the parties before it.

636. The justification for permitting an unnamed defendant was explained as follows:

> The problem of the defendants' identities is met, I believe, by the fact that copies of the summons, complaint, and restraining order itself will be served on all. A similar case is reported from *New Zealand in Tony Blain Pty. Ltd. v. Splain and Other Persons* (1994, FSR 497), where the plaintiff asked for an ex parte order enjoining the sale of products associated with the popular entertainers Metallica and Paul McCartney. During the dates of their concerts, the High Court of New Zealand enjoined John Doe and Jane Doe defendants. The

court based its order on the plaintiff's reasonable apprehension that these John Doe and Jane Doe bootleggers would hawk their goods outside the concert venues and the persons from whom Billy Joel merchandise is seized on the night of the concert. These parties will be informed that whether or not they reveal their names they may appear in court on 16 July 1980, to contest the seizures. Plaintiffs, meanwhile, have posted a bond to cover any damages that may be incurred.

637. The court noted the fact that persons who cannot be identified at this stage of the proceeding is no bar to relief against persons who may be identified at a relevant time. It is not the name but the identity and identification of infringing persons which is relevant. The identity may not be immediately established but persons infringing will be identified by their act of infringement. Jane Doe and John Doe will be known by their works.

In *EMI Records Ltd. v. Kudhail* (1985, FSR 36), a court in the UK passed a restraining order against a class of defendants who were all music cassette counterfeiters avoiding the attention of trading standards officers. There was a common interest among them in preventing anybody from finding out where the counterfeit cassettes came from. Since the secrecy of the defendants' network prevented the plaintiff from finding out the source of infringement, the court held that a class action was justified.

638. Based on these overseas legal rulings, Ten Sports argued that Indian law is flexible enough to provide for an order in the John Doe style. For example, Order 7 Rule 1C of the Civil Procedure Code (CPC) required that the defendant's name and address be stated, only 'so far as they can be ascertained'. Similarly, Order 1 Rule 8 of the CPC permits the filing of a 'class action', thereby justifying an order against a class of infringers. The plaintiffs also argued that the practice of obtaining orders against unknown persons in criminal matters is fairly common. A civil proceeding is far less intrusive than a criminal one and therefore it is only right and proper that this concept of unknown parties be extended to civil proceedings as well. Finally, the plaintiffs relied on the inherent powers of the court to make the orders necessary for justice to be done.

C. Order of General Application or John Doe Order

639. After taking into account the various case laws and commentaries from other jurisdictions cited by the plaintiffs, the court found that Indian law did permit an order similar to a John Doe. However, owing to the unique nature of the cable industry in India and the rampant abuse of IP rights by cable operators, the judge found it necessary to go beyond a traditional John Doe order. In the court's words: 'Undoubtedly the cable operators in India have a long history of violating copyrights. A very large number of court orders are testimony to this. The cable operators are encouraged owing to the unique nature of the cable piracy and the unstructured nature of the cable industry, the speed with which any trace of infringement can be erased by the cable operators, enforcement of rights in conservative nature is unlikely to redress effectively the plaintiff's grievance.'

640. The court passed an order that applied to the cable industry in general, without restricting it to a specified number of unknown defendants. It must be remembered that in the US only ten John Doe defendants can be named in a single suit and in Canada only twelve. The broad reach of the courts' order was softened by the absence of seizure powers in respect to equipment found at the premises of the John Does. Thus, though the court commissioner can seize infringing material at the premises of named and identified defendants, he cannot do so at the John Doe premises. With regard to this, the court commissioner's powers are limited to entering any premises and recording evidence of infringing activities, including taking video or photographic evidence. The court also ensured a fair execution of the order by appointing a retired joint registrar of the court as the commissioner.

D. Specialists Required

641. In order to give teeth to the order, the commissioner was permitted to use technical experts and the police. On the basis of evidence recorded by the commissioner at the premises of various unauthorized cable operators, the court would, after issuing notices and hearing the parties, consider taking appropriate action, both civil and criminal. The court commissioner was at liberty to issue warnings to prospective violators.

The uniqueness of the Ten Sports Order lay in the fact that while deriving inspiration from John Doe orders in other jurisdictions, it went further in the following ways:

- the court did not stipulate any geographical limitations or limitations in the number of parties to which the order may apply;
- the commissioner was invested with the power to record evidence including the taking of video films, photographs and so on, which could then be used as evidence against the infringing cable operators, either in civil or criminal proceedings; and
- the commissioner could issue warning letters including placing a cautionary notice in a newspaper, which in itself could have a tremendous effect on piracy.

The tricky problem of jurisdictional complexity, normally inherent in a John Doe order, was eased out in this case because, under the Indian copyright regime, a plaintiff could file a copyright infringement claim in its own jurisdiction. Plaintiff number two, HMA Udyog, which was the exclusive distributor for the Ten Sports channel in India, was based in New Delhi. The Delhi High Court therefore would have jurisdiction over any violators of the plaintiffs' copyrights in any part of India.

E. Enforcement of the Order

642. The enforcement of the Ten Sports Order began with the enforcement team visiting the premises of a known defendant. This defendant caught red-handed telecasting the Ten Sports channel, immediately offered to take a licence from the plaintiffs. In accordance with the court's order, the commissioner seized all equipment used to transmit the channel illegally, including the demodulator, amplifier and other equipment. Following the defendant's signing of an undertaking that he would forthwith desist from stealing the Ten Sports signal, and would produce the infringing equipment before the court when called on to do so, the commissioner offered to release the seized equipment. Within a few minutes of the raid on this defendant's premises, all other unauthorized cable operators shut off their relay immediately. In the circumstances, the commissioner did not see the need for visiting the premises of the other defendants.

F. Mumbai Infringement

643. After receiving information that a number of operators in Mumbai were transmitting the Ten Sports signal without permission, the commissioner and his team visited Mumbai. Their first target was a five-star deluxe hotel. They checked into a room and found they could watch the World Cup quarter-final between England and Brazil on television. The hotel claimed that it was receiving the signals from an MSO in Mumbai. While the evidence was being recorded, the Ten Sports transmission came to a halt and was replaced by the blurred signal of a Chinese channel, CCTV. Apparently, CCTV had the exclusive rights for China, but owing to its failure to encrypt its signals; these 'free-to-air' signals were spilling over into India and were being captured by cable operators. Of course, these signals were far from clear and worse still; the commentary was in a language incomprehensible to most Indians. The commissioner immediately visited the premises of the MSO and confirmed that the CCTV channel was being telecast from their control room.

G. Parallel Importation

644. It is worth asking whether an Indian court would be prepared to restrain cable operators from distributing free-to-air signals originating in other countries but not intended to flow over to India. If such signals cannot be restrained, the plaintiffs' exclusive territorial rights over an international event would be deeply eroded as cable operators would use the free-to-air signals as a means to circumvent licence fees. The principle of parallel importation may apply here. A similar situation arose in the UK in *R. v. Mainwaring* (2002, FSR 325), where decoders supplied for a Netherlands satellite television broadcast were held to have been sold without authorization in the UK. The court, in finding for the prosecution, observed that a contrary interpretation of the law would frustrate the right of the broadcaster to control access within a certain territorial area. Given the nature of cable piracy and the ease with which traces of infringement can be erased, this groundbreaking order has helped enforce broadcast rights in a more effective manner and consequently helping broadcast companies recover the huge licence fees that they normally pay for the right to telecast big events and shows. In fact, as a result of the Ten Sports Order, a large number of cable operators signed up with the plaintiffs and there was an immediate increase in business.

H. Help to IP Owners

645. The Ten Sports Order has come as a boon to intellectual property owners, especially those who own rights with a limited shelf life. In fact, the Ten Sports Order also holds the distinction of being one of the first cases of the enforcement of a BRR under section 37 of the Copyright Act of 1957. This order also heralds the growth of sports law in India, a legal domain that until now has found few takers.

646. In the case of *Prasar Bharti v. Sahara TV Network Pvt. Ltd.* (CS (OS) No. 1523 of 2005) the contention raised on behalf of defendant, before the Delhi High Court was that the injunction order passed by the court was seriously prejudicing their interest. They further prayed that at least for the remaining two matches of India-South Africa Series, the interim order may be varied.

The court ruled that 'the parties have raised serious issues of facts and law. It may not be possible to conclude the hearing and pronounce the orders today itself. Furthermore the court is of the considered opinion that this matter involves certain technical notices in regard to capacity of Prasar Bharti to frame its regulations, BCCI's power to put an absolute bar or any other such bar, which may be unfair. The BCCI having given its rights for the two series in question to the Prasar Bharti has retained its copyright, is not really raising any serious objections either way. It must be noticed that the news channels cannot be treated at parity with total commercial channels and they must act in a larger interest of the public in ensuring that the cricket news reaches all parts of the country or even overseas. Learned counsel for the Prasar Bharti without prejudice to their rights and contentions has in fact vehemently argued that the restriction imposed by them under the New Access Rules is just, fair and proper and they are legally competent to do so and agreed to enhance the time (cap time to four minutes). Further with a qualification that a news channel will not prefix or even run scroller before, during or after by adding commercial advertisements by a scroller or otherwise and will not carry out any programming of the entire time'.

647. Alternately, learned counsel appearing for the defendants submitted that Prasar Bharti has no legal or any other right to impose such restriction, while taking the plea of discrimination, the DD News Channel has no such restriction and is given time for 102 minutes (as per the documents by the plaintiff itself). It is also contended on behalf of the plaintiff that they are paying more than INR 1 crore per hour of match and as such they cannot without commercial interest permit the defendants to use any further time and DD News is their channel as such that can permit them any time limit. Learned counsel for plaintiff submits that they have no intention so as to restrict totally the news channels even from reasonably depicting the news in relation to the matches. It was contended on behalf of the defendants that there is apparent discrimination made by the plaintiff between the news channels itself. The DD News Channel has no restriction while upon all other channels, this restriction has been imposed. It is also their contention that the defendants are also protected under section 39 of the Copyright Act being a fair dealing. However, according to the plaintiff, there is no unreasonable restriction imposed by them and the action of the defendants cannot be termed as fair dealing in accordance with the provisions of section 39, the transaction in question being entirely a commercial transaction.

648. In the circumstances of the case, the court felt that some interim arrangements are to be made so as not to totally frustrate the right of the news channels to give news in relation to cricket matches, as was said during the course of the hearing that the news channels give news every half an hour. It cannot be stated to be in public interest that news must be repeated every half an hour. The news channels can certainly regulate giving such news so as to put certain restrictions even if their contentions have some merit. Without prejudice to the rights and contentions of the parties and keeping in view that the learned counsel appearing for the parties have not seriously opposed passing of interim directions, it is directed as under:

(a) The news channels would be regulated in terms of the same clause as stated in the rules of the Prasar Bharti on record except to the extent that the maximum cap-limit of two minutes shall stand extended to seven minutes in 24 hours.
(b) The use of this time shall only be for giving cricket news without any commercial programme, advertisements before, during and after the cricket news. However, they would be at liberty to show any news or important events during that period as well.

IV. The Right to View Important Sports Events

649. In *Ten Sports v. Citizen Consumer and Civic Action Group* ((2004) 5 SCC 351), the court deliberated at length on the right to view sports event and declared that it is part of the fundamental right of freedom of speech and expression. Broadcasting is one of the means of communication and, therefore, a medium of speech and expression. Therefore in a democracy, neither any private individual, institution or organization nor any government or government organization can claim exclusive right over it. The Constitution forbids monopoly on print and electronic media as these are mediums of speech and expression. Therefore public cannot be denied this right with respect to seeing sports events on television.

650. The claim for monopoly by the government is to utilize the public resources in the form of the limited frequencies available for the benefit of the society at large. It is justified by the government to prevent the concentration of the frequencies in the hands of rich few who can monopolize the dissemination of views and information to suit their interests and thus in fact to control and manipulate public opinion which results in smothering of the right to freedom of speech and expression and freedom of information of others (paragraph 47 of the judgment).

This claim may lose all its rationale if either any section of the society is unreasonably denied an access to broadcasting or the governmental agency claims exclusive right to prepare and relay programmes. The ground is further not available when those claiming an access either do not make a demand on the limited frequencies controlled by the government or claim frequency which is not utilized and is available for transmission. The government sometimes claims monopoly also on the ground that having regard to all pervasive presence and impact of the electronic media, it may be utilized for purposes not permitted by law and the damage done by private broadcasters may be irreparable. There is much to be said in favour of this view and it is for this reason that the regulatory provisions, including those for granting licences to private broadcasting where it is permitted, are enacted. Alternately if the government is vested with an unbridled discretion to grant or refuse to grant the licence or access to the media, the reason for creating monopoly will lose is validity. For then it is the government which will be enabled to effectively suppress the freedom of speech and expression instead of protecting it and utilizing the licensing power strictly for the purposes for which it is conferred (paragraph 47). It is for this reason that in most democratic countries an independent autonomous broadcasting authority is created to control all the aspects of the operation of the electronic media. Such authority is representative of all sections of the society and is free from control of the political and administrative executive of the State (paragraph 47).

651. As regards the rights of viewers and listeners it has been aptly stated in Red Lion Broadcasting case: ‘But the people as a whole retain their interest in free speech by radio and their collective right to have the medium function consistently with the ends and purposes of the first amendment. It is the right of viewers and listeners, not the right of the broadcasting, which is paramount’ (paragraph 39).

V. Right of the Viewers

652. Viewing the matter from the aspect of the right of viewers, there can be no dispute with the proposition that the freedom of speech has to be viewed also as the right of viewers which has paramount importance, and this view has significance in a democratic country which India is. To safeguard the rights of the viewers, it is necessary to regulate and restrict the right to access to telecasting. This right of the viewers is also relevant in another context. When the electronic media is controlled by one central agency or few private agencies of the rich, there is a need to have a central agency to represent all sections of the society. Hence, to have a central agency to ensure the viewers’ right to be informed adequately and truthfully is a part of the right of the viewers under Article 19(1)(a). Therefore, an independent autonomous public authority is to be established which is representative of all sections and interests in the society to control and regulate the use of airwaves (paragraph 122(iii)).

653. In the case of Secretary, Ministry of Information and Broadcasting, Government of India and Others v. Cricket Association of Bengal and Others (AIR 1995 SC 1236: (1995) 2 SCC 161; (1995) 1 SCR 1036) it was brought out that:
The law on the subject – makes it clear that the fundamental right to freedom of speech and expression includes the right to communicate effectively and to as large a population not only in this country but also abroad, as is feasible. There are no geographical barriers to communication. Hence every citizen has a right to use the best means available for the purpose. At present, electronic media, namely, TV and radio, is the most effective means of communication. The restrictions which the electronic media suffers in addition to those suffered by the print media, are that (i) the airwaves are a public property and they have to be used for the benefit of the society at large, (ii) the frequencies are limited and (iii) media is subject to pre-censorship. The other limitation, namely, the reasonable restrictions imposed by law made for the purposes mentioned in Article 19(2) is common to all the media. In the present case, it was not and cannot be the case of the Ministry of Information and Broadcasting (MIB) that the telecasting of the cricket matches was not for the benefit of the society at large or not in the public interest and, therefore, not a proper use of the public property. It was not the case of the MIB that it was in violation of the provisions of Article 19(2).

654. It was further held that:

> there was nothing to be pre-censored on the grounds mentioned in Article 19(2). As regards the limitation of resources, since the DD was prepared to telecast the cricket matches, but only on its terms it could not plead that there was no frequency available for telecasting. The DD could also not have ignored the rights of the viewers which the High Court was at pains to emphasize while passing its orders and to which we have also made a reference. The CAB/BCCI being the organizers of the event had a right to sell the telecasting rights of its event to any agency. Assuming that the DD had no frequency to spare for telecasting the matches, the CAB could certainly enter into a contract with any agency including a foreign agency to telecast the said matches through that agency's frequency for the viewers in this country (who could have access to those frequencies) as well as for the viewers abroad. The orders passed by the High Court in effect gave a right to DD to be the host broadcaster for telecasting in this country and for the TWI, for telecasting for the viewers outside this country as well as those viewers in this country who have an access to the TWI frequency. The order was eminently in the interests of the viewers whatever its merits on the other aspects of the matter.

655. In *Citizen, Consumer and Civic Action Group and Another v. Prasar Bharti and Others* ((2006) 5 Comp LJ 74 (Mad), the court made some pertinent observation as to right of the viewers and position of law. The facts of the case were as follows:

> Ten Sports', a business concern, had acquired the global radio and television rights of the series from Pakistan Cricket Board, where the matches were to be

played. In lieu of the grant of the said rights to telecast through satellites, Ten Sports has already parted with its rights to Pakistan to telecast the matches by Pakistan Television (PTV) for an agreed price. Now, the public in Pakistan can view the matches through a public service provider. Whereas, the global rights, including India, have been acquired by Ten Sports, of course, for a whopping cost of around S10 million paid to Pakistan. But even though the telecasting rights to Pakistan Television have been given by Ten Sports for an agreed price, the Union Government and its agent, Prasar Bharti, are struggling hard to get those terrestrial rights to telecast through Doordarshan and, in fact, are pleading helplessness to intervene in the matter.

656. The court observed as follows:

> Airwaves are a public property and the transmission is regulated by the government and now it is entrusted with an Authority. Primarily, rights vest in the Indian public, over the Indian territory, and they are regulated under the relevant Acts, be it Indian Telegraph Act, 1885, Prasar Bharti Act, 1990 or the Telecom Regulatory Authority of India Act, 1997. Any rights given to an intermediary to transmit or retransmit are secondary rights.

657. Law on this aspect is not so clear as it is so evident from the plea of the respondents in requesting the third respondent to part with its rights of transmission so far as Indian subcontinent is concerned, offering some price, which, it seems, is not acceptable to the third respondent Ten Sports for obvious commercial reasons. There is only one leading judgment on the point, as on date, i.e., *Secretary, Ministry of I & B v. Cricket Association of Bengal* which held in no uncertain terms that right to have access to the electronic media is a fundamental right to speech and expression coming within the ambit of Article 19(1)(a) of the Constitution and which can be restricted reasonably only for the reasons enumerated in Sub-Article (2) of Article 19 of the Constitution. No grounds are made out to attract Article 19(2) of the Constitution. On the other hand, the respondents support the cause espoused by the petitioners in these two writ petitions. But the third respondent is a loner in the fight. However, his roots are strong in contractual field, which cannot completely be uprooted by this public law remedy forum.

658. In *K.M. Natraj, Advocate and Another v. State of Karnataka and Another* (AIR 1997 Kant 36) the petitioners contended that non-supply of electricity during the time when Wills World Cup Cricket 1996 was being telecast would amount to seriously affecting the RTI guaranteed under Article 19(1)(a) of the Constitution. The facts of the case are as follows:

> The petitions are presented as public interest litigation by the lovers of the game of cricket, before this Court and who are interested in viewing the 'Wills World Cup' Cricket, 1996. Though in these petitions they have prayed for a direction to the respondents not to apply power cut/load shedding during the telecast hour of the 'Wills World Cup' Cricket, 1996, commencing from 14 February 1996 to 17 March 1996; at hearing of the petitions learned counsel

appearing for the petitioners in W.P. No. 3292/96 (hereinafter referred to as the 'learned counsel for petitioners') and Advocates appearing in person (hereinafter referred to as the 'petitioners') submitted that they would confine their relief in these petitions only for a direction to the respondents for reschedule of power cut/load shedding during the cricket telecast hours.

659. The petitioners submitted that the power cut notified by the respondents, if given effect to during the telecast hours of the 'Wills World Cup' Cricket, 1996, which commenced between 14 February 1996 and 17 March 1996, would seriously affect their RTI guaranteed under Article 19(1)(a) of the Constitution of India and the said right cannot be infringed except by imposing reasonable restrictions as provided under subclause (2) of Article 19 of the Constitution of India. They submitted that the freedom of speech and expression guaranteed under Article 19(1)(a), guarantees the RTI and right to receive knowledge through electronic media relating to telecast of 'Wills World Cup' Cricket, 1996. It is submitted that imposition of power cut or depriving the public of their right to view the telecast of 'Wills World Cup' Cricket, 1996, which is a mega event, without properly rescheduling the timings relating to power cut to enable the public to view the World Cup Cricket would amount to depriving the citizens of this country who are residing in this State, the right to freedom of information guaranteed to them under Article 19(1)(a) of the Constitution of India. It is also urged that if for any reason, the direction as sought for by the petitioners cannot be granted, at least a direction may be given to the respondents to adhere to the proposal made by the second respondent to reschedule the supply of electricity as per the notification issued, which has been published in the local dailies on 13 February 1996, the copy of which has been made available to the Court.

660. The court held as follows after considering administrative aspect of notification issued for power cuts:

> it is not permissible – to interfere with the policy decision taken by the State by issuing Notification dated 26 October 1995 regulating the imposition of power cut/regulating the supply of power, which is being implemented by the second respondent. So far as the contention – that RTI and right to acquire knowledge about the game of Cricket through electronic media is a right guaranteed to the petitioners under Article 19(1)(a) of the Constitution of India is concerned, there cannot be any dispute on this proposition, and the decision in the case of 'Secretary Ministry of Information and Broadcasting and others' supports this contention. However, I am of the view that the said decision has absolutely no bearing on the facts of the present case and the nature of the right sought to be enforced by the petitioners. That was a case where the right of the Cricket Association to telecast the sporting event came up for consideration before the Supreme Court, and in that background the Supreme Court took the view that the promotion of sports also includes its popularization through all legitimate means like Radio and Television. That is not the position in the present case. – I do not find any merit in the contentions – that the power cut imposed by the State or refusal to reschedule the supply of electricity during

the telecast hours of 'Wills World Cup', 1996, entirely deprives the petitioners or others, of their RTI guaranteed to them under Article 19(1)(a) of the Constitution. Even otherwise, I am of the opinion that the restrictions imposed in regard to the use of power by virtue of the notification dated 26 October 1995 issued by the respondent state in exercise of its powers under section 22B of the Indian Electricity Act must be considered as reasonable restriction imposed within the meaning of Article 19(2) of the Constitution. Further, the petitioners do not have a higher or better right than other members of the public who are consuming electricity and whose rights are also affected on account of the power cut/reschedule of supply of electricity introduced by the respondents. On this ground also, the petitioners are not entitled for the relief.

661. So far as the additional contention of the petitioners – that the second respondent had relaxed the power cut during the sports meet in Hubli organized by the second respondent and therefore, there should not be any difficulty for the second respondent to reschedule the supply of electricity as prayed for by the petitioners, it is unnecessary for me to go into the correctness of the said statement made by the petitioners relying upon a paper publication, a copy of which has been produced on the short ground that if the second respondent having regard to the availability of power during the month of January 1996, had relaxed the power cut in the month of January 1996, it will not give any right to the petitioners to seek for a direction to regulate the power cut during the telecast hours of 'Wills World Cup Cricket' 1996, as sought for by the petitioners. Further, even if the action of the second respondent in relaxing the power cut during the sports meet organized is arbitrary or illegal, that will not give any right for the petitioners to seek for direction before this Court to regulate the power cut or reschedule supply of electricity in exercise of – power under Article 226 of the Constitution of India, so long as there is a shortage of power in the State, as made out by the respondents.

662. 'With regard to the submission – that the respondents may at least be directed to adhere to the proposal made for rescheduling of supply of electricity as per the notification published in the local daily dated 13 February 1996 is concerned, I am of the view that it is not permissible for me to direct the respondents to stick to the reschedule of supply of electricity as notified in the paper publication referred to above. The respondent – KEB must be left with the discretion to suitably alter the timings having regard to the availability of power and need of the other consumers. The fact that the respondent – KEB has come forward with a proposal is a clear indication that earnest efforts are being made by the respondents to respond to the sentiments expressed by the petitioners and other lovers of the game of cricket.'

The petitions were dismissed. However, notwithstanding the dismissal of these petitions the court desired that the 'Wills World Cup' Cricket, 1996, being a mega event, if the power is available and if it is possible to be made available, the respondents would certainly respond to the public sentiments to reschedule the supply of electricity to enable the public to watch the 'Wills World Cup' Cricket, 1996.

VI. Policy and Provision with Respect to Uplinking

663. The Ministry of Information and Broadcasting has notified the consolidated 'Guidelines for Up Linking from India'. These have come into effect from 2 December 2005 and would be applicable to existing channels as well. As per the new guidelines, the company seeking permission to set up an uplinking hub/ teleport should have minimum network ranging from INR 1 crore to INR 3 crores depending on channel carrying capacity of the teleport. For news & current affairs TV channels, foreign equity holding including FDI/Foreign Institutional Investor (FII)/Non-resident Indians (NRIs) investments should not exceed 26% of the paid-up equity of the applicant company. However, the entity making portfolio investment in the form of FII/NRIs deposits shall not be 'persons acting in concert' with FDI investors, as defined in Securities and Exchange Board of India (Substantial Acquisition of Shares and Takeovers) Regulations, 1997.

Special conditions/obligations related to non-news and current affairs TV channels are as under:

(a) The applicant company permitted to uplink shall operationalize the channel within a period of one year from the date the permission is granted by the Ministry of Information & Broadcasting failing which the permission is liable to be withdrawn, after affording an opportunity of being heard.
(b) The sports channels/sports rights management companies having TV broadcasting rights shall with immediate effect share their feed with Prasar Bharti for national and international sporting events of national importance, held in India or aboard, for terrestrial transmission and DTH broadcasting (free-to-air) under the following conditions:
   - The events of national importance shall be determined by the Ministry of Information & Broadcasting in consultation with Ministry of Sports & Youth Affairs, Prasar Bharti and the concerned sports channels/sports rights management companies. In case of cricket events, these shall include all matches featuring India and the semi-finals and finals of international competitions.
   - The above conditions shall apply to all future events including those covered by existing contracts of broadcasting rights. However, in the case of cricket events whose broadcasting rights have been obtained by sports channels/right management companies prior to the issue of the notification in the matter the rights holders will be obliged to share the feed for all matches featuring India and finals of international competitions.
   - Prasar Bharti shall transmit the feed, free-to-air, on its terrestrial channel and carried through the terrestrial network and/or the satellite/DTH mode.
   - The marketing of the events' rights (terrestrial as well as satellite/DTH) will be decided through mutual negotiations between Prasar Bharti and the rights holder. The marketing rights should go to the party which offers to maximize the revenue.
   - Revenue-sharing formula of 75:25 in favour of rights holders without any minimum guarantee/opportunity cost should be applied.

664. Foreign news channels/agencies seeking permission for temporary uplinking may be granted permission up to one year at a time for temporary uplinking from time to time through a predesignated teleport, subject to the following conditions:

– The applicant is accredited with the PIB, Government of India.
– The applicant undertakes to conform to the Programme and Advertisement Codes.
– The applicant has a binding agreement with the relevant teleport for the period of permission.
– The applicant pays a processing fee of INR 10,000 and temporary permission fee of INR 50,000 per year.

665. The news/footage so unlinked shall be primarily for the usage abroad by the foreign news agency or channel and shall not be broadcast in India without downlinking permission and registration of the channel. Ministry of I&B had notified the 'Guidelines for Up Linking from India' in July 2000 followed by 'Guidelines for Up linking of News and Current Affairs TV Channels from India' in March 2003, which were amended in August 2003. 'Guidelines for use of SNG/DSNGs' were issued in May 2003 and addendum dated 1 April 2005 to the uplinking guidelines. These were further amended on 20 October 2005. The new guidelines supersede all previous guidelines.

VII. Policy for Information Flow

666. The Ministry of Information & Broadcasting has taken several policy initiatives to smoothen the flow of information. New downlinking guidelines were put in place while uplinking policy was revised. The second phase of private FM Radio was launched for 337 radio stations spread over 91 towns across the country. Print media policy was revised in tune with the changing times. With a view to promote the film industry, the Ministry signed a film co-production agreement with several countries.

A. Downlinking of Television Channels

667. Policy guidelines for downlinking all satellite television channels downlinked, received or transmitted and retransmitted in India for public viewing have been put in place. Consequently, no person or entity shall downlink a channel, which has not been registered by the Ministry under these guidelines. Henceforth, all persons or entities providing Television Satellite Broadcasting Services (TV Channels) unlinked from other countries to viewers in India as well as any entity desirous of providing such a Television Satellite Broadcasting Service, receivable in India for public viewership, shall be required to obtain permission from Ministry of Information & Broadcasting. Major Provisions of the new guidelines are:

(a) The entity applying for permission for downlinking a channel, unlinked from abroad, must be a company registered in India and must have a commercial presence in India with its principal place of business in India.
(b) The applicant company must either own the channel it wants to be downlinked for public viewing, or must enjoy, for the territory of India, exclusive marketing/distribution rights for the same, inclusive of the rights to the advertising and subscription revenues for the channel and must submit adequate proof at the time of application.
(c) The downlinked channel must be licensed or permitted for being broadcast by the regulatory or licensing authority of the country of transmission, proof of which would have to be submitted at the time of application.
(d) No news and current affairs channel shall be permitted to be downlinked if it does not meet certain additional conditions:
   - Companies whose channels are being downlinked at present will be required to comply with all formalities of registration of these channels within 180 days from the date of issue of these guidelines.
   - The company permitted to downlink registered channels shall comply with the programme and advertising code prescribed under the Cable Television Networks (Regulation) Act, 1995.
   - The sports channels/sports rights management companies having TV broadcasting rights shall with immediate effect share their feed with Prasar Bharti for national and international sporting events of national importance (to be determined by the Ministry of Information & Broadcasting), held in India or abroad, for terrestrial transmission and DTH broadcasting (free-to-air). In case of cricket events, these shall include all matches featuring India and the finals and semi-finals of international competitions.
   - Prasar Bharti shall transmit the feed, free-to-air, on its terrestrial channel and carried through the terrestrial network and/or the satellite/DTH mode. Revenue-sharing formula of 75:25 in favour of rights holders without any minimum guarantee or opportunity cost should be applied.
   - The applicant company shall provide the necessary monitoring facility at its own cost for monitoring of programmes or content by the representative of the Ministry of Information & Broadcasting or any other government agency as and when required.

B. Guidelines for Uplinking from India

668. Consolidated ‘Guidelines for Up Linking from India’ have been notified. As per the new guidelines, the company seeking permission to set up an uplinking hub/teleport should have minimum network ranging from INR 1 crore to INR 3 crores depending on channel carrying capacity of the teleport. For news and current affairs TV channels, foreign equity holding including FDI/FII/NRI investments should not exceed 26% of the paid-up equity of the applicant company.

The sports channels/sports rights management companies having TV broadcasting rights shall with immediate effect share their feed with Prasar Bharti for national and international sporting events of national importance, held in India or aboard. For terrestrial transmission and DTH broadcasting (free-to-air) mandatory sharing of feed is on certain conditions.

669. Foreign news channels/agencies seeking permission for temporary uplinking may be granted permission up to one year at a time for temporary uplinking from time to time through a predesignated teleport, subject to some conditions. The news/footage so unlinked shall be primarily for the usage abroad by the foreign news agency/channel and shall not be broadcast in India without downlinking permission and registration of the channel.

C. Policy on FM Radio

670. Under the new policy, additional 337 private FM radio channels will be available across the country, spread over ninety-one cities/towns of A., A, B, C and D categories. Besides, thirty-six channels of IGNOU and fifty-one others are also earmarked for educational purposes. Eight towns in the north-east region would be covered under the scheme with forty FM radio stations, including thirty-two private operators and eight dedicated for educational purposes.

Similarly, in Jammu & Kashmir nine channels (seven for private broadcasting and two for education) are planned in the cities of Jammu and Srinagar.

671. In order to overcome the drawbacks of Phase-I, the bidding process has been made closed bid type to restrict speculative bidding of the open bidding. Second, the fixed annual fees have been replaced with the revenue-sharing pattern, whereby the private operators will have to pay 4% of their revenue as annual fees. Third, withdrawal clauses have been made more stringent to ensure that those who bid for a particular frequency do come up with the radio station.

Under the new policy provisions, care has been taken to ensure that a single large entity does not monopolize the airwaves. Accordingly, no entity can own more than one FM radio station in the same city/town, and no single entity will be allowed to own more than 15% of the total airwaves frequencies in the country.

D. Guidelines for Foreign Investment in Print Media

672. FDI (which includes FDIs by NRIs, PIOs) and portfolio investments by recognized FIIs, together up to a ceiling of 26% of paid-up equity capital, in Indian entities publishing newspapers and periodicals dealing with news and current affairs has been allowed. Such investment would be permissible by foreign entities having sound credentials and international standing, subject to certain conditions.

Facsimile editions, in whole or in part(s), of foreign newspapers, by Indian entities, with or without foreign investment, and also by foreign companies owning the original newspapers is allowed, provided they get incorporated and registered in India under the Companies Act, 2013. Any foreign company owning the original foreign newspaper will be permitted to publish the facsimile edition of its newspaper. However, the facsimile edition shall not carry any advertisements aimed at India readers in any form. The facsimile edition shall not carry any locally generated content/India-specific content, which is not simultaneously published in the original edition of a foreign newspaper.

673. Permission will be granted only in cases where equity held by the largest Indian shareholder is at least 51% of the paid-up equity, excluding the equity held by public sector banks and public financial institutions, in the new entity. At least 50% of the FDI will have to be inducted by issue of fresh equity. The balance, namely up to 50% of the FDI, may be inducted through transfer of existing equity.

674. The twenty-fifth State Information Ministers Conference (SIMCON) was held wherein ministers/participants from thirty-four States/UT took part. The conference deliberated on the issues of piracy, entertainment tax and other issues related to the entertainment sector. The major points of consensus included:

– More effective implementation of anti-piracy law with adequate powers to officials of State government and local authorities.
– Licensing or registration of video libraries by State government to bring it under regulatory regime of local area.
– To work towards further reduction of entertainment tax so as to bring it in the range of 25%–30%. To revive cinema industry and to encourage multiplexes.

To organize sensitization and training of State Government Officers by the Government of India for monitoring cable operators.

VIII. Broadcasting of Sports Events

675. The duty of State to protect the right of freedom of speech and expressions to all its citizens creates an obligation upon it to ensure that the broadcasting media is not monopolized, dominated or hijacked by privileged, rich and powerful interests. Such monopolization or domination should not be prejudicial to the freedom of speech and expression of citizens in general.

In this respect mention of a government order can be made according to which private firms were asked to share broadcasts with non-cable companies to let more people watch the game. However, it was felt that with no exclusivity of content, broadcasts of top cricket matches in India look likely to lose their monetary value massively and there will be loss of revenue to cricket boards as many of these boards heavily depend on television revenue.

A. Collective Selling of Broadcasting Rights

676. From the standpoint of Article 19(1)(a) of the Constitution of India, what is paramount is the right of the listeners and viewers and not the right of the broadcaster – whether the broadcaster is the State, public corporation or a private individual or body. A monopoly of broadcasting, whether by government or by anybody else, is not consistence with the free speech right of the citizens. State control really means governmental control, which in turn means, control of the political party or parties in power for the time being. Such control is bound to colour the views, information and opinions conveyed by the media.

The free right speech of the citizens is better served in keeping the broadcasting media under the control of the public. Control by public means control by an independent public corporation or corporations, as the case may be, formed under a statute. Broadcasting provides an essential service in a democratic society and could legitimately be reserved for a public institution, provided certain conditions are met. The corporation(s) must be constituted and composed in such a manner as to ensure its independence from government and its impartiality on public issues. When presenting or discussing a public issue, it must be ensured that all aspects of it are presented in a balanced manner, without appearing to espouse any one point of view (*Ten Sports v. Citizen Consumer and Civic Action Group* ((2004) 5 SCC 351, paragraph 194).

B. Exclusive Broadcasting Rights

677. The question related to monopoly as to exclusive broadcasting rights of the government and its national broadcaster in sport viewing was considered by the Honourable Supreme Court of India in *Ten Sports v. Citizen Consumer and Civic Action Group* ((2004) 5 SCC 351) and the issue was deliberated at length as given below:

> 'In *LIC v. Manubhai Shah* ((1992) 3 SCC 637), the court held that the freedom of speech and expression guaranteed to the citizens of this country includes the right to propagate one's views through print media or any other communication channel, e.g., the radio and the television. Every citizen of this free country, therefore, has the right to air the views through the printing and/or the electronic media subject of course to permissible restrictions imposed under Article 19(2) of the Constitution'. To the same effect is the holding in Odyssey Communications. Once this is so, it follows that no monopoly of this media can be conceived for the simple reason that Article 19(2) does not permit State monopoly unlike Clause (6) of Article 19 *vis-à-vis* the right guaranteed by Article 19(1)(g) (paragraph 198).

678. The constitutional courts of Europe have taken the uniform view that in the interest of insuring plurality of opinions, views, ideas and ideologies, the broadcasting media cannot be allowed to be under the monopoly of government or of an individual, body or organization. Government control in effect means the control of the political party or parties in power for the time being. Such control is bound to colour and in some cases, may even distort the news, views and opinions expressed through the media. It is not conducive to free expressions of contending viewpoints and opinions which is essential for the growth of a healthy democracy. In India, All India Reporter (AIR) and DD enjoy a monopoly in the matter of broadcasting and telecasting. They cannot think of any other agency doing the same job.[29]

C. *Government Monopoly on Broadcasting*

679. The government monopoly of broadcasting media in India is the result of historical and other factors. This may be true of every other country, to start with. Until recently, the broadcasting media has been in the hands of public/statutory corporations in most of the West European countries. Private broadcasting is comparatively a recent phenomenon. The experience of Italy of allowing private broadcasting at local level (while prohibiting it at national level) has left much to be desired. It has given rise to powerful media empires whose development is certainly not conducive to free speech right of the citizens.[30]

680. Broadcasting media is affected by the free speech right of the citizens guaranteed by Article 19(1)(a). Hence the monopoly of this medium (broadcasting media), whether by government or by an individual, body or organization is unacceptable. Clause (2) of Article 19 does not permit a monopoly in the matter of freedom of speech and expression as is permitted by Clause (6) of Article 19 vis-à-vis the right guaranteed by Article 19(1)(g).[31]

681. The right of free speech and expression includes the right to receive and impart information. For ensuring the free speech right of the citizens, it is necessary that the citizens have the benefit of plurality of views and a range of opinions on all public issues. A successful democracy posits an 'aware' citizenry. Diversity of opinions, views, ideas and ideologies is essential to enable the citizens to arrive at informed judgment in all issues touching them. This cannot be provided by a medium controlled by a monopoly – whether the monopoly is of the State or any other individual, group or organization. As a matter of fact, private broadcasting stations may perhaps be more prejudicial to free speech right of the citizens than the government-controlled media.

682. The broadcasting media should be under the control of the public as distinct from the government. This is the command implicit in Article 19(1)(a). It should be operated by a public statutory corporation or corporations, as the case may be, whose constitution and composition must be such as to ensure its/their impartiality in political, economic and social matters and on all public issues. It/they

29. *See* paras 199, 128 and 159 of the Secretary, *Ministry of Information & Broadcasting v. Cricket Association of Bengal & Anr.* (1995 AIR 1236) (1995 SCC (2) 161).
30. *Ten Sports v. Citizen Consumer and Civic Action Group* ((2004) 5 SCC 351, para. 201(2)).
31. *Ibid.*, para. 201(3)(a)).

must be required by laws to present news, views and opinions in a balanced way ensuring pluralism and diversity of opinions and views. It/they must provide equal access to all the citizens and groups to avail of the medium.[32]

IX. Outdated Legislation

683. The means of communication, broadcasting and telecasting media has undergone a complete change and means of communications have been revolutionized, however legislation to deal with the emerging situations remains age-old. The court observed on this behalf that 'Now, coming to the Indian Telegraph Act, 1885, a look at its scheme and provisions would disclose that it was meant for a different purpose altogether. When it was enacted, there was neither radio nor, of course, television, though it may be that radio or television falls within the definition of "telegraph" in section 3(1). Except section 4 and the definition of the expression "telegraph", no other provision of the Act appears to be relevant to broadcasting media since the validity of section 4(1) has not been specifically challenged before us, we decline to express any opinion thereon. The situation is undoubtedly unsatisfactory. This is the result of the legislation in this country not keeping pace with the technological developments. While all the democracies in the world have enacted laws specifically governing the broadcasting media, this country has lagged behind, rooted in the Telegraph Act of 1885 which is wholly inadequate and unsuited to an important media like radio and television, i.e., broadcasting media. It is absolutely essential, in the interest of public, in the interests of the freedom of speech and expression guaranteed by Article 19(1)(a) and with a view to avoid confusion, uncertainty and consequent litigation that Parliament steps in soon to fill the void by enacting a law or laws, as the case may be, governing the broadcasting media, i.e., both radio and television media. The question whether to permit private broadcasting or not is a matter of policy for the Parliament to decide. If it decides to permit it, it is for the Parliament to decide, subject to what conditions and restrictions it should be permitted (This aspect was been dealt with *supra*). The fact remains that private broadcasting, even if allowed, should not be left to market forces, in the interest of ensuring that a wide variety of voices enjoy access to it.'[33]

684. It is, therefore, imperative that Parliament makes a law placing the broadcasting media in the hands of a public or statutory corporate or the corporations, as the case may be. This is necessary to safeguard the interests of public and the interests of the law as also to avoid uncertainty, confusion and consequent litigation.[34]

In 2007, the Sports Broadcasting Signals (Mandatory Sharing with Prasar Bharti) Act was passed. The objective was to provide access to large numbers of listeners and viewers, on a free-to-air basis, of sporting events of national importance through mandatory sharing of sports broadcasting signals with Prasar Bharti. Any

32. *Ten Sports v. Citizen Consumer and Civic Action Group* ((2004) 5 SCC 351, para. 201(3)(b)).
33. Paragraph 82 AIR 1995 SC 1236: (1995) 2 SCC 161; [1995] 1 SCR 1036.
34. (Paragraphs 201(4) and 200) *Secy., Ministry of Information and Broadcasting, Govt. of India v. Cricket Assn. of Bengal* (1995) 2 SCC 161: AIR 1995 SC 1236.

content right owner or holder, television or radio broadcasting service provider shall not carry a live television broadcast on any cable or Direct-to-Home network or radio commentary broadcast in India of sporting event of national importance, unless it simultaneously shares the live broadcasting signal, without its advertisements, with the Prasar Bharti to enable them to retransmit the same on its terrestrial networks and Direct-to-Home networks in such manner and on such terms and conditions as may be specified.

§2. Sponsoring

685. In these days of mass media, sponsorship plays a major role in organizing the sports events. The sponsorship has become related to the most important aspect that is how much could be earned from an event. The quantum of earning not only affects but also determines the scale on which a sporting event is organized. Recently when Indian Cricket Board signed a kit sponsorship deal with Nike, worth around GBP 25 million over five years, one official of ICB said that India had now become the world's 'most valued brand in team sponsorship' and the aim of sponsorship was 'to maximize the gains for the benefit of the game'. It would be worth mentioning that BCCI is the richest Cricket Board in the world. The ICC negotiates global TV rights for the World Cup, held every four years, and ICC Champions Trophy held every alternate year. But if a country hosts a test series, it can sell the TV rights accordingly – and these normally attract a lot of money through advertising, sponsoring and viewing of the match if the match involves India.

686. The Indian sports sponsorship market – comprising on-air, on-ground, team, franchise fee and endorsements has grown tremendously. Many corporates today are betting big on sports to build brands, primarily due to its ability to attract a large number of viewers. For instance, digital wallet and e-commerce player Paytm has committed INR 500 crore over 2015–2019 to the sports category and is likely to target upcoming leagues in the country. Cricket dominates sports sponsorships with 51% share in on-ground sponsorship, 61% in team sponsorship and 64% in endorsements. Sponsorship money raised by other sports is also on the rise. India has witnessed the entry of multiple start-ups in sports over the past few years. These include companies involved in sports infrastructure, data/content aggregation, education and training, online retail, technology and online ticket booking.

I. Purpose of Sponsorship

687. In India, companies sponsor particular sport or sportspersons or sport kit. The purpose is generally to get publicity for the goods through exposure to the spectators who come to see the sporting event and its coverage through electronic and print media. The sponsored parties and items act as vehicle of publicity, obliged to accomplish certain tasks and to enhance the sponsor's image, no doubt in exchange for remuneration.

II. Advertising

688. Sponsorship has an element of advertising but advertising by sportspersons encompasses designating brand ambassadors and direct advertising of a product on radio and TV. The remuneration depends on name, fame and reputation of the sportsperson. It is a fact that in some cases sportspersons and sport organizations earn more from promotion of products through advertising than they directly earn from the sport activity itself.

The sponsorship of sports can extend the advertising budgets, and research shows that it gives more mileage than routine airtime spends of an equivalent value. However, the extent of the multiplier effect depends on effectively leveraging the association between advertising and sponsorship.

III. Sponsorship as an Atypical Contract

689. The sponsorship contracts do not follow a single or set pattern. These differ from case to case and are the product of peculiar facts and circumstances of a given situation and opportunity available to a sportsman.

IV. Contents of Contract and Obligations of the Parties

690. The contents of the sponsorship contracts depend on the object for which sponsor is sponsoring. If it is development of sport in the country, then there can be less emphasis on promotion of the brand name. But in majority of cases business houses or companies sponsor want that on all the items used by the sportsperson their logo or brand name is used so that they can get maximum publicity. In case sponsor has contract with the event organizer then there can be terms allowing sale of product of the sponsor or provision for organizing demonstration for promotion of their product. There can be display of the brand name of the company in the sport arena, on the clothing, etc. There can be reasonable restriction on the right so that sportsperson or organizer may not enter into a similar type of contract with the competitor of the sponsor.

V. Linkage Contracts

691. The linkage contracts entail change in or integration of the name of the sport club which allows the sponsor to convey its message by exhibiting its name directly to tournament spectator as well as through other means of communication to sports lovers. This contract is signed with the team and not with the individual player.

VI. Sponsorship of Individual Players

692. Sponsorship of individual player is a complex issue because of the fact that player may be member of sporting club or might be member of national squad in case of team. There may be clash of interests so far as conditions or restrictions on being member of a club and contract entered into, if any, with the club is concerned. In case of reputed and famous players, they generally may get more reward and remuneration from sponsors than whatever payment is made by the club.

There is also sponsorship for training ahead of an event like Olympics. The sponsor provides assistance so as to meet training, coaching and other expenses. The player enters into an agreement for sponsorship containing detailed terms and conditions.

VII. Sponsorship of Events and Constitution of the Pools

693. In those cases and eventualities when a large amount is required for organizing the sport event then more than one sponsor is required to raise the money. Thus a pool of sponsors is formed, and they enter into contract directly with the sponsored party which may be a club or sports federation.

In the field of cricket, there are long-term sponsorship contracts with the world governing body of cricket namely ICC. ICC enters in 'ICC Members Playing Agreement' for this purpose. This long-term sponsorship agreement addresses a number of issues and in Indian context BCCI is insisting that it must also address issues of catering, accreditation and security which are unique to the Indian subcontinent.

§3. Merchandising

I. The Merchandising Contract: An Atypical Contract

694. Merchandising contract is an arrangement by which the owner of a trademark allows its use to another who uses it for the promotion of a different product other than for which it is registered. Thus the mark is used on the product which may increase its sale because of reputation of trademark and thus a relationship of mutual benefit is developed which tries to protect the interest of both the parties through entering into a contract.

There is a lot of insecurity in the business of sports marketing with legal wrangles about acquisition rights, cut-throat competition and new terms such as ambush marketing. Further, conditional access system will open a new chapter in sports marketing.

II. Personality and 'Corporate' Merchandising

695. The name and fame of a sportsperson can be used for establishing a relationship of trust with the product promoted by using the name of such sportsperson. This merchandising can be by the club or by the person himself.

A renowned brand is protected from its use even for totally different items for which it is not known. This is the attribute of exclusive and absolute right in the mark which implies that it cannot be used by anybody else to put goods in the market and get the benefit out of reputation which such mark enjoys. The resemblance with such mark is also not allowed, but there is a very thin line when and where resemblance starts and when and where it ends.

696. As per reports the BCCI is looking at exploring new sources of revenue and will soon open itself to product merchandising, ground sponsorship and other licensing part of its strategy to market the game. Television is no doubt the main spark that captured the imagination of sports marketers as well as merchandisers and was responsible for driving the growth of sports in the world. The television had great impact and is responsible for inducing exultation, joy and anguish amidst the sports lovers. Television is mainly responsible for driving the growth of sports in the world as sport came to the drawing rooms from the field. This phenomenon has resulted in a multitude of opportunities in terms of merchandising and endorsements.

697. Sports consumption in India depends on viewer interests, team affiliation, aspiration and level of competition. In India, the excessive focus on cricket is unique and the audiences here are different from the rest of the world. However positive movement in the arena of sport is possible only when the framework of legislation changes.

698. The government must see that the associations develop and peruse long-term goals, for instance, eight- to ten-year plans for sports such as hockey and football. Also, the government and broadcasters must promote those sports where India has good prospects of winning Olympic medals or World championships. The private channels and the public broadcaster must promote local and national level sporting events, especially in sports such as tennis, hockey and chess where India is doing well. Nationwide talent hunts and local infrastructure has to be organized with government and corporate support. The print media must also give prominence to achievers and role models in other sports. The government must initiate a legislation wherein advertisers who spend on cricket must contribute a certain percentage of their spends on other sports.

699. Advertisers believe that they can ignite consumer passion through sports. It is one of the few mediums that actively engage consumers. Other media are passive. Advertisers are buying an audience. They do not care whether sports or films or serials get them that audience. Research shows that several industries such as tourism and hospitality get a fillip when international sporting events take place in a city or country. Sports associations and marketers need to package the propositions well in order to convince media planners and buyers. There must be a single window with whom the advertisers and agencies can negotiate (as in cricket). It is necessary to ensure that proper studies are conducted prior to and after the sports events.

700. Advertisers and media planners need to create a knowledge base to have a benchmark. This would ensure that the association is a long-term effort rather than being a random one. The business is too tactical and has a handful of serious advertisers. Little efforts are made to integrate efforts into marketing. Talented sports achievers needed proper marketing, the current era is driven by commerce and television propelled sports into the limelight. Marketing sports properties and events was a natural progression. Certain sports have a natural advantage as they are visually appealing – they are interesting to watch in terms of colour, arenas, physicality and personalities. The sports marketers must endeavour to promote other sports on television. Several games such as bowling and darts have become popular on television in the developed nations as sports marketers managed to package them well. In the UK, billiards captured the imagination of the women audiences who loved to watch well-attired handsome men. Passion for the game of cricket is a strange phenomenon and a one-off case. All the anguish that fans feel when the team loses is forgotten with a single win.

701. Advertisers who wish to associate themselves with sports need to ask themselves three important questions:

(1) Will the association help in building the brand, communicating the core values and proposition?
(2) Will the association help in innovating?
(3) Is the association being effectively leveraged?

702. There is a need for sports associations to change their approach and way of functioning. The sports associations need to become more professional, package better, present concepts better, negotiate from a position of strength. The sports associations need a long-term vision and everyone needs to contribute to the process wherein self-sufficiency can be developed. The key is proper packaging and then the advertising bucks will come to non-cricket sports. The under-utilized sports marketing opportunities – such as merchandising – must be explored. The problem with sports associations and administrators is that they are ill equipped to allow the sportsperson's talent to blossom beyond a certain degree. They do not have the tools or the capabilities to enhance talent and convert it to medals.

§4. Ownership of Clubs

703. Owning a sports club of one's own is the newest status symbol in India. The sport of cricket through IPL has been very popular and is a household name. IPL has generated USD 3.2 billion (in sponsorship fees and broadcasting revenues) over the years. Reliance Industries picked up the Mumbai Indians cricket franchise for more than USD 110 million in 2008. The team is worth an estimated USD 200 million. Other billionaire IPL team owners are G.M. Rao, who owns the Delhi Daredevils, and media magnate Kalanithi Maran owns the Sunrisers Hyderabad. The Ambanis are backing what they see as the next big thing: soccer. The newly launched Indian Super League, in partnership with sports management firm IMG, debuts in October with Brijmohan Lall Munjal's Hero MotoCorp as the title sponsor. Electronics magnate Venugopal Dhoot and Sanjiv Goenka are among the eight franchise owners. Kabaddi, an ancient Indian contact sport, recently got a fresh lease on life when Anand Mahindra created the Pro Kabaddi League. The inaugural edition garnered 435 million TV viewers over the thirty-seven-day event as teams with names like the Telugu Titans, Bengaluru Bulls and Jaipur Pink Panthers went at it. It's now the country's second-most-viewed sporting tournament.

In the arena of football Mohun Bagan and East Bengal are supporter-based clubs and run by the members of the club. Vijay Mallya owned United Breweries bought 50% stake in both clubs naming the Mcdowell's Mohun Bagan and Kingfisher East Bengal. After shares of UB were bought by Diageo, the ownership of East Bengal was passed to them. Mohun Bagan is still under UB Group. Bengaluru FC, on the other hand, is owned by JSW Group. Mumbai FC is owned by Essel Group. Pune-based DSK Shivajians are owned by DSK Group, a construction business company. Goa-based Salgaocar is owned by VM Salgaocar Group. Sporting Goa is owned by Goan businessman, Peter Vaz. Aizawl FC is owned by Robert Royte owned NECS. Shillong Lajong FC is owned by AIFF Vice President, Larsing Ming. In case some investment company or other entity control different sports club, then such company or entity will promote its own interest and not act always in the interest of sport. Multiple ownerships can result in limitation on freedom of action of a club whereas investors should ensure their legitimate aim, i.e., to protect the uncertainties of results in the interest of the public.

Chapter 2. Private Regulations

704. The sport governance in the country is mostly in the hands of autonomous clubs, federations and associations. The Ministry of Youth and Sports has a moderating effect and lays down guidelines and frames promotional schemes and incentives which can be availed by sport bodies. The sportspersons are employed by railways and other government department's public sector undertakings and private sector on contract basis or as regular employees. There is also a sport quota for admissions in colleges and universities.

705. There is no separate or specific legislation dealing with sports matters but the constitutional documents of clubs, federations and associations, and rules made by them regulate various aspects of the sports. For example, IOA lays down norms, governs as well as guides the sport activities of the individual players and federations on an all India basis.

706. The sport discipline is dealt by the regulations of the club, federations and association of which a sportsperson is a member. Thus it is semi-government bodies or private bodies like sports club which regulate sports in India. Any activity which results in bodily injury or damage to property may fall under the law of tort which is not very developed in India with respect to quantum of damages as the amount of compensation allowed is on lower side. Besides, the assault and bodily violence being criminal in nature, are also dwelt with under the criminal law which prescribes punishment and penalties but not compensatory in nature. The Disciplinary Rules of IOA have been applied to ban some cricketers for life because of allegations of match-fixing against them. With respect to broadcasting and telecasting matters, the law on the subject is very old and as it cannot deal with new situations and circumstances; therefore, Ministry of Information and Broadcasting has issued certain guidelines which deal with the uplinking and downlinking matters.

707. Since the sport falls in State List of the Constitution and only State can legislate on sport and related matters; hence, Central Government efforts to bring any uniform legislation for the development of the sport in the whole country have been resisted by the States. In view of this, there is a move to bring 'sports' in the Concurrent List so that both centre and State can legislate on it. This will pave the way for a uniform legislation applicable throughout India and development of sport activity in a systematic manner. It can have space for private regulation as well. The Central Government, acting under Entries 13 and 97 of the Union List in the Seventh Schedule to the Constitution of India, has brought a National Sports Development Bill, 2013. The Entry 13 deals with and brings in the ambit of legislative power of the Central Government, participation in international conferences, association and other bodies. Further, the regulation of National Olympic Committee and NSFs, which enjoy national jurisdiction, falls within the jurisdiction of the Union Government under its residuary powers under Entry 97 of the Union List in the Seventh Schedule read with Article 248 of the Constitution of India. The passage of this legislation may pave the way for more systematic development of sports law in India and bring uniformity so far as actions by different sports clubs are concerned.

Part VI. Sport and Covid

Introduction

708. Covid-19 pandemic has spread to almost all countries of the world and governments have imposed social and physical distancing measures, complete or partial lockdowns and overall curtaining of social life so as to prevent the spread of the disease. These actions have disrupted many regular aspects of life, including sport and physical activity. Covid-19 has also posed challenges to the sporting world and to physical activity. The impact of Coronavirus (Covid-19) has been acute and far-reaching. The response to the pandemic requires concerted action from all areas of society, including leaders and policy makers in the sport sector. The high level of contact between participants and spectators means sporting events can heighten the risk of spreading coronavirus. Government sports agencies, governing bodies and leagues have therefore made difficult but necessary decisions to shut down or restrict professional and community sports activities. So sportsman have less opportunities to be physically active and enjoy the social interaction sport provides. Many people working in the field have lost their livelihood. To help sports policymakers and officials make good decisions about sport and exercise during the pandemic the Commonwealth has launched a sport, exercise and physical activity.

§1. Government Measures

I. Constitutional Background

709. The COVID-19 pandemic being a global medical emergency required immediate and stringent action by the government to control human loss. The Constitutional provisions related to health are contained in Part IV dealing with the Directive Principles of State Policy. Article 39(e) mentions the State's responsibility to ensure that health and strength of workers, men, and women and the tender age of children are not abused. Article 41 imposes a duty on the State to provide public assistance in cases of old age, sickness and disablement. Article 47 deals with the level of nutrition and the standard of living of people and improving public health. Both the Central Government and the States are empowered to make laws related to public health. Items related to public health are mentioned in all three lists of the Indian Constitution. Quarantine, including all issues related to seamen's and marine hospitals and medical institutions, are mentioned in items 28 and 81 of the

Union List. The States can make legislation related to 'healthcare, sanitation, hospitals, dispensaries and prevention of animal diseases' under item 6 of the State List. The Union and States can make laws related to the health profession and the prevention of the extension from one State to another of infectious or contagious diseases or pests affecting people, animals, or plants under entries 26 and 29 of the Concurrent List.

II. Other Legislation Related to Pandemic

A. The Epidemic Diseases Act, 1897

710. The Epidemic Diseases Act, 1897 (EDA) was enacted during the British colonial era to tackle the bubonic plague. This Act is 125 years old, with only four sections but proved was vital in containing Cholera (1910), Spanish Flu (1918–20), Smallpox (1974), Swine flu (2014) and the Nipah Virus (2018). The EDA is the only act that provides for legal interventions in the case of a national or regional epidemic. It deals with the power to take special measures and prescribe regulations during times of dangerous diseases by the central and State governments. Under section 2 of the act, the State government may take or empower to issue notices or regulations to be observed during the outbreak. Section 2A empowers the Central Government to take precautions and issue regulations for the inspection of ships and vessels and also to regulate any person who intends to sail. The disobedience to the directions of public servants under the act is considered an offence and punishable under section 188 of the IPC 45 of 1860.

1. Amendment in EDA after Covid-19

711. On 22 April 2020, the government issued an ordinance to amend the EDA, as there had been incidents of attacks on healthcare workers. The ordinance amended section 3 of the EDA. If anyone causes damage or loss to the property, then they may be punished with imprisonment for a term of three months to five-years and with a fine. In case of violence and physical attack on healthcare workers, they can be imprisoned 'for a term of six months to seven years and with a fine. In addition, "the offender shall also be liable to pay compensation to the victim and twice the fair market value for damage of property"'.

B. Issue of Guidelines

712. The Ministry of Health and Family Welfare (MoHFW), which is a nodal agency for issuing guidelines and bulletins to other ministries in the Central Government and State governments, is actively involved in directing and advising the States on Covid-19. The State/UT governments under section 2 of the EDA issued regulations and notifications related to measures to be taken for containing the spread of Covid-19.

1. Government of Odisha and Telangana

713. The Odisha State government has brought in an ordinance, which provides that any person violating the epidemic regulation shall be imprisoned for a period of two years and given a fine. Telangana, a south Indian State, invoked the EDA by issuing a regulation called the Telangana Epidemic Disease (COVID-19) Regulation 2020. The regulation empowers the Director of Public Health (DPH), the Director of Medical Education, all the District collectors, Commissioner of Police, District Superintendent of Police, and all Municipal Commissioners of Corporations in the State to take measures to control and contain COVID-19. The regulation brings all hospitals, both public and private, under the purview of the regulations and directs them to report all cases to the State Integrated Surveillance Units and Collector of the District or the Commissioner of Corporations. The empowered officials can take action on persons who refuse to comply with the regulation under section 188 of the IPC. The regulation also prohibits the spread of misinformation on social media and in print media, and necessary action may be taken on violators.

2. Government of Karnataka

714. The Karnataka State government brought Epidemic Diseases, Covid-19 Regulations, 2020, using the powers under the EDA. The regulations bar private laboratories from conducting Covid-19 testing. All samples must be collected by the designated laboratory by the District Nodal Officer of the Department of Health and Family Welfare of the concerned district. The samples are collected according to guidelines issued by the Central Government. The interesting point of the regulation is that it makes the District Disaster Management Committee headed by the Deputy Commissioner the main authority for preparing strategies regarding containment measures at the district level. Similarly, many State governments have issued regulations according to their institutional set-up and strategized their plans to counter Covid-19.

3. Other State Governments

715. Prior to the Covid-19 pandemic, some State governments had their own public health acts or had amended the EDA to include certain provisions at the State level. The Madras Public Health Act, 1939 in the State of Tamil Nadu, is one example of comprehensive public health law at the State level. The act includes a Public Health Board being constituted at the State level that includes a Minister of Public Health, other coordination ministers, the surgeon general, Director of Health Services, Sanitary Engineer and other members nominated by the State government. The Board's role is to advise the State government. The act also includes prevention, notification and treatment of diseases. There is a similar act in the State of Madhya Pradesh, namely the Madhya Pradesh Public Health Act, 1949. In the State of Kerala, the Travancore-Cochin Public Health Act, 1955 and the Malabar Public

Health Act, 1939 are both in place in the case of any major public health issue. Compulsory provision of vaccinations is included by the State government of Himachal Pradesh under the Himachal Pradesh Vaccination Act, 1968.

716. The EDA is not comprehensive and left to State governments to devise their own public health laws. However, only some State governments like Madhya Pradesh and Bihar have their own laws related to public health. Though the EDA has been invoked during the COVID-19 pandemic by various State governments after directions from the Central Government, there is a need for an integrated, comprehensive, actionable and relevant legal provision for the control of outbreaks in India. The EDA in the present form is not sufficient to face health emergencies like COVID-19 as it is silent on technical and operational mechanisms of the control and management of epidemics.

C. Disaster Management Act, 2005

717. Under the Disaster Management Act (DMA), the nationwide lockdown of twenty-one days was declared on 25 March 2020 by the government and was then extended until 31 May 2020. The DMA was enacted in 2005 with the objective 'to provide for the effective management of disasters and for matters connected therewith or incidental there to'. This act established the National Disaster Management Authority, State Disaster Management Authority, District Disaster Management Authority and contain measures to be taken by the governments during the disaster, penalties and offences of the violators.

718. The Central Government acting under DMA imposed the lockdown and restricted all kinds of transportation. Section 62 of the DMA gives powers to the Central Government to issue directions to all ministries or departments of the Government of India and State/UT governments. Unlike the other laws, this act 'provides for an exhaustive administration set-up for disaster preparedness'. Violators are punishable up to one year in jail or a fine or both under sections 51 to 60 of the Act. The law describes the offence as obstructing any officer or employee from performing their duty or refusing to comply with directions. For the better execution of the national lockdown, numerous States likewise summoned section 144 of the Cr.P.C.

719. One of the major issues with the DMA is whether epidemic or pandemic can be considered 'disaster' as per its definition. Section 2(d) of the DMA States that: 'Disaster means a catastrophe, mishap, calamity or grave occurrence in any area, arising from natural or man-made causes, or by accident or negligence which results in substantial loss of life or human suffering or damage to, and destruction of, property, or damage to, or degradation of, environment, and is of such a nature or magnitude as to be beyond the coping capacity of the community of the affected area.' One can interpret that a health emergency of the kind created by the COVID-19 pandemic falls under 'grave concerns', but such interpretation will not serve any purpose in effectively managing the epidemic.

D. Other Legislative Provisions

720. Terms like 'quarantinable disease' and 'isolation', have been defined under the Indian Aircraft (Public Health) Rules, 1954 as yellow fever, plague, cholera, smallpox, typhus and relapsing fever. It also provides definitions of various other words such as 'Health Officer', 'Infected Aircraft', 'Infected Area', 'Infected Person'. Similar restrictions are found under the Indian Port Health Rules, 1955, framed under the Indian Port Act, 1908, for the quarantining and isolation of passenger ships, cargo ships and cruise ships. It further provides for the provision, which states that the Central Government has the power of inspection of any ship or vessel leaving or arriving at the port at any point of time which comes under its jurisdiction. The Drugs and Cosmetics Act, 1940 provides provisions related to public health on the grounds of availability of and distribution of vaccines and drugs during an outbreak of dangerous and infectious disease.

III. Government Guidelines

721. The global outbreak of Covid-19 has brought governmental restrictions and resulted in complete or partial closure and regulation on functioning of gyms, stadiums, pools, dance and fitness studios, parks and playgrounds. Many players were not able to actively participate in regular individual or group sporting or physical activities. Under such conditions, many tend to be less physically active resulting in weight gain and loss of physical fitness. Even organizing training camps have become a task. Some athletes are not keen on taking risks and are happy to train at their home or in nearby academies. Training in contact sports, especially, has become a task, with norms of social distancing in place.

722. Government has issued general guidelines and instructions from time to time after the outbreak of pandemic like quarantine requirements, movement restrictions from foreign countries, etc. On 1 March 2021 Government of India Ministry of Health & Family Welfare issued Guidelines on Preventive Measures (Guidelines) to contain spread of Covid-19 in Yoga Institutes and Gymnasiums (in supersession of guidelines issued earlier dated 3 August 2020).Various generic precautionary measures have been suggested in addition to specific measures to be taken at yoga institutes and gymnasiums. The guidelines aim to minimize possible physical contacts between staff, members and visitors and maintain physical distancing.

A. Containment Zone

723. All yoga institutes and gymnasiums in containment zones shall remain closed for public. Only those outside containment zones will be allowed to open up. All yoga institutes and gymnasiums shall comply with all health-related guideline/SOP/notification issued by the Union/State government from time to time. Persons above 65 years of age, persons with co-morbidities, pregnant women and children below the age of 10 are advised to take necessary precautions in terms of maintaining physical distancing, wearing mask properly, etc. Organizations managing the yoga institutes and gymnasiums shall advise all members, visitors and staff accordingly.

B. Preventive Measures

724. The generic preventive measures include public health measures that are to be followed to reduce the risk of Covid-19. These measures need to be observed by all in these places at all times. These include:

(i) Individual sportsman must maintain a minimum distance of 6 feet as far as feasible.
(ii) Use of face covers/masks at all times. They must be worn properly to cover nose and mouth except during exercise.
(iii) Practice frequent hand washing with soap (for at least 40-60 seconds) even when hands are not visibly dirty. Use of alcohol-based hand sanitizers (for at least 20 seconds) can be practised wherever feasible.
(iv) Respiratory etiquettes to be strictly followed. This involves strict practice of covering one's mouth and nose while coughing/sneezing with a tissue/handkerchief/flexed elbow and disposing off used tissues properly.
(v) Self-monitoring of health by all and reporting any illness at the earliest to State and District helpline.
(vi) Spitting should be strictly prohibited.
(vii) Installation and use of Aarogya Setu App shall be advised to all.

C. Instructions for Opening and Functioning

725. Before opening the yoga institutes/gymnasiums Processes and premises redesigning including proper placement of equipment

(i) Plan yoga/gymnasiums floor area based on 4 m2 per person.
(ii) Place equipment including cardio and strength machines, 6 feet apart, wherever feasible, by moving equipment to facilitate physical distancing.
(iii) Where available, utilize any outdoor space by relocating equipment outside.
(iv) Create specific pathways for entering and exiting exercise areas within closed spaces using floor or wall markings.
(v) Ensure queue management, inside and outside the premises, with specific markings on the floor with a gap of 6 feet.
(vi) Promote card-based/contactless payment.
(vii) For air-conditioning/ventilation, the guidelines, the temperature setting of all air-conditioning devices should be in the range of 24–30°C, relative humidity should be in the range of 40–70%, intake of fresh air should be as much as possible and cross-ventilation should be adequate.

(viii) Limit the number of staff and members within the general gymnasium floor, specific workout areas and change rooms by: a. restricting the number of members allowed in specified areas; b. implementing 'fitness sessions' for particular exercise areas with requirements for members to register (ideally online) for specific sessions.

(ix) Spas, Sauna and Steam Bath shall function in accordance with the SOPs issued by the State/UT concerned. Swimming pools shall function in accordance with SOP issued by MYAS.

D. Sanitizing the Area

726. All areas within the premises shall be disinfected using clinically approved disinfectants. The areas to be disinfected include but are not limited to:

(i) entrances to premise, building, rooms;
(ii) all open areas used by staff and visitors;
(iii) washrooms and toilets;
(iv) shoe baths (members will be encouraged to carry separate workout shoes);
(v) all other frequently touched surfaces (doorknobs, handles, etc.).

E. Planning and Scheduling of Activities

727. With respect to planning and scheduling of activities in yoga centres/ gymnasiums and other institutions following has been provided:

(i) After calculating the maximum capacity per session based on redesigned spaces, the session should be scheduled.
(ii) Implement staggering class session times and allowing minimum of 15-30 minutes between classes to avoid overlap between members arriving and leaving. Group fitness classes should be organized online, wherever possible.
(iii) Ensure sessions are tailored to include only exercises that do not require physical contact between the trainer and the sportsman including set-up and use of equipment.
(iv) Staff residing in the containment zone shall not attend the facility till containment zone is de-notified.
(v) All employees who are at higher risk i.e., older employees, pregnant employees and employees who have underlying medical conditions to take extra precautions. They should preferably not be exposed to any frontline work requiring direct contact with the clients.

F. Availability and Management of Supplies

728. With respect to availability of supplies, the following must be adhered to:

(i) Appropriate personal protection gears like face covers/masks, visors, hand sanitizers, etc. shall be made available by management to the members, visitors and staff.
(ii) Provide an adequate supply of disinfectant wipes or disinfecting solutions and disposable paper towels for members/staff to wipe exercise equipment clean before and after use.
(iii) Ensure availability of pulse oximeters to record oxygen saturation of members prior to the exercise. Entrance to have mandatory hand hygiene (sanitizer dispenser) and thermal screening provisions. Only asymptomatic persons (including staff) be allowed in the premises.
(iv) All persons to be allowed entry only if using face cover/masks.
(v) All members, visitors and staff may consider using Aarogya Setu application for risk identification at all times inside the yoga institute/gymnasiums.
(vi) Posters/standees on preventive measures about Covid-19 to be displayed prominently. Audio and Video clips to spread awareness on preventive measures for Covid-19 may be regularly played.
(vii) Proper crowd management in the parking lots, in corridors and in elevators – duly following physical distancing norms shall be organized by the management/any outsourced agencies.
(viii) Staggering of members/visitors to be done, with separate timing slots, to allow for adequate physical distancing and disinfection of premises and equipment.
(ix) Ensure that the equipment has been disinfected, particularly the frequently touched surfaces before each use.
(x) Those having oxygen saturation below 95% should not be allowed to exercise. Call central/State helpline/ambulance and refer such persons to the nearest health facility.
(xi) Common exercise mats should be avoided, and members should preferably bring their own exercise mats which they may take back with them.
(xii) Stop the exercise if you feel difficulty in breathing. Check oxygen saturation level. Those having oxygen saturation below 95% should not be allowed to continue exercise. Call central/State helpline/ambulance and refer such persons to the nearest health facility.
(xiii) After exercise and in common areas ensure proper disposal of face covers/masks/used towels in covered bins. The shower areas/washrooms should be sanitized before and after use.
(xiv) The floor cleaning shall be taken up between exercise sessions. At the time of closure, shower rooms and lockers/changing areas need to be properly sanitized. Deep cleaning of all washrooms shall be ensured. Before closure, the entire premises will be disinfected.
(xv) Additional precautions are to be followed in case of a suspect case in the premises. Place the ill person in a room or area where they are isolated from others. Provide a mask/face cover till examination by a doctor. Immediately

inform the nearest medical facility (hospital/clinic) or call the State or district helpline. A risk assessment will be undertaken by the designated public health authority (District Rapid Response Team/treating physician) and accordingly further action be initiated regarding management of case, his/her contacts and need for disinfection. Disinfection of the premises is to be taken up if the person is found positive.

§2. Sports Associations (Federations, Leagues, Clubs)' Measures

729. The promotion and development of sports has been severely affected as many academies and schools have stopped organizing tournaments and training camps for the fear of Covid-19. Sports activities also depend on the flow of funds down from major events and from philanthropy which are facing major challenges. The future is hard for sports and the stakeholders, whether the athletes, the academies, boards, organizers, broadcasters, etc. When BCCI, the richest Cricket Board in the world, talks about cancelling their domestic tournaments due to Covid-19, one can easily gauge the effect of the pandemic on other sports.

730. The United Nations system, through its sports policy instruments and mechanisms such as the Intergovernmental Committee for Physical Education and Sport, as well as through its research and policy guidance provides support. Governments, UN entities and other key stakeholders should ensure the provision of capacity development and technical cooperation services to support the development and implementation of national policies and approaches for the best use of sport to advance health and well-being in the age of Covid-19.

I. Guidance by Organizations

731. Governments and intergovernmental organizations provide sports federations, clubs and organizations guidance related to safety, health, labour and other standards and protocols that would apply to future sport events and related safe working conditions. This allows all stakeholders to work and cooperate as a team with the objective to address the current challenges and to facilitate future sports events that are safe and enjoyable for all. The sport business, comprising of producers, broadcasters, fans, businesses, owners and players among others, need to find new and innovative norms to mitigate the effects of COVID19 on the world of sport. This includes finding ways to engage with fans in order to ensure safe sport events while maintaining the workforce, creating new operating models and venue strategies.

II. World Health Organization

732. The sport associations and other organizations have shown their solidarity with efforts to reduce the spread of the virus. For example, FIFA has teamed up with the World Health Organization (WHO) and launched a 'Pass the message to kick out coronavirus' campaign led by well-known football players in thirteen languages, calling on people to follow five key steps to stop the spread of the disease focused on hand washing, coughing etiquette, not touching one's face, physical distance and staying home if feeling unwell. Other international sport for development and peace organizations have come together to support one another in solidarity during this time, for example, through periodic online community discussions to share challenges and issues. Participants in such online dialogues have also sought to devise innovative solutions to larger social issues, for example, by identifying ways that sporting organizations can respond to problems faced by vulnerable people who normally participate in sporting programmes in low income communities but who are now unable to, given restriction to movement.

III. Standing Operating Procedure Issued by SAI

733. The SAI has issued Standard Operating Procedures (SOPs) to deal with Covid-19 cases. These measures will be strictly implemented at the various National Centres of Excellence (NCOE) as well as the ongoing national coaching camps. Upon arrival at the training centres, all athletes will undergo a mandatory Rapid Antigen Test (RAT). If the result comes negative, they will train and dine separately until the sixth day of joining. A repeat of the RAT would take place on the fifth day. The ones who get a positive result would undergo an RT-PCR test and be treated in isolation, while the athletes testing negative would continue normal training. Isolation facilities have been earmarked for Covid-positive or symptomatic athletes across camps. The facilities would be sanitized twice a day. There will also be a micro bio-bubble, where the athletes will be divided into small groups for training and dining. The athletes have also been strictly asked to avoid interacting with other groups.

Besides, random testing of athletes, coaches, support staff and non-residential staff in the NCOE will be carried out once every fifteen days. It has also been recommended that athletes would be participating in only those competitions recommended by the respective NSFs and the SAI HQ officials, the nodal sports body said in a release. For invitational tournaments and non-Olympic qualifying events, recommendations would be made by the respective Regional Directors of the NCOEs.

734. As far as players and coaches supported by Sport Authority of India (SAI), no financial curtailment has been resorted to. Further, during the lockdown period, players have been provided with the facilities to continue their training. Regular online training/class were conducted for athletes by the coaches to keep them motivated and fit during lock down period. Athletes were provided with online training module for daily practice. Regular interaction with the athletes was done in order to boost their morale and keep them motivated in these tough times. Seminars and workshops by experts in sports psychology, sports science/medicating, nutrition in

COVID 19, strength and conditioning, high performance sports environment, anti-doping have been organized online to educate athletes about how to cope with stress and depression during tough times and focusing on their objectives so that the training is not hampered.

§3. CONCLUDING REMARKS

735. Sport is a major contributor to economic and social development. Its role is well recognized by governments, including in the Political Declaration of the 2030 Agenda, which reflects on the contribution sports make to the empowerment of women and of young people, individuals and communities, as well as to health, education and social inclusion objectives. With no competitions happening, the livelihoods of athletes have been affected. With the economy severely affected, sponsorship revenue in non-cricket sports has suffered a lot. The role of foundations, institutions, boards is significant here as such a crisis may have a generational impact on athletes. The role will be to look at the non-obvious and to do the difficult things, including sustaining livelihoods, keeping talent (sporting, coaching, off-field) in sport through the next 2-3 years. Otherwise a short-time crisis could have a generational impact. With economy in distress and economists doubting quick recovery in the coming months, the budget for sports in India may also be reduced hugely, with the government looking to focus on other key areas during or in a post-pandemic. COVID19 impact challenging times ahead for Indian sports as hosting tournaments grassroots development continue to suffer

Selected Bibliography

Urvashi, Agrawal & Sharan A. Gupta, 'Issues Plaguing the Sports Arena', JMI 3 (2018) p 143-166.
Annual Report, 2017–2018, 2020–2021 of Ministry of Youth Affairs and Sports, Government of India.
Anti-Doping Rules, 2021 (Revised as per 2021 WADA Code).
Comprehensive Sports Policy 2007, (draft) Ministry of Youth Affairs and Sports, Government of India.
Anti-Doping Bill 2021.
Draft National Sports Development Bill, 2013.
Draft Prevention of Sporting Fraud Bill, 2013.
National Sports Ethics Commission Bill, 2016.
Subhrajit, Chanda, *Handbook: Developing Sports Law in India: Challenge Ahead.* INSC International Publishers, Chikkamagaluru, 1st ed. 2021, ISBN: 978-1-68576-121-9.
Abhimanyu, Chattree. 'Sports Laws in India: A Critical Analysis', *Cosmos* 10, no. 1 (July–December 2020).
Lovely, Dasgupta & Shameek Sen (eds). *Sports Law in India, Policy, Regulation and Commercialization.* SAGE Publications, 2018.
Raizada, Shaifali, Ekta Gupta & Nain Bhavya. *Handbook on Sports Law*. Satyam Law International, 2018.
National Code Against Age Fraud in Sports.
National Development Code of India, 2011, Department of Sports, MYAS.
Gardiner, Simon, et al. *Sports Law*, 2nd ed. London: Cavendish Publication Limited, 2001.
'Sports Fans Rights and Remedies: The Liability of Sports Teams, Ticket Sellers and Sporting Event Tour Operators for Defaults, Performance Failures and Physical Injuries'. www.sportsmanagement.in/www.classactionlitigation.com.
'Sports Law: An Overview'. www.law.cornell.edu/topics/sports.html.
'Contact Sport Exception Allows for Participant Negligence'. *NRPA Law Review*, May 1998, Parks and Recreation.
Mark, James. 'Liability for Professional Athletes Injuries: A Comparative Analysis of Where the Risk Lies'. http://usir.salford.ac.uk/1058/1/james1.pdf.
'Sports in India'. www.sports.indiapress.org.

Selected Bibliography

Index

The numbers here refer to the paragraph numbers.

www.ingramcontent.com/pod-product-compliance
Ingram Content Group UK Ltd.
Pitfield, Milton Keynes, MK11 3LW, UK
UKHW020135290926
15471UKWH00003B/510

9 789403 500362